9-22

# HOW WE LEARN

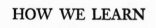

# How We Learn

*by*

BOYD HENRY BODE

PROFESSOR OF PRINCIPLES AND
PRACTICE OF EDUCATION
*The Ohio State University*

GREENWOOD PRESS, PUBLISHERS
WESTPORT, CONNECTICUT

# Preface

THIS BOOK began as a revision of an earlier volume entitled *Conflicting Psychologies of Learning*. As it turned out, however, well over half of the present document consists of entirely new material, and the rest was so extensively revised and reorganized that it seemed more appropriate to select a new title and let the earlier effort achieve oblivion by the shortest possible route.

Developments in the field of psychology are making it increasingly apparent that studies in the learning process derive their chief significance for education from the conceptions of mind which lie back of them. What we conceive or assume the mind to be is of determining influence, both in the field of method and in the realm of values or goals. Perhaps the most effective way to become intelligent about the business of education, in both its narrower and its broader aspects, is to explore the problem of learning with reference to its implications regarding the nature of mind. The discussion is centered on four distinct theories of mind and of learning, all of which continue to exert a strong influence on present-day education and which, taken together, present a development that has both a historical and a logical aspect. The last of these theories is intimately associated with the name of John Dewey, to whom I am profoundly indebted. On the negative side this theory means a break with the past. On the positive side it means a new perspective on educational theory and practice, and a new interpretation of American democracy and American life.

BOYD H. BODE

*Columbus, Ohio*

# Contents

# HOW WE LEARN

# CHAPTER I

## *Introductory*

In approaching the problem of learning it is appropriate, first of all, to ask why learning should be regarded as a problem at all. It is not a problem, in any significant sense, for the average man. He takes the fact that we learn from experience as a matter of course. One of Kipling's heroes, for example, in relating his experiences with women of all kinds and degrees, pauses occasionally to remark: " And I learned about women from her "; and there is no indication that to him there was anything problematical about the business of learning. Of course, we learn from experience, so why not let it go at that?

This is not to say that puzzling questions may not be asked about learning. The learning process can be made to look mysterious, as can so many other things. If a person is so disposed, he may ask, for example, how visual perception takes place. What happens when we see an object on the horizon? Does the mind reach across the intervening space to lay hold of the distant object, or do we have merely a subjective impression which may or may not resemble the object that we think we see? This is a question that has troubled many an inquiring soul. To the common-sense person, however, this is likely to be a dubious kind of question. What profit is there in questions like that? We know well enough that we can see things, so why go looking for trouble? Similarly with respect to learning; we know that learning goes on and this should be enough to satisfy us. Raising academic questions about learning may be left to people who have no important occupation in life. Or if we wish to be harsh, we may quote the Scriptural saying that a fool can ask more questions than seven wise men can answer.

There is no denying the fact that throughout the ages practical people have demonstrated their competency to deal with learning situations without troubling themselves as to the precise nature of the learning process. They not only learned, but they also managed to teach others. The apprenticeship system of teaching, for example, seems to have worked fairly well, without requiring any extensive educational equipment on the part of the teacher. The master trained the apprentice by telling him things occasionally, by showing him how certain things were done, and perhaps by rapping his knuckles at intervals as an antidote to carelessness. The master had no theories about learning and no training in method, but he generally managed to make the apprentice a qualified member of the craft. A teacher of this kind could hardly be expected to appreciate the desirability of devoting himself to a serious study of the learning process.

The master craftsman, however, was not the only kind of teacher, even in his own day. If his apprentices were to learn the three R's, some other kind of teaching and of equipment had to be provided. The three R's are different from such occupations as farming or carpentry in that they cannot be taught so directly in connection with everyday work. A pupil can hardly be expected to learn to read by getting a job on a newspaper or in a printing establishment; he needs a primer containing the alphabet, perhaps, and easy words especially chosen for him. The situation is similar with respect to the learning of mathematics. The school, in brief, is a special environment for the facilitation of learning. But how is this environment to be set up? In reading, shall we begin with the memorizing of the alphabet, then follow this with short syllables, like ab, ac, ad, to be combined later into words, which are finally arranged into sentences? This has been advocated and practiced, on the ground that learning should proceed from the simple to the complex. Eventually this procedure was generally discarded, because it was maintained that learning does not take place in this fashion. This pitches us into the middle of the problem. How, then, do we learn and how should reading be taught? The problem is not an academic but an eminently practical one.

The teaching of number relations lands us in pretty much the same place. How should number work be taught? Is it primarily a matter of establishing connections in the nervous system, so that 6 x 7 will almost automatically evoke the response, 42? If so, then repetition and drill will loom large in the program. Or is the teaching of mathematics primarily a matter of developing the reasoning faculty? In that case the procedure will be correspondingly different. Or, again, should we guard against the danger of abstractness, by stressing the importance of teaching number relations as incidental to projects which require this kind of knowledge? This, in turn, points to a still different procedure. Back of it all lies the question of how we really learn.

No matter where we turn in the schoolroom, this question rises to confront us. What about history or literature? How we teach it is conditioned by what we assume the nature of learning to be. Perhaps learning is physiological habit-formation; perhaps it is the training of some faculty; perhaps it is the enrichment of present experience.  Perhaps history should be taught backwards; perhaps literary appreciation requires the " conditioning " of certain involuntary responses, such as are involved in the emotions of anger and fear.  As soon as we undertake to create a special environment, in the form of a school, for the special purpose of promoting learning, we become involved in the question of what learning is.  Our conception of learning has a direct bearing on method.  It also has a bearing on educational aims or objectives, because the question of what learning is can be answered only in terms of what the mind is; and our conception of the mind, in turn, will decide what we consider to be " good " for the mind, in terms of an educational program.  Thus if the mind has faculties, it is desirable that these should be trained; if the mind is some kind of function, as present-day psychologists are disposed to hold, then education will set itself some other purpose.  It seems evident, therefore, that a teacher who seeks to become as intelligent as possible about his work is bound to explore the problem of learning.

There is another reason why such exploration is necessary.  Various theories of mind have been developed in the past, with corresponding diversities in the conception of learning.  The newer theories, however, never managed to displace their predecessors, but merely competed with them.  As the successive theories came along, the water became more and more muddied.  It is likely that teachers generally have a less clear conception of what learning is than they had a century ago.  The average teacher tends to adopt different features of different theories without being aware that these do not harmonize with one another and without even clearly realizing that he is proceeding eclectically. The problem of learning must be explored, partly to enable the teacher to straighten out his own thinking and partly to enable him to understand the confusion that prevails in present-day education.

Since the problem of learning is tied up with problem of mind, the approach to the problem in this book is through certain theories of mind which have proved of outstanding importance for education, for the purpose of determining their significance in terms of the learning process. This is done in the belief that a semihistorical approach offers the best opportunity to analyze the present situation, which is a product of all these theories in combination, to show what conception of learning is necessitated in the light of present-day knowledge, and to point out the bearing of this conception on educational practice. Our first task, therefore, will be to trace the historical development of the contrast between mind and matter, in order to get a closer look at a conception of mind which holds the distinction of being the earliest in theoretical formulation, the most widespread, both in the past and in the present, and the most powerful in its influence on education.

# CHAPTER II

# The Contrast between Mind and Matter

To the average person the distinction between mind and body is a familiar and obvious fact. The body is an object that makes itself known to the senses; the mind is an immaterial reality inside the body, presumably in the head, which thinks and feels and wills, and which is in control of the activities of the body. The outstanding difference between a human being and an inanimate object lies in the fact that human beings have minds, whereas inanimate objects do not. Consequently there is an enormous difference in behavior in the two cases. Inanimate objects are merely dead matter, whereas human beings are alive and responsible for what they do.

The distinction is so self-evident that it hardly occurs to our average person to make any difficulty about it. Though some people, and especially his pastor, may have talked to him about his mind or soul,[1] he was never taught, as far as he can remember, to distinguish between mind and body. This distinction is thrust upon him by the facts themselves. The distinction itself is almost as inevitable as the distinction between a house and a tree. We notice the difference as soon as we are capable of intelligent observation.

[1] The reader is requested to note that the terms *mind* and *soul* are used interchangeably throughout this book. They are treated as synonyms because, as far as our present purpose is concerned, they mean the same thing.

The fact that this is, in general, the attitude of the
common-sense man shows how easy it is to identify the
familiar with the self-evident. That the distinction between mind and matter, far from being self-evident, was
slowly wrought out through ages of reflective thinking
scarcely occurs to the average person. Nor is he likely
to realize that this distinction is full of obscurities and
difficulties. He simply accepts or absorbs this distinction, which has become an integral part of his spiritual
heritage, in much the same way as he acquires a knowledge of the number system or of his mother tongue. All
these things are as much a part of his environment as the
ground on which he treads or the flowers of the field.
Consequently he takes them all for granted. By the time
he is grown he has built up certain habits of thinking
which have become so easy and familiar that any other
ways of thinking are apt to strike him as strange and un-
natural.

The point of the foregoing comments is that the concepts of mind and matter, as they come down to us, represent *achievements* of thinking and not starting points of
thinking. We are now in possession of these concepts,
not because they are self-evident, but because the thinking has been done for us. If we take a glance at the more
primitive levels of culture, we find there is no such distinction between mind and matter as we have today. Let
us consider first the notion of matter. We talk of matter
as " dead " or " mechanical." No matter acts purely in
and of itself, but only in relation to other forms of matter. This notion has been made familiar to us by the
physical sciences, which have traced out in considerable
detail the laws or conditions under which material bodies
act. The time was, however, when very little was

known about all this. Consequently material bodies were supposed to act quite spontaneously, without reference to other bodies. There was no " dead " matter, but all things were " animated "; i.e., they acted for reasons of their own and in response to inward prompting. Every object in nature was supposed to act from essentially the same causes and motives as human beings. This belief or attitude is sometimes known as *animism*.

It is easy to see now that this attitude was inevitable. Primitive man did not know why the river rose and became a flood, why the winds blew, why the sun moved about in the sky, or why the lightnings descended to rend and destroy. Consequently he explained these actions in terms of his own behavior, which was the only explanation accessible to him. In other words, he took for granted that these things were all done " on purpose." Animism means that " man recognizes in every detail of his world the operation of personal life and will." [2] His world was not a universe, i.e., a system of interrelated facts, but a collection of independent things. These independent things, he assumed, operated spontaneously and not in accordance with universal and immutable laws. In other words, primitive man did not have a conception of " dead " matter to set over against the conception of a free and purposive mind.

In the case of the lower animals it was perhaps to be expected that the distinction between them and man would not be as clearly drawn in the past as it is at present. It is related that in France, in 1457,

A sow and her six young ones were tried on a charge of their having murdered and partly eaten a child; the sow, be-

<hr>

[2] E. B. Tylor, *Primitive Culture*, Vol. I, p. 285.

ing found guilty, was condemned to death, the young pigs were acquitted on account of their youth and the bad example of their mother.[3]

Primitive man, however, went far beyond this point in explaining events as expressing " the operation of personal life and will." The behavior of inanimate things was viewed in much the same light.

The wild native of Brazil would bite the stone he stumbled over, or the arrow that had wounded him. Such a mental condition may be traced along the course of history, not merely in impulsive habit, but in formally enacted law. The rude Kukis of Southern Asia were very scrupulous in carrying out their simple law of vengeance, life for life; if a tiger killed a Kuki, his family were in disgrace till they had retaliated by killing and eating this tiger, or another; but further, if a man was killed by a fall from a tree, his relatives would take their revenge by cutting the tree down, and scattering it in chips. A modern king of Cochin-China, when one of his ships sailed badly, used to put it in the pillory, as he would any other criminal. In classical times, the stories of Xerxes flogging the Hellespont and Cyrus draining the Gyndes occur as cases in point, but one of the regular Athenian legal proceedings is a yet more striking relic. A court of justice was held at the Prytaneum, to try any inanimate object, such as an axe or a piece of wood or stone, which had caused the death of anyone without proved human agency, and this wood or stone, if condemned, was in solemn form cast beyond the border.[4]

In the course of time, however, certain distinctions were bound to be made. Even our remote ancestors pre-

[3] E. Westermarck, *The Origin and Development of the Moral Ideas*, Vol. I, p. 257, quoted by Dewey and Tufts, *Ethics*.
[4] Tylor, *op. cit.*, p. 286.

sumably noticed certain differences, even though they were unable to account for them. It could hardly have escaped their notice that if a tool or an article of clothing is put down somewhere, it will stay where it is put until it is picked up again. On the other hand, a small child or a pup that is left in this fashion is likely to be somewhere else by the time we return. To work out an adequate explanation of the difference, however, required a long, long time.

Viewed in retrospect, the explanation that was gradually developed can be easily pointed out. Inanimate objects move only as they are pushed or pulled; their movements are due to a force operating on them from the outside, and it is not at all necessary to make any reference to " the operation of personal life and will " in explaining what they do. Punishing inanimate objects for their behavior consequently went out of fashion. The explanation for their behavior lies in something outside of them. Floods do not occur because of evil intent on the part of the river, but because of rainfalls or melting snows. Storms became linked with the facts of meteorology; epidemics were discovered to be the result of certain unfavorable health conditions; sunrise and sunset were referred to the rotation of the earth; and lightning was identified with electrical phenomena which occur elsewhere and which are subject to specifiable laws. Things behave as they do because they cannot help themselves. Inanimate objects are *inert*, and they act only in response to an external push or pull. Objects move because they are set in motion by other objects, which in turn are acted upon by still other objects, and so ad infinitum.

This type of explanation is exemplified in the solar system, which operates in accordance with a simple, inclusive principle, viz., the law of gravitation. Within this system other motions are generated, as when a meteor strikes the atmosphere of the earth and thus produces motions connected with light and heat. What is thus exhibited on a grand scale by the solar system is supposed to provide an indication of what takes place in every tiny molecule. The molecule is likewise a system, with relatively vast spaces between the constituent atoms. What is sometimes referred to nowadays as *classical* physics is the explanation of all the fulness and variety of the material universe in terms of the movements which take place among the constituent atoms. Such explanation is called *mechanistic*, because it accounts for everything by reference to a few simple laws of motion.

When any phenomenon was reduced to motion, it was "explained." The temperature of a body rises? This is "because" there has been an increase in the rate of molecular vibration. A billiard ball moves? This is "because" another billiard ball in motion has hit it and imparted its motion; fundamentally, because of the impacts of the innumerable atoms that make up the billiard balls. This sugar tastes sweet? This is because "the rapidly moving molecules of the sugar set the molecules composing various taste buds" into motion of a certain sort, and thence spring other motions along the nerves to the cerebral cortex.[5]

All this constituted a great advance. In the first place, it gave man an astonishing power over the forces of nature, as is attested by the growth of our modern material civilization. In the second place, it provided a clear-cut conception of matter and thus prepared the way for a sharp contrast between the conceptions of matter and

[5] Burnham and Wheelwright, *Philosophical Analysis*, p. 214.

mind. Stated negatively, the idea of matter is transformed because the element of personification, which is
characteristic of animistic beliefs, is eliminated from it.
Matter came to be regarded as inert or " dead " and as
reducible to mass and motion. Every atom had its place
in an interlocking system, in which every event is theoretically predictable because it is determined in rigidly
mechanical fashion. To the scientist the notion that each
planet is guided through the heavens by an angel or
spirit, or that there is such a thing as " music of the
spheres," is either merely poetry or else silly superstition,
according to his temperament or mood. In either case he
wants it distinctly understood that he does not take such
suggestions seriously. His idea of explanation is to trans-
late the phenomena of the heavens into terms of the law
of gravitation, which can be stated in quantitative form,
and which can be made the basis of prediction by means
of mathematical calculations. This type of explanation
is not merely a more dependable formulation of causal
connections; it is also an elaboration or refinement of our
ideas regarding the nature of matter.

Given this conception of matter which was worked
out with overpowering cogency, the nature of mind obviously becomes a serious problem. The conception of
the material universe as a vast machine was, indeed, a
great stimulus to the construction of machines by human
beings, but it did not at once have the effect of making
men think they themselves were likewise nothing but
machines. On the contrary, a strong conviction was
generated that reality does not consist entirely of matter.
Except in the case of a few avowed materialists, it seemed
altogether obvious that there is a fundamental difference
between the potter and the clay, between the man who

makes a machine and the machine itself. Man's most intimate knowledge of himself is as a being capable of having purposes, of making decisions, of shouldering responsibility for what he does. These are precisely the qualities which are lacking in machines. Having these qualities, man cannot be regarded as merely a part of the mechanical system which constitutes the material universe. Moreover, the entire system of religion and ethics would collapse, and this would be too high a price to pay. It became necessary, therefore, to round out the picture of the universe by making provision for a second kind of reality in addition to matter, a reality which is usually designated as spirit or mind or soul.

In a vague way the distinction between matter and spirit was foreshadowed or anticipated far back in the remote past. As a well-known writer says: " A certain crude distinction between soul and body, combined with the idea that the soul may act where the body is not, is suggested to the most savage races by familiar psychical phenomena, particularly those of dreams." [6] The distinction was crude, because the soul or spirit was assumed to be a very thin and elusive or evanescent kind of matter. In dreams this soul was supposed to leave the body temporarily and go off on adventures of its own. The physical nature of this soul is indicated by the practice of providing food at burial places for departed souls, or perhaps seeing to it that a deceased warrior was accompanied into the spiritland by his favorite wife or horse or slave. It is further indicated by the synonyms for soul, such as *spirit*, from the Latin word *spiritus*, meaning breath, and *shade*, which is still perpetuated in exclamations like " shades of our ancestors! "

[6] R. W. Smith, *The Religion of the Semites*, p. 86.

For rigorous and exact thinking, however, a distinction of this kind is scarcely adequate. Thin matter is still matter; it operates exclusively on the principles of mechanics, and it affords no room whatsoever for " spiritual " values. The saying, " No matter how thin you slice it, it's still baloney," covers the point entirely. If the facts and values represented by the terms " mind " and " soul " are to receive appropriate recognition, it is necessary to make a clean break with the whole system of mechanics. Since every existing thing that occupies space is, by virtue of that fact, subject to the principles of mechanics, there is no way of placing the mind outside of the realm of mechanics except by declaring that it has no extension, that it does not occupy space at all. There can be no compromise at this point. But this makes the concept of mind highly mysterious. How are we to frame a concept of mind under such conditions?

In brief, then, classical physics gives us a definite conception of matter and it also lays down the conditions that must be met if we are to have a defensible concept of mind. Perhaps it is no exaggeration to say that the conception of mind which has been developed by theology and philosophy finds its strongest argument and its strongest support in classical physics. With a different conception of matter, our conception of mind would presumably be correspondingly different. At any rate, the conception of matter offered to us by classical physics being what it is, we have no alternative but to infer that mind is an existence of a wholly different order, an existence which is a real existence despite the fact that it has no spacial qualities whatsoever.

For the average man the concept of matter presented here is perhaps not entirely familiar. It is reasonably certain that the implication of this theory for a concept of mind is anything but familiar. The fact that the mind is usually located in the head indicates that it is not sharply contrasted with matter, since immaterial realities are not located in space at all. The failure to see that mind must be taken out of space altogether, if we are to believe in it at all, is responsible for much of the vagueness that clusters about the notion of mind. The average man does, indeed, distinguish between matter and mind, but he is mistaken in the notion that the distinction is self-evident; and he is further mistaken in the assumption that his concepts about matter and mind are reasonably clear. The distinction between matter and mind is undoubtedly a familiar distinction, since we make it constantly. But familiarity and clarity are not the same thing. When we scrutinize these concepts, we are forced to the conclusion that they have behind them a long period of development and that the distinction which they represent has become so deeply embedded in our cultural heritage as to make it take on the appearance of being a self-evident fact.

It is evident that the conceptions of matter and mind go hand in hand. A basic change in the conception of matter is bound to result in a corresponding change in the conception of mind. Hence the revisions which the physical sciences are making in their conception of matter are bound to have repercussions far beyond the limits of these sciences. It is no accident, therefore, that psychology is likewise in a state of upheaval. Traditional notions regarding the nature of mind are being sharply challenged, and established beliefs are going by the board. Our present concern is with these developments in their bearing on education. Every significant change in our thinking about mind is bound, eventually, to be reflected in educational practice. At present the confusion in psychology is duplicated in our conceptions of the nature of the learning process and of educational aims or ideals. In the succeeding chapters our first task will be to present the traditional conception of mind more in detail, together with its implications for education, and then to survey the rival theories which are seeking to displace it as a guide to practice.

## Bibliography

BURNHAM and WHEELWRIGHT, *Philosophical Analysis*, Chap. VII. Henry Holt & Co.

SMITH, R. W., *The Religion of the Semites*, Chap. III. A. and C. Black.

STALLO, J. B., *The Concepts and Theories of Modern Physics*, Chaps. I and II. Appleton and Co.

TYLOR, E. B., *Primitive Culture*, Vol. I, Chaps. VIII and XI. Henry Holt & Co.

WESTERMARCK, E., *The Origin and Development of the Moral Ideas*, Vol. I, Chap. X. Macmillan Co.

# CHAPTER III

# The Mind as a Substance or Entity

IN THE preceding chapter the discussion centered on the proposition that the conception of mind was developed concomitantly with the conception of matter. The conception of matter, as held by classical physics, was the result of brilliant scientific genius and centuries of cumulative effort. It was no simple task to get behind the endless diversity of the material world and reduce all this diversity to the motions and groupings of invisible atoms. When the task was finally achieved, the great bulk of qualitative differences in the world of matter had been traced back to a small variety of atoms, which, by comparison, were all pretty much alike. This reduction made it possible to think of the material world as a thoroughgoing mechanism, in which everything could theoretically be figured out in advance, since all action could be dealt with in terms of mass and motion. As this went on, everything that could not be so dealt with was moved over into a separate and distinct realm, viz., the realm of the mind. This was the realm of freedom and purpose, of hopes and fears, of joys and sorrows, a realm in which all this talk about mass and motion has no relevancy and no meaning.

In philosophy this point of view is commonly referred to as dualism. By dualism is meant the doctrine that reality comprises two kinds of " things," or " existences," or " substances," viz., matter and mind. In the case of matter we usually have no trouble in identifying what it is that we are talking about. Anything is matter which has mass, extension, motion, and impenetrability. If the properties of atoms are limited to such qualities as these, it follows by definition that activity among atoms is analogous to what happens when marbles are shaken in a bag. We get motions, collisions, rearrangements, and nothing else.

With the realm of matter thus defined and limited, it seems necessary to say at once that matter is not the whole of reality. There are facts in this world of ours which are not reducible to terms of motion and arrangement, however much they may be connected with material processes. Such facts are our aches and pains, our aspirations and frustrations, our appreciations and purposes and volitions. These are not just by-products of matter; by definition they cannot be produced by matter at all. They have their source or " ground " in a different kind of reality. This reality exists in its own right, so to speak, which means that it cannot be reduced to a form of matter and that it can operate in relative independence of the laws of mechanics. For convenience this immaterial reality is here designated as " mind " or " mind-substance." In ordinary usage we sometimes distinguish between mind and soul and consciousness, but these distinctions all come within the boundaries of this immaterial reality and so they may be disregarded for the purposes of the present discussion. Our concern just now is with the broad distinction between material and immaterial reality, and as a designation of this immaterial reality in its entirety the term mind or mind-substance is presumably as good as any.

To call the mind a " substance " may cause some difficulty. We have become so accustomed to identifying the term substance with material reality that the application of this term to something which does not occupy space at all may seem like a misuse of language. But if we undertake to deal with " mind " as something that exists and operates in relative independence of matter, we need a term that will confer upon it this status. It is for this reason that scholars in the past have insisted on calling the mind a substance. This term was sometimes used interchangeably with the term " entity," which comes to the same thing. In using these terms they meant to emphasize that mind is just as real as matter, that it has a nature of its own, and that it operates in its own distinctive fashion.

. While the terminology may be somewhat technical, the general idea conveyed by this terminology has become an integral part of our tradition. We are profoundly convinced that man is made of different stuff from the inanimate things by which he is surrounded. In the language of Holy Writ, he was created a " living soul." Inanimate objects are the slaves of circumstance, but man can choose his goal and bend circumstances to his will. He can foresee the future and shape his present conduct with reference to what is yet to come. To him, accordingly, it is given to have dominion over the earth and to be master of his own destiny. As Voltaire once remarked, this little being, five feet tall, can undertake to constitute himself an exception to the laws of the universe. We may add that he can undertake this because he is an exception from the start. Instead of being simply a product and plaything of the forces of nature, he possesses freedom and the power to initiate activity. He can discover the laws of nature and make them the servants of his desires.

It is time, however, to come to closer grips. Granted that there is a mind-substance, a reality that operates in its own peculiar way, how is this mind-substance related to our momentary experiences, our aches and pains, our perceptions and emotions, which come and go in an endless flow? Is mind-substance just a name for this whole heterogeneous collection, or must we distinguish between the mind-substance and the experience of the moment? Common sense is not very clear on this point, which is to say that it sometimes identifies the mind with the stream of changing experiences and at other times distinguishes between them. It may seem quite proper to say that our passing emotions, thoughts, and acts of volition are what we mean by mind. They, then, are the mind. But there are also situations where this identification is a bit too simple. What shall we say, for example, when a person is in a dead faint or in a dreamless sleep? Has his mind left him, or would it be more correct to say that he still has a mind, although it does not happen to be functioning at the moment? Here common sense inclines to the view that the mind is still present, although temporarily inactive. The mind is a more or less permanent thing, which is active at some times, but not necessarily active all the time.

This latter view is in accordance with historic doctrine. Realities are not supposed to pop into and out of existence in the lighthearted fashion in which our experiences come and go. These experiences are merely the " states " or " attributes " of a reality that abides, a reality that is different from matter. Otherwise we should have to conclude that matter can produce mind. If we may trust our classical physics, however, matter can do no such thing. All that matter can do is to produce new arrangements of atoms and new forms of motion. At most the processes of matter can stimulate the mind, but it is the mind, and not matter, that produces our experiences. So it seems necessary to distinguish between the mind-substance and the experiences of the moment. These experiences are qualities or momentary activities of the mind in somewhat the same way that arrangements and motions are qualities of the atoms by which they are produced.

This distinction is clearly drawn by Bishop Berkeley, one of the great figures in the history of philosophy. As Berkeley puts it:

Besides all that endless variety of ideas or objects of knowledge, there is likewise *something which knows or perceives them, and exercises diverse operations* — as willing, imagining, remembering — about them. This perceiving, active being is what I call *mind, spirit, soul* or *myself*. By which words I do not denote any one of my ideas, but a thing entirely distinct from them, wherein they exist, or, which is the same thing, whereby they are perceived — for the existence of an idea consists in being perceived.[1]

The point so far is that, since matter is conceived in such a way as to make it incapable of producing experiences, we have no alternative but to have recourse to a mind-substance. Experiences can occur only when the activities of the nervous system impinge on the mind or mind-substance. As long as the mind-substance is left out of the picture, the activities of the nervous system involve nothing but matter and motion. Put in a mind-substance to receive the impact or stimulations of these physiological processes and the situation is very different. Experiences then take place, but they take place because

[1] G. Berkeley, *Principles of Human Knowledge*, Sec. 2.

they are produced by the mind in its reaction to the physiological stimulation. For that matter, the initiative may be taken by the mind; it may start activities which lead to further activities within the nervous system, instead of waiting passively for the nervous system to act. In either case, our experiences are far from being just products of physical activity.

This dependence of experiences on a mind-substance points to a distinction between mind and its experiences which the scholastics described as a distinction between *substance* and *attributes*. Our experiences are attributes for precisely the same reason that colors and shapes and movements are attributes, viz., because they cannot exist by themselves. They necessarily depend on something else in which they inhere or to which they belong. Self-dependence is the mark of a substance. The mind is a substance because it does not depend upon anything else, but exists in its own right.

At this point we have trenched upon the question of the relation between mind and body. A further consideration of this question will serve to emphasize the fundamental contrast or opposition between the two. As a point of departure we may refer briefly to the theory of the French philosopher, Descartes. According to Descartes, whose name is associated with the beginnings of modern philosophy, the human soul is a substance or entity that has its seat in the brain, and more specifically in the pineal gland. The brain being composed of two hemispheres which are bilaterally symmetrical to each other, nearly all its parts or constituents are arranged in pairs, one member of the pair being found on each of the hemispheres. Near the center of the brain, however, is found the pineal gland, which is an exception to the general rule. From the fact that it has no duplicate and that it is somewhat centrally located, Descartes inferred that it is probably the habitation of the intelligent power which gives direction to conscious behavior. The living body, in his view, is an elaborate and cleverly contrived mechanism, and the function of the brain is to connect the impulses coming in from the peripheral sense organs with the nerves that control the muscles. The brain, to use a modern figure of speech, is the central switchboard in a complicated telephone system. To a certain extent this switchboard is operated on the principle of the automatic telephone. The incoming currents work their way out in the form of motor discharges, without the help of a supervising intelligence. This form of activity is known as reflex action. In some cases, however, appropriate response is possible only if the incoming excitation first calls up " central " stationed at the pineal gland, in order to get the right connections. The soul then sees to it that purposive activity occurs by deflecting the currents in such a way that the sensory stimulus is followed by the correct motor response.

It may be remarked that this view still represents with reasonable accuracy the popular notion of the soul. Such words as *soul, mind, consciousness* are commonly associated with an entity or spiritual substance that resides somewhere in the head. By means of this hypothesis the explanation of intelligent behavior becomes fairly simple, or at least apparently so. The stimulations or currents coming in to the brain from the sense organs are like so many knocks on a door to arouse the sleeper within. The soul thereupon takes cognizance of the situation and decides what is to be done, and in conformity with this decision it switches the cerebral energy into the neural centers that control the muscles for the appropriate response.

In its general outlines this doctrine presumably offers a reasonably adequate picture of the way in which the average man of today still thinks about the relation of mind and body, when he thinks about it at all. As an explanation of how the mind guides and directs the body, it is peculiarly fitted to satisfy the imagination. The nicely adapted movements of a sailing vessel tacking into the wind or of an automobile winding its way through a crowded thoroughfare are amply explained when we discover the function of the pilot at the helm or of the driver at the wheel. Our average man is likely to have hazy notions as to what constitutes a scientific explanation, and so the theory that there is an agent seated in the brain which directs the activities of the body is perhaps the simplest and most adequate explanation for him. " ' Herr Pastor, sure there be a horse inside,' called out the peasants to X after their spiritual shepherd had spent hours in explaining to them the construction of the locomotive. With a horse inside truly everything becomes clear, even though it be a queer enough sort of horse — the horse itself calls for no explanation." [2]

Now the horse itself is the very thing that calls for explanation in the present case. It is, indeed, a " queer enough sort of horse." In the first place, since the mind is nonspacial, the statement that it is located in the brain is merely a figure of speech. If it is nonspacial, it cannot be located anywhere, any more than we can locate honesty or justice or the square root of a given number. Secondly, the way in which spacial and nonspacial things can lay hands on each other, so to speak, in order to produce action, is past finding out. The problem seems to

[2] W. James, *Principles of Psychology*, Vol. I, p. 29.

be entirely different from a problem of interaction which is confined wholly to material things. In the world of matter, causation is by definition a process of rearrangement among atoms and of changes in motion. It has nothing to do with any other kind of fact. The opposition between mind and matter is so sharp and so complete that there is no way of bringing the two together again. A gulf is fixed between them which no scientific explanation can bridge.

The passage from the physics of the brain to the corresponding facts of consciousness is inconceivable as a result of mechanics. Granted that a definite thought, and a definite molecular action in the brain, occur simultaneously; we do not possess the intellectual organ, nor apparently any rudiment of the organ, which would enable us to pass, by a process of reasoning, from the one to the other. They appear together, but we do not know why. Were our minds and senses so expanded, strengthened, and illuminated, as to enable us to see and feel the very molecules of the brain; were we capable of following all their motions, all their groupings, all their electric discharges, if such there be; and were we intimately acquainted with the corresponding states of thought and feeling, we should be as far as ever from the solution of the problem, " How are these physical processes connected with the facts of consciousness? " The chasm between the two classes of phenomena would still remain intellectually impassable. Let the consciousness of love, for example, be associated with a right-handed spiral motion of the molecules of the brain, and the consciousness of hate with a left-handed spiral motion. We should then know, when we love, that the motion is in one direction, and, when we hate, that the motion is in the other; but the " why? " would remain as unanswerable as before.[3]

[3] J. Tyndall, *Fragments of Science*. Vol. II, Chapter on " Scientific Materialism."

Here then we are confronted by a mystery which merely deepens the more we try to solve it. Matter is matter and mind is mind, and they have no common denominator. As Kipling says: East is East and West is West, and never the twain shall meet. The appalling gap between the mind and the material universe is too wide to be bridged. Our wisest course, perhaps, is to be philosophical about it and remind ourselves on occasion that this mystery is the price that we have to pay in order to safeguard what we sometimes call spiritual values. From the standpoint of classical physics, this appears to be a reasonable conclusion. If we could trace the whole series of causes, as the physicist deals with them, from the incoming stimulations to the overt action, without reference at any point to a non-mechanistic factor, our scientific demand for explanation would indeed be satisfied. Such an explanation, however, would either leave the mind entirely out of the picture or else would drag it into this unbroken sequence of causes and make it just as much a passive link in the chain as any other member of the sequence. Freedom, initiative, personal responsibility, all would vanish.

There must be a break in the chain if these things are to have any meaning. The mind is, indeed, dependent on the body for stimulations from the outside world. But when these stimulations are once received, it can act independently. The man confronted by a bear may decide to run, or to fight, or to try to stare the brute out of countenance through the " power of the human eye." The decision, whichever it is, comes from the inside and not from the outside. The mind acts " on its own," and not through any compelling power of outside causes. This is why it is free. This is what makes possible the introduction of values and ideals and standards through which human living is sharply marked off from the realm of mechanical causation.

This is dualism, unashamed and unadorned. The realm of matter and the realm of mind stand side by side, with nothing to join them except a profound mystery. The scientific mind does not like to let it go at that, but there seems to be nothing else to do. Our acceptance of this dualism is not merely the result of wishful thinking, but is forced upon us by the development of the concept of matter. The end result is indeed disturbing, but there seems to be nothing that we can do about it. Mind and matter constitute the strangest team that is to be found anywhere. Practically anything that may be said of either member of the pair turns out to be inapplicable to the other member. Matter is spacial; the mind is nonspacial. Matter is subject to the rigid and universal laws of nature; the mind is free and responsible for its acts. Matter is corruptible; the mind is incorruptible. Matter is confined to the present; the mind can live in the past and in the future. Matter is a collection of atoms, with no destiny but blind, unending movement; the mind is an indivisible unit and an independent source of goodness, beauty, and truth.

Can we doubt that the mind is an independent, creative source of concepts? What, for example, shall we say of a concept like causation? We do not see it directly; what we observe is at most certain sequences of events. Since the concept is not given from without through the sense organs, it must necessarily be supplied from within, by the mind itself. The same holds for concepts like force and energy, which are basic in the physical sciences, or for concepts like freedom or right and wrong, which we can scarcely pretend to derive from immediate observation. The concept of infinity is likewise a case in point. We may believe that space, for example, is infinite, but no one has ever *seen* the infinity of space. The concept of infinity is a construct of the mind, a product of creative activity. It is not derived by the simple process of adding spaces together. The addition of spaces can never give us anything which is not measurable; it does not get us off the level of the finite. The concept of infinity, therefore, must have its source within the mind and not outside; in other words, the fact that we have a concept like infinity points to the existence of a substantive mind.

That we possess knowledge which we do not derive through the senses must be evident to all who will consider the matter. Our idea of space, for example, is not merely the sum of all the spaces embraced in our experience, but it transcends all possible experience. So of the idea of time. We can acquaint ourselves with things that are very great in extent — the earth, the distances of the heavenly bodies, the profound abysses penetrated by the telescope, but still we know that all these are limited, finite, and we cannot help believing that there is something more, the unlimited, the infinite. No experience can show us that two straight lines cannot enclose a space, or that two parallel lines will never meet, and yet we know that such is the case. We may, indeed, have no adequate conception of the absolute or the infinite, of a creation, of God, or of immortality; but certainly we have ground for thinking that there is something uncaused, something unlimited, that the universe had a beginning, that God is, and the human spirit is immortal. In every direction the intuitions of the Reason overlap the boundaries of experience, and furnish, at least, a ground for enlightened faith. As the Reason is the source of the kind of knowledge now referred to, it may be called rational knowledge.[4]

The situation is similar when we consider a concept like substance or identity. The senses present us with a succession of impressions, but nothing more. They cannot give us *thinghood* or substance.

Take, for example, this piece of wax: it is quite fresh, having been but recently taken from the bee-hive; it has not yet lost the sweetness of the honey it contained; it still retains somewhat of the odour of the flowers from which it was gathered; its colour, figure, size, are apparent (to the sight); it is hard, cold, easily handled; and sounds when struck upon with the finger. In fine, all that contributes to make a body as distinctly known as possible, is found in the one before us. But, while I am speaking, let it be placed near the fire — what remained of the taste exhales, the smell evaporates, the colour changes, its figure is destroyed, its size increases, it becomes liquid, it grows hot, it can hardly be handled and, although struck upon, it emits no sound. Does the same wax still remain after this change? It must be admitted that it does remain; no one doubts it, or judges otherwise. What, then, was it I knew with so much distinctness in the piece of wax? Assuredly, it would be nothing of all that I observed by means of the senses, since all the things that fell under taste, smell, sight, touch, and hearing are changed, and yet the same wax remains.[5]

In many cases, it is true, the content of our concepts seems to come directly from the outside world through sense perception. It is through sense perception that we become acquainted with qualities like hardness, fragrance, whiteness, and sweetness. As long as we limit ourselves to sense experience, however, we get only par-

4 J. P. Wickersham, *Methods of Instruction*, pp. 44-45.
5 R. Descartes, *Meditations*, Meditation II.

ticular cases of such qualities.  The fact that we have abstractions, e.g., whiteness which is not any particular whiteness, but whiteness as such or in general, remains to be accounted for.  In order to explain such abstractions it is necessary once more to bring in a *mind* as an agency which performs the act of abstraction.  Abstract ideas do not just drop in from nowhere; they presuppose a certain activity.  As Locke says:

> The mind makes the particular ideas received from particular objects to become general; which is done by considering them as they are in the mind, such appearances, separate from all other existences, and the circumstances of real existence, as time, place, or any other concomitant ideas.  This is called abstraction, whereby ideas taken from particular beings become general representatives of all of the same kind, and their names general names, applicable to whatever exists conformable to such abstract ideas.  Such precise, named appearances in the mind, without considering how, whence, or with what others they came there, the understanding lays up (with names commonly annexed to them) as the standard to rank real existences into sorts, as they agree with these patterns, and to denominate them accordingly.  Thus the same colour being observed today in chalk or snow, which the mind yesterday received from milk, it considers that appearance alone makes it a representative of all of that kind; and having given it the name whiteness, it by that sound signifies the same quality, wheresoever to be imagined or met with, and thus universals, whether ideas or terms, are made.[6]

Concepts, then, are made either by sheer creative activity or by a process of abstraction.  In either case they presuppose an agency such as the substantive mind.  To

[6] John Locke, *Essay on the Human Understanding,* Book II, Chap. XI, Sec. 9.

the casual eye, at any rate, the explanation of concepts by means of a substantive mind has an undeniable simplicity and plausibility.

Whether or not we regard these arguments as conclusive, it is evident that the belief in a substantive mind is not an exhibition of sheer wilfulness or prejudice. The development of physical science seemed to leave no alternative. By assuming the existence of a substantive mind we can apparently give a satisfactory account of various experiences with which physical science is wholly unable to cope. We can readily understand, therefore, why it is that this conception of mind should have been adopted so widely. It seems entirely safe to say that the great bulk of mankind still holds to this belief.

For good measure we may add a reference to the belief in immortality. The question of immortality is of perennial interest. Most people would grant that immortality is not a demonstrated fact, like the roundness of the earth or the existence of other planets in the heavens. It is a fact, however, that the belief in immortality is very widely held. The fact that this belief is so widespread is often regarded as giving it at least an antecedent presumption of being true. This presumption is strengthened if we accept the doctrine of a substantive mind. It has even been argued that this doctrine guarantees immortality. To destroy a thing means to tear it apart, to cause its disintegration. Since the mind or soul is simple and indivisible, it is as indestructible as the atom. As Berkeley says:

We have shown that the soul is indivisible, incorporeal, unextended, and it is consequently incorruptible. Nothing can be plainer than that the motions, changes, decays, and dissolutions which we hourly see befall natural bodies (and which is what we mean by the *course of nature*) cannot possibly affect an active, simple, uncompounded substance; such a being therefore is indissoluble by the force of nature; that is to say — the soul of man is *naturally* immortal.[7]

Whether or not we regard Berkeley's argument as convincing, it seems clear that the doctrine of a substantive mind not only affords a basis for the belief in immortality but gives a very simple interpretation of the phenomenon of death. According to this point of view, death is simply a separation of mind and body. The body disintegrates; the mind or soul goes to its eternal reward. In other words, death is simply a name for the fact that the temporary union between body and mind has been dissolved. If we do not accept the belief in a substantive mind, it is less simple and easy to believe in immortality.

It is not supposed, of course, that this argument demonstrates the existence of a substantive mind. It does not count as an argument at all, except on the basis of a previous assumption that immortality is a fact. If the belief in immortality is denied, then this argument disappears altogether. If we grant, however, that the belief in immortality has an antecedent presumption in its favor, then it would appear that we have another reason for the belief in the existence of a substantive mind.

Perhaps this whole question of mind and matter has the appearance of being just another of those academic problems which the average intelligent person who is not a specialist in this field can afford to leave to persons who, for some inscrutable reason, enjoy worrying about such matters. Philosophical and psychological opinions,

[7] G. Berkeley, *Principles of Human Knowledge,* Sec. 141.

however, have a way of " cashing in " eventually by of-
fering themselves as guides to belief and practice, and
particularly so in the field of education. If we accept the
theory of mind presented in the foregoing discussion, it
soon appears that we have given hostages to the future.
We find ourselves committed to certain educational aims
and ideals that are of far-reaching significance.

To be more specific, this theory of mind gives an answer to the question as to the nature of learning. All
learning is a process of developing or training the mind,
and it can be nothing else. We learn to see objects as
objects by applying concepts like substance and causation to them; we develop our powers of imagination,
memory, will and thought, by exercising them. In other
words, education is a process of inner development.
When all is said and done, there is precious little, educationally speaking, that the individual gets from the mechanistic environment in which he lives. The concepts
with which he operates in scientific investigation, the
moral standards which he applies to conduct, the notions
of art by which he discriminates between the beautiful
and the ugly, are all derived from his own bosom. Even
the sense qualities which we perceive are not merely
picked up out of the environment, as we pick apples out
of a basket, but are created by the mind in response
to incoming stimulations. Education, therefore, should
be made a process of self-development or self-cultivation. As over against crude utilitarianism or intellectual and spiritual regimentation, it emphasizes what has
been called " the dignity and worth of the individual."
Self-development or self-realization, in some form or
other, becomes the only defensible goal of education.
This conception of education has loomed large in the

past and it still has a powerful appeal. The attempts to apply this conception to educational practices furnish interesting material for determining whether the doctrine of mind-substance is an adequate basis for an acceptable system of education.

## Bibliography

BERKELEY, G., *Principles of Human Knowledge*, Sections 1–9, 135–144. Open Court Publishing Co.
DESCARTES, R., *Meditations*. Meditation II. Open Court Publishing Co.
HAVEN, JOSEPH, *Mental Philosophy*, Part IV, Chaps. I, II.
HILL, O. A., *Psychology and Natural Theology*. Macmillan Co.
LOCKE, J., *Essay on the Human Understanding*, Book II, Chaps. XII, XXIII; Book IV, Chap. IX. Open Court Publishing Co.
MOORE, J. S., *The Foundations of Psychology*, Chap. V. Princeton University Press.
NORLIE, O. M., *An Elementary Christian Psychology*, Chaps. I, II. Augsburg Publishing Co.
PATRICK, G. T. W., *Introduction to Philosophy*, Chap. XVI. Houghton Mifflin Co.
WICKERSHAM, J. P., *Methods of Instruction*, pp. 44–45. Lippincott.

# CHAPTER IV

# Education as "Development from Within"

IN OUR discussion up to this point the emphasis has been on the irreconcilable difference between mind and matter. Apart from mind the world is just a vast machine operating blindly and heedlessly according to mechanical laws. When mind appears on the scene, an entirely new set of phenomena enters into the picture. The mind chooses and rejects, loves and hates, admires and despises, remembers and forgets, makes guesses and blunders — in short, it does things of which there is in the material world not a trace.

> The world rolls round forever like a mill
> It grinds out death, and life, and good and ill;
> It has no purpose, heart, or mind, or will.
>
> Man might know one thing were his sight less dim,
> That it whirls not to suit his petty whim,
> That it is quite indifferent to him.[1]

Mind is capable of creating a world of values because it has an original nature of its own. It is endowed with an innate capacity for beauty, goodness, and truth. Hence education is, indeed, a process of inner development. But this still leaves the problem how this capacity

[1] James Thomson, *The City of Dreadful Night*, Sec. VIII.

is to be developed properly; and this is a problem about which there is a difference of opinion. It is a real problem, because innate capacity may be developed in a right way or in a wrong way.

To illustrate, every normal human being has the capacity of making esthetic discriminations. This capacity, however, may be so developed as to result in atrocious taste. Thus squaws are said to have a lively appreciation of gaudy colors and to take delight in combinations that jar the sensibilities of better educated people. Development must be guided by the right standards or patterns. " I once knew a church in a small town which worshipped in a plain rectangular old building with colonial windows. When a rival denomination erected a monstrous building with a huge circular stained-glass window facing the street, the group which worshipped in the old structure became dissatisfied. After much difficulty in securing the money, a committee was sent to a near-by city and purchased a quantity of gaudily-colored translucent paper similar to that one used occasionally to see on the front door of a saloon. This paper the congregation proudly pasted on its colonial window panes." [2] The problem confronting the educator in this connection is the problem of distinguishing between good and bad esthetic patterns.

The same type of problem occurs in other fields. The fact that a person is developing a keener sense of discrimination between right and wrong is no guarantee that his discriminations are of the right kind. He may honestly believe, for example, that a man should be relentless and unforgiving towards his enemies, or that lying and stealing are permissible and even admirable, as

[2] E. D. Martin, *The Meaning of a Liberal Education*, p. 148.

long as one gets away with it. Standards of this kind are not unknown to the historian. Such standards undoubtedly involve development through practice, since babies are not born with them. On what basis is the educator to draw the distinction between good and bad patterns of conduct?

To add one more illustration, people may go completely wrong with respect to matters of truth and falsehood. Thus one of the earliest of the Greek philosophers, Thales, is remembered chiefly for his doctrine that everything in the universe consists of water. He achieved fame by this doctrine, not because it is true, but because he had the insight to postulate identities back of the endless diversities of experience. In other words, he had trained his powers of observation and reasoning. This is likewise true of persons who figure out that human destiny is influenced by the stars, or by witches, or by black cats and unlucky numbers. Every process of reasoning involves a certain development. It would hardly do in education, however, to say that the direction of the development does not matter. There must be correct patterns or standards for proper development with respect to beauty, goodness, and truth.

How are such patterns or standards to be obtained? The problem is full of difficulty. Standards of some kind are, indeed, present and operative in every form of group life, no matter how low it may be in the scale of culture. Every social group distinguishes in some way between the beautiful and the ugly, between the good and the bad, between the true and the false. How the standards are secured is perhaps not easily shown, but they do come and they tend to take on sanctity or authority with the passage of time. The trouble is, of course, that different groups hold widely divergent views as to what is beautiful, or good, or true, which indicates that we cannot be content simply to let nature take its course. It may be added that these standards, however they may be obtained, become the basis on which each group builds its way of life. They are socially approved, and they are transmitted to young people through a process of education, which may consist wholly in direct participation in the life of the community or may be supplemented by schools.

As long as there is no serious question with respect to the authority of these standards, education becomes identified with the process of transmitting a way of life; or, as it is sometimes put, education is concerned with conserving the values of the past. The trouble with this conception of education is that, even if a way of life seems satisfactory or adequate at one time, it may not continue to be so at a later time. Our notions of what constitutes the true, the good, and the beautiful do not remain constant. The Greeks, for example, accounted for the movement of the sun in the heavens by the myth that Apollo transported the sun from east to west in his chariot; and they saw nothing seriously wrong with the institution of slavery. We hold different views at the present time. There must be some other way of arriving at standards for the true, the good, and the beautiful than simply borrowing them from the past.

The inadequacy of such borrowing was precisely what provided Rousseau with a theme and the impetus for social and educational reform. The old way of life had become, in the hands of stupid conservatism and selfish interests, an instrumentality for exploiting and degrading great masses of people, who are described by a French writer as " wild animals, male and female, scattered over the fields, black, livid, all burnt by the sun, bound to the earth that they dig and work with unconquerable pertinacity; they have a sort of articulate voice, and when they rise on their feet, they show a human face, and, in fact, are men." [3] This maiming or mutilation of human nature is a natural outcome of the tendency to regard the customs and institutions of a particular period as a final and immutable pattern or standard.

What is to be done about it? To this question Rousseau provided an answer that was both simple and tremendously influential in education. The whole trouble, so he maintained, could be traced to the fact that we try to derive our standards for truth, goodness, and beauty from the social order, instead of deriving them directly from the individual. Wrong development results from the insistence that individuals must grow up in accordance with standards set by the social order and not in accordance with standards set by the nature of the individual himself. Since man is created in the image of God, there is no necessity for the imposition of standards from without. Such imposition means that children are victimized by the prejudices and superstitions and the greed of others. In contrast with all this Rousseau advocated a system of education based on the proposition that sound development is a process of unfolding from within, instead of imposition from without. Patterns or standards for development were asserted to inhere in the nature of the individual. Pupils, therefore, were to learn in accordance with the promptings of their own interests and desires, without coercion or prescription. This was

[3] Quoted by P. Monroe, *A Text-book in the History of Education*, pp. 547–575.

called education according to nature. Follow nature and the capacities of the individual for truth, goodness, and beauty will automatically come to full fruition.

The effects of this doctrine on Rousseau's own day and age were momentous, and the reverberations of his impact on social and educational doctrine extend down to the present day. It is generally recognized, however, that Rousseau's solution of our difficulties was too simple, and so we need not examine it in detail. From the standpoint of modern psychology the trouble with Rousseau's point of view lies in the doctrine that minds are provided with fixed inner patterns which will direct development if they are permitted to do so. There is a vast difference between saying that man has capacity for beauty, goodness, and truth, and saying that the development of this capacity is directed from within, as the process of hatching an egg is directed by the nature of the egg. This latter view is equivalent to saying that every random impulse has a divine origin and so has the right of way. In practice this leads to the kind of thing exemplified by some of the heroes of the romantic movement in literature. Consequently many writers have taken pains to warn us against " enthusiasts " and reformers, who are usually people that let some one idea run away with them. Sound development requires constant restraint, regulation, direction, which must be supplied by the individual himself, as a matter of conscious effort and through the exercise of intelligence. We can permit an egg to hatch in its own way, because this is not an educational process. To transform an egg into a chick is very different from transforming a small boy into a well-developed or well-educated person. For this latter process nature provides no pattern. Man is equipped with reason or intelligence for the very purpose of enabling him to take charge of his own destiny.

Even if all this be granted, however, we have not disposed of Rousseau's contention that sound development must be directed from within.  If mind and matter are so completely opposed to each other, then the material environment obviously can serve only as a stimulus for evoking the potentialities of the individual; it cannot set standards.  Now it appears that the social environment is not a suitable source for standards either, which means development must be directed from within.  So far Rousseau appears to be in the right.  His mistake lay in the assumption that the removal of social pressures would automatically ensure right development.  To repeat the point made just above, however, there is another alternative.  Direction may be provided from within, not by yielding to the behests of every chance impulse, but by following a principle which the individual himself formulates and lays down for the guidance of his conduct.

This is the position taken by the great rival of Rousseauism, which is sometimes referred to as the classical tradition in education.  In order to arrive at this guiding principle, the first step is to take an inventory of the capacities or powers that inhere in the individual.  For practical purposes it is perhaps sufficient to say with Matthew Arnold that when we " set ourselves to enumerate the powers which go to the building up of human life," these may be listed as " the power of conduct, the power of intellect and knowledge, the power of beauty, and the power of social life and manners." [4]

This inventory gives us the raw material, so to speak, which education must take into account.  Provision must

[4] Matthew Arnold, *Literature and Science*.

be made for the development of all these powers. More-over, these various powers must be developed in relation to one another. Moral zeal, for example, must be tempered by intelligence to prevent it from developing into fanaticism. Conversely, intelligence must draw on the moral sense to keep it from growing into the purblindness either of the mere pedant or of the person who, for all his learning, finds it possible to be " terribly at ease in Zion." Moreover, both intellect and the moral sense must be infused with the spirit of beauty and of " social life and manners " in order to avoid the harshness and crudeness so frequently exhibited by otherwise admirable characters.

Here, then, we seem to find the guiding principle that we need. In Arnold's language, " perfection," i.e., ideal development, " is a harmonious expansion of *all* the powers which make the beauty and worth of human nature and is not consistent with the over-development of any one power at the expense of the rest." [5] What constitutes harmonious development must obviously be decided in the light of circumstances as they arise. What restraint must be placed on impulses so as to provide room for the exercise of intelligence or for the infusion of " beauty and sweetness," which are " essential characters of a complete human perfection," cannot be decided in advance. This is a matter for which the individual must assume responsibility. He must meet each situation with due regard for the requirements of harmonious development, which is to say that the final test lies within the individual himself. The principle to be followed is an inner principle. Self-perfection is the final standard. Socrates is quoted approvingly as saying:

[5] Matthew Arnold, *Sweetness and Light.*

" The best man is he who most tries to perfect himself, and the happiest man is he who most feels that he *is* perfecting himself." [6]

Does such an ideal appear to be too self-centered or individualistic? If so, let it be borne in mind that

Because men are all members of one great whole, and because the sympathy which is in human nature will not allow one member to be indifferent to the rest or to have a perfect welfare independent of the rest, the expansion of our humanity to suit the idea of perfection which culture forms, must be a *general* expansion. Perfection, as culture conceives it, is not possible while the individual remains isolated. The individual is required, under pain of being stunted and enfeebled in his own development if he disobeys, to carry others along with him in his march towards perfection, to be continually doing all he can to enlarge and increase the volume of the human stream sweeping thitherward.[7]

General education, then, as distinguished from vocational or technical education, is, first of all, a matter of self-cultivation. In Arnold's words, culture is a " study of perfection." But since no man liveth unto himself, perfection is both individual and social; the individual is required to " carry others along with him in his march towards perfection." Secondly, culture requires a constant struggle with raw impulse or spontaneous desire. Harmonious development can be achieved only through arduous effort and stern self-discipline, Rousseau to the contrary notwithstanding. Man's most distinctive possession is this power to regulate himself. This power has been called by later writers the " inner check " or " the will to refrain " or " the law of measure." It is man's

[6] Matthew Arnold, *Hebraism and Hellenism.*
[7] Matthew Arnold, *Sweetness and Light.*

distinguishing characteristic in that it lifts him indisputably above the level of ordinary cause and effect by which everything else in nature is determined.  Lastly, the cultured person controls his own destiny; he is both the author and the interpreter of the standards by which his judgments and his conduct are determined.  His favorite precepts are: " Decency, moderation, measure, common sense, the normal and representative, the centralized, discipline, standards, humility, self-control, vital restraint, proportionateness, decorum, stability.  His thoughts circulate around these words: they constitute the magnetic portion of his vocabulary." [8]

This general point of view, besides being called the classical tradition, is also sometimes designated as humanism, a name which has been revived of late years in this country.  We are told that " the word humanist was applied, first in the Italy of the fifteenth century, and later in other European countries, to the type of scholar who was not only proficient in Greek and Latin, but who at the same time inclined to prefer the humanity of the great classical writers to what seemed to him the excess of divinity in the mediaevals."  The earlier writers who deserve to be called humanists " actually caught a glimpse of the fine proportionateness of the ancients at their best.  They were thus encouraged to aim at a harmonious development of their faculties in this world rather than at an other-worldly felicity.  Each faculty, they held, should be cultivated in due measure without one-sidedness or over-emphasis, whether that of the ascetic or that of the specialist.  ' Nothing too much ' is indeed the cen-

[8] G. Munson, *The Dilemma of the Liberated*, p. 271.  Cf. also Chap. III.  See also E. D. Martin, *The Meaning of a Liberal Education*, Chap. VII.

tral maxim of all genuine humanists, ancient and modern." [9]

Whether it be called classicism or humanism, we can
readily understand why this ideal of culture leans heavily
on the past.   In the first place, there was a long period
during which the personalities and writings which best
exemplified this ideal were contributed almost exclusively by Greece and Rome.   Consequently Socrates,
Plato, Aristotle, Virgil, Horace, and others were constantly pointed to as models, not for slavish imitation, but
for inspiration.   Secondly, these earlier examples of this
ideal have probably never been surpassed.   Time was,
therefore, when a knowledge of Greek and Latin was indispensable for a liberal education, and this is perhaps still
the case.   It may be remarked, however, that this fact is
no excuse for the crude mistake of assuming that a knowledge of Greek and Latin automatically imparts this type
of culture.   Nor is it intelligent to assume that the ancients had a monopoly of this culture.   True representatives of its spirit may appear in any age.   Later periods,
for example, have produced personages like Erasmus and
Montaigne and Matthew Arnold.   Genuine culture is
sensitive to the fact that modern civilization has produced
literary masterpieces of its own.   There are modern as
well as ancient classics, although the greater number of
classics appear to have been produced in the remote past.

Natural science too has a place in classical education,
since culture requires us " to know the best that has been
thought and said."   In itself, however, science is necessarily of subordinate importance, since it deals with inanimate nature and not with the life of the spirit.   Hence,

[9] Irving Babbitt in " Humanism: An Essay at Definition," from
*Humanism and America,* p. 26.   Edited by Norman Foerster.

while the classics of literature, and particularly the ancient classics, do not constitute the whole content of liberal or general education, they constitute the heart of it. As one writer puts it, " science deals with facts that have no human quality, that came raw from the great whirl of the cosmic machine. As a discipline, then, for the ordinary man, the study of science tends not a whit towards refinement, toward temperamental regeneration; it tends only to develop an accurate trick of the senses, fine observation, crude intellectual strength. . . . Literature nourishes the whole spirit of man; science ministers only to the intellect." [10]

This, then, is in rough outline the classical tradition in education. It starts with the assumption of a sharp contrast between mind and matter.. On the basis of this contrast it is useless to look anywhere for standards of excellence except in the mind itself, which means, ultimately, the mind of the individual person. The kingdom of heaven is *within* us. To this proposition the irreconcilable opposition between mind and matter gives a special and impressive meaning. Man must look inward into his own bosom, and not outward to the realm of dead matter, for clues to conduct. In the words of Emerson, which our modern representatives of the classical tradition are fond of quoting:

> There are two laws discrete
> Not reconciled, —
> Law for man and law for thing;
> The last builds town and fleet,
> But it runs wild,
> And doth the man unking.

[10] L. E. Gates, *Selections from Matthew Arnold*, Introduction.

Education as self-cultivation according to the pattern of the classical tradition has long dominated our institutions of higher learning and is still a potent ideal. Its outlines, however, are frequently blurred, because of the inroads made by the demands of practical life into the life of our colleges. All kinds of subjects have forced their way into the curriculum, and in so doing they have diluted the ideal of harmonious development. We have tended to identify education with any and all development, instead of limiting it to the ideal of *self*-perfection or *self*-development. Students innocently think that they are getting a liberal or cultural education when they are merely learning how to run a machine, how to make slides for a microscope, how to plot statistical curves, or how to track down historical sources in a library.

The students are confused because the colleges themselves are confused. They have lost their sensitiveness to the living ideal embodied in the classical tradition. All too often the literary expressions of this ideal are used as material for mechanical manipulation and memorization, on the assumption that this provides a kind of " discipline " which automatically imparts the spirit of culture. The modern college with its impressive wealth of offerings is in the position of being all dressed up and no place to go. It has neither remained loyal to the ideal of classicism nor provided an adequate concept of liberal education to take its place.

It is not surprising that this same confusion should be reflected in our secondary and elementary schools. One might reasonably have expected that the " progressive " movement in education, with its emphasis on growth and development, would contribute to greater clarity of thinking, but its effect has been to muddy the waters still more. The issue, with respect to the doctrine of growth and development, seems fairly clear. In the first instance, at any rate, it calls for a choice between Rousseau and classicism. This issue has never been met squarely. There has been a lot of chatter about inner motivation and creative activity and about the " dignity and worth of the individual " but the movement has consistently refused either to ally itself openly with Rousseau or to advocate the rigid self-discipline of classicism, or else to present a distinctive program of its own. In most cases it seems unable to get its mind off the individual pupil long enough to reflect on what it is that it is trying to do. These comments are in no sense intended to disparage the real contributions of the progressive movement towards the improvement of the conditions of learning in our schools. With reference to the question of controlling ideals, however, it has scarcely achieved sufficient intellectual respectability to be classed as a movement at all.

The need of reorientation in education is both great and urgent. From the standpoint of the dualism between mind and matter, we seem to be committed to the conclusion that a choice must be made between Rousseauism and classicism. If neither alternative is acceptable, there is no escape from the necessity of re-examining and revising the dualism out of which these alternatives have grown, as a preliminary step towards the reformulation of our educational aims and ideals.

### Bibliography

ARNOLD, M., *Essays: Sweetness and Light, Literature and Science, Hebraism and Hellenism.*
BABBITT, I., *Humanism and America*, Chap. II. Edited by Norman Foerster. Farrar and Rinehart.

MARTIN, E. D., *The Meaning of a Liberal Education*, Chaps. VII, XI, XII. W. W. Norton and Co.

MUNSON, G., *The Dilemma of the Liberated*, Chaps. III, VI. Coward-McCann.

ROUSSEAU, J. J., *Émile.* For a summary sketch see MONROE, P., *A Text-book in the History of Education*, Chap. X. Macmillan Co.

# CHAPTER V

# The Aristocratic Origin of the Classical Tradition

A COMPARISON of Rousseau with the classical tradition shows that the two have in common a fundamental thesis, viz., that the appropriate concern of education is with the full development of the individual and not with conformity to an external standard. The " inside " and the " outside " were placed in sharp opposition to each other. Since Rousseau believed that this full development would take care of itself if it got a reasonable chance, he proposed to secure " freedom " for the pupil by withdrawing him from social pressures. The classical tradition, on the other hand, rejected this idea of freedom. It insisted that freedom cannot be bestowed on the pupil, but that it must be acquired by his own efforts. Freedom is not to be identified with absence of external restraint but with the exercise of internal restraint, applied by the individual himself, in accordance with the requirements of his own harmonious development. Through this internal restraint the individual becomes a free spirit even in the midst of public clamor or the hurly-burly of the market place. He becomes free because freedom means " emancipation from herd opinion, self-mastery, capacity for self-criticism, suspended judgment, and urbanity." [1]

It requires no great power of imagination to see the

[1] E. D. Martin, *op. cit.*, Preface.

significance of such a point of view for progress. Primitive societies stress conformity to the social patterns that
happen to prevail, and they are intolerant of deviations.
The same may be said of our modern dictatorships. By
contrast, this theory stresses the right of the individual to
inner self-determination. It is jealous of any invasions of
this right, and it places all the emphasis on the worthy
exercise of freedom. The standard for right conduct is
to be found inside the individual and not outside him.
In thus defending the individual against the tyranny of
" herd opinion," classicism keeps open the door for spiritual progress and has frequently taken pride in identifying itself with liberalism. The final obligation of the individual is to himself and to himself alone. He has social
obligations only in so far as these are bound up with this
obligation to his ideal of self-perfection. Social obligation is, in a sense, a by-product. It must be recognized
indeed, but solely for the reason that " the individual is
required, under pain of being stunted and enfeebled in
his own development if he disobeys, to carry others along
with him in his march towards perfection."

Up to this point, then, the issue between Rousseau and
classicism is not whether the guiding principle for conduct and for education is to be derived from the individual, but is rather a question concerning the nature of the
principle that is thus derived. The classicists are doubtless justified in rejecting the doctrine of Rousseau. This,
however, is not the same as saying that the principle of
harmonious development is our only alternative. There
is always the possibility that the basic assumption of dualism is wrong. There is room for serious doubt as to the
principle of harmonious development.

To be specific, let us assume that a man is the head of

a large family and is able only by dint of unremitting struggle to provide his dependents with the bare necessities of life. If he were to take seriously the admonition to regulate his conduct by the principle of his own harmonious development — what then? It is not denied, of course, that he must continue to be sensitive to the needs of his family. This sensitiveness is required by the obligation to develop his " power of conduct." The other powers, however, have an equal claim. There would appear to be an equally solemn obligation to divert some of the money that he earns towards subscriptions to a high-grade magazine or two, towards tickets for the opera, towards social entertainment, and perhaps towards buying a dress suit. No " power," it must be remembered, may be developed at the expense of the rest.

It seems reasonably clear that the requirements of harmonious development cannot be determined by the simple process of looking into one's own bosom in order to see whether the various powers are properly balanced or harmonized. No one can tell, by such a process of self-inspection, whether he should have contributed more or less to the city relief fund; whether he should have been more or less courteous to the passing stranger; whether his taste in dress is too sombre or too flamboyant; or whether he should devote more or less of his leisure time to crossword puzzles or to problems in higher mathematics. There is no mental gadget inside us to indicate whether we are moving towards a greater harmony of development or away from it. The real test is not something inside the individual in any such crude sense. The standards of conduct are derived from a social ideal in relation to the circumstances in which we are placed.

What is this social ideal which is tacitly assumed by

classicism as a standard? A clue is provided if we take a look at the life of the ancient Greeks, who are supposed to provide such excellent examples of harmonious development. Even a casual inspection of this life shows that no mysterious principle of harmonious development is required to explain it. Greek society was founded on the institution of slavery. The consequence of this was that the aristocrats of that day were automatically debarred from participation in gainful pursuits. As in all other forms of aristocracy, manual work and trade were regarded as degrading and as fit only for slaves and for the baser elements in the community. Since there was a lack of science and machinery at that time, this view of work may have had a certain justification. It is likely that Millet's picture of " The Man with the Hoe " and Edwin Markham's poem on the same theme have a special significance in reference to that earlier period. At any rate, work, in the ordinary sense of the term, was believed to disfigure both the body and the mind. Plato's view of the matter is reported by Arnold as follows:

The base mechanic arts and handicrafts, says Plato, bring about a natural weakness in the principle of excellence in a man, so that he cannot govern the ignoble growths in him, but nurses them, and cannot understand fostering any other. Those who exercise such arts and trades, as they have their bodies, he says, marred by their vulgar businesses, so they have their souls, too, bowed and broken by them. And if one of these uncomely people has a mind to seek self-culture and philosophy, Plato compares him to a bald little tinker, who has scraped together money, and has got his release from service, and has had a bath, and bought a new coat, and is rigged out like a bridegroom about to marry the daughter of his master who has fallen into poor and helpless estate.[2]

[2] *Literature and Science.*

It would be unjust to dismiss Plato's scorn for practical occupations as snobbery. He was honestly convinced that these occupations were incompatible with living a good life. For Plato a good life did not consist in self-indulgence or the pursuit of pleasure, but in self-cultivation. The controlling purpose of the true aristocrat was to raise himself to the highest possible level of perfection. His business in life was not with trades or handicrafts, but with himself. Intellectual and artistic interests, social graces and manners, must be cultivated in order that he might become "a gentleman and a scholar," a splendid specimen of human nature, a living work of art.

By contrast with a leisure class devoted to mean pleasures and excitements, Plato's ideal has much to commend it. Whether such preoccupation with one's personal development is the last word, however, is a different matter. To put it unkindly, the "gentleman" is always aware of being on a pedestal. He must never fail to be conscious of himself as a superior person; he must never be caught off balance; he must insist on maintaining his poise under all circumstances. Emotions, passions, and excitements are always a threat to poise and so must be guarded against in all matters, great or small. "It must be admitted," as a distinguished classicist says, "that even a true religious enthusiasm is hard to combine with poise." [3] As someone else once remarked, a gentleman hastens, but he is never in a hurry. No matter what the circumstances, the man of poise maintains an attitude of cool, detached, critical appraisal; which gives point to the comment attributed to R. L. Stevenson, when informed of Matthew Arnold's death: "Well, he won't like God."

[3] Irving Babbitt in "Humanism: An Essay at Definition," from *Humanism and America*, p. 42. Edited by Norman Foerster.

Time has, indeed, brought certain changes since the days of the ancient Greeks. The position of the aristocrat in the general scheme of things is different from what it was then. Plato's attitude towards trade and handicraft and the professions, which Arnold calls " fantastic," is out of tune with the spirit of our own times. It would require some hardihood to claim that practical affairs, as conducted under modern conditions, lead necessarily and inevitably to spiritual and physical ruination. This change in conditions, however, has slight bearing on the matter under discussion. The question remains whether a person should be concerned chiefly with his own personal self-development or with something else. On this point the position of the classicists is unmistakable. Irving Babbitt, a leading spokesman of present-day classicism, maintains the historic contrast between culture and vocation when he assures us that a good life requires a type of education that has " the idea of leisure enshrined at its very center." [4] E. D. Martin is of the opinion that " a leisure class is a social necessity, for it serves as an example to other people, showing them how to enjoy their idle hours. The English aristocracy with its horse races and other outdoor sports has done much to make life interesting in that otherwise factory-ridden country." [5]  Matthew Arnold, as previously noted, agrees with Socrates that " the best man is he who most tries to perfect himself, and the happiest man is he who most feels that he *is* perfecting himself." [6]

Self-perfection or harmonious development is supposed to be achieved by acting in accordance with an inner principle, but is in fact derived from the principle of aristocracy, and it traces back to the model set by the

---

[4] *Ibid.*, p. 51.                    [6] *Hebraism and Hellenism.*
[5] E. D. Martin, *op. cit.*, p. 79.

Greeks. Taken by itself, " harmonious development " is an empty phrase. It acquires content only in terms of the contrast between the life of the aristocrat and the life of the common man. This contrast finds expression, first of all, in the contrast between the devotion of the aristocrat to self-perfection and the absorption of the common man in other ends. It is for the purpose of maintaining this distinction that Aristotle regards it as unbecoming for a gentleman to achieve as high a degree of proficiency with musical instruments as that of the paid public entertainer. To rival the expert in this respect is to set an ideal other than that of being a gentleman. By refusing to compete with the expert he shows that he *is* a gentleman. For the gentleman the principle which Babbitt calls the " law of measure " is the final criterion. Courage, for example, is the mean between rashness and timidity; generosity is the mean between extravagance and parsimony; politeness is the mean between rudeness and servility. But the only practical way of determining the mean in any given situation is by the test which distinguishes the gentleman from the man of common clay.

It is not surprising, therefore, to find that the present-day classicist is generally a gentleman with a predilection for the study of letters and a keen consciousness of his superiority to the " masses " or the " pack " or the " herd." The classicist is the old-time aristocrat doing his turn on a twentieth-century stage. The claim that his conduct is dictated by a hypothetical principle of " harmonious development " or " law of measure " is sheer self-deception. The classical tradition presupposes the social ideal or standard of aristocracy by which harmonious development is measured and then makes the preposterous claim that harmonious development dictates the ideal.

While the changes in general conditions have not succeeded in weaning the classicist from the individualistic
ideal of self-cultivation, they have succeeded in throwing
into relief a different and competing ideal. This ideal rejects the assumption that a good life must necessarily be
divorced from the affairs of a sweating, struggling humanity. In Plato's view, as previously noted, the base
mechanic arts and handicrafts "bring about a natural
weakness in the principle of excellence in man"; the
body is marred and the soul is "bowed and broken by
them." This view precludes in advance the possibility of
setting up an ideal of a social order in which every member may have the opportunity to achieve a "more abundant life" by sharing progressively and according to capacity in common interests and purposes. The modern
world, however, has become more sympathetic to the
notion that the world of practical affairs can be made
over into a means of grace; in other words, that practical
affairs can be so organized as to promote relationships of
co-operation based on mutual recognition of interests,
and thus provide for continuous growth in the spiritual
stature of those who are engaged in them. Genuine culture, in this case, becomes part and parcel of everyday
practical living and not something apart from it. An
ideal of this kind, called by contrast the democratic ideal,
is, of course, sheer nonsense if we start with the assumption that practical affairs are of such a nature that body
and soul are marred and broken by them.

The classicist of our own day is prepared to make concessions to the spirit of democracy to the extent of admitting that culture, as he understands it, should not be made
a special privilege for any limited social group. The
ideal of culture, however, remains pretty much the same.

It is still the ideal of individualistic self-cultivation and it maintains its traditional association with the idea of leisure. The chief difference is that now everyone is to be encouraged to play at being an aristocrat when he is off the job. In his youth the common man should have free access to culture in connection with his schooling; and as an adult he should have opportunity to cultivate literature and music and poetry and art during those hours when his attention is not taken up by his butter-and-egg business.

Democracy, from this standpoint, is not a different ideal, but means a chance for everybody to cultivate the classical ideal. The scenery of the stage has been shifted, but the backdrop remains the same. The contrast is no longer between the aristocrat and the serf, but has become a contrast between " culture " and practical affairs within the life of each individual. Those unfortunates who are lacking in capacity to learn from books are out of luck. About all that our system of education can hope to achieve, on any level, is to cull out from the masses those who are potential aristocrats. " Adult education is selective. Its aim is . . . to select out of the undifferentiated mass those who are capable of becoming something more than automatons. . . . Such persons are different from the common lot. It is not that they may possess some secret information which the others may not have. They have a different *goal*." [7]

In general, the classicist manages to make peace with the concept of democracy because he treats it as a form of political organization and not as a competing way of life. In a political sense democracy is good or bad in proportion as it favors the classical view of a good life. De-

---

[7] E. D. Martin, *op. cit.*, pp. 317, 318.

mocracy is good when it gives the individual a large measure of self-government; it is bad when it fails to do so. " If the people or their representatives should vote to establish a censorship of books, or to prohibit smoking tobacco, or to compel church attendance on Sunday, that would be democracy; but it would not be a gain for freedom." [8] It would still be democracy if it did these things; which is to say that democracy is not a social ideal but a name for majority rule.

The classical ideal requires leisure or a certain degree of emancipation from the necessity of engaging in gainful pursuits; and so it is not surprising that the classicist tends to be conservative with respect to property rights and labor movements. The following quotation is indicative of this attitude:

As a result of the concentrated mental effort of the gifted few, an effort displayed either in invention or else in organization and management, the common laborer may today enjoy comforts that were out of the reach even of the opulent only two or three generations ago. If the laborer wishes to add to these comforts or even to keep them, he should not listen to the agitator who seeks to stir up his envy of every form of superiority. He should be the first to recognize that exceptional capacity should receive exceptional rewards.[9]

Still more outspoken is another representative of classicism who takes the position that " to the civilized man *the rights of property are more important than the right to life.*" Social justice is, for him, " such a distribution of power and privilege, and of property as the symbol and instrument of these, as at once will satisfy the distinctions of reason among the superior, and will not outrage

[8] *Ibid.*, p. 143.
[9] Irving Babbitt, *Democracy and Leadership*, p. 193.

the feelings of the inferior." It is in this connection that the teacher has an important duty to perform, which is to educate in such a way that people

. . . will accept with equanimity the fatal fact that social justice must include a considerable amount of that disposition of Nature in dealing with her own which we, judging by the standard of the individual soul, are so ready to call injustice. The first step towards the equipoise of a soul just within itself is to recognize the necessity of a measure of injustice in the relation of man with man and with the world. We must learn from the god of realities how " ill is our anger with things, since it concerns them not at all." [10]

It must be admitted, of course, that the aristocratic origin of the classical ideal does not, in itself, dispose of its claim to validity. It may be admitted, further, that this ideal has various admirable traits. Whether the ideal is acceptable must be determined on other grounds than that of origin or of " harmonious development." The classicist has still a further reason, as we shall presently see, for his claim that self-cultivation or self-perfection is both a tenable and a desirable ideal in education.

## Bibliography

ARNOLD, M., *Essay on Philistinism.*
BABBITT, I., *Democracy and Leadership*, Chap. VI. Houghton Mifflin Co.
MARTIN, E. D., *The Meaning of a Liberal Education*, Chap. VIII. W. W. Norton and Co.
MORE, P. E., *Aristocracy and Justice*, Chaps. on " Justice " and " Property and Law." Houghton Mifflin Co.
MUNSON, G., *The Dilemma of the Liberated*, Chap. X. Coward-McCann.

[10] P. E. More, *Aristocracy and Justice*, chapters on " Justice " and " Property and Law." ' In fairness it should be added that not all classicists are so smugly conservative. Cf. G. Munson, *op. cit.*, Chap. X.

CHAPTER VI

# A Critical Examination of the Classical Tradition

In the preceding chapter it was argued that the ideal of harmonious development, or self-cultivation, is not, in fact, an inner principle at all, but a social pattern borrowed from an aristocratic tradition and masquerading under a false name. Neither Rousseauism nor classicism has succeeded in deriving an ideal of conduct wholly from " within the individual." But a social pattern needs some justification besides the fact that certain people happen to like it. Why be a classicist at all?

It is obvious that holding the world of practical affairs in contempt is not the same thing as prizing the ideal of self-perfection. Perhaps the game is not worth the candle. There is always another alternative. Why not live for the moment and grasp what pleasures we may, in accordance with the sentiment: Enjoy life while you live, for you will be a long time dead. As Omar Khayyám has it:

> A Book of Verses underneath the Bough,
> A Jug of Wine, a Loaf of Bread — and thou
> Beside me singing in the Wilderness —
> Ah, Wilderness were Paradise enow!

There are two ways of meeting a challenge of this kind. One is to become abusive, and to say with Martin that " educational opportunities are for people who are worth educating," the test of worth-whileness being whether a person has a desire to become a classicist. A classical type of education, according to the same authority, enables us to " select out of the undifferentiated mass those who are naturally capable of becoming something more than automatons " — which means, presumably, that anyone who questions classical education demonstrates thereby that he is still an automaton. The other way is to take the challenge seriously. If the ideal represents something more than an individual preference, such as a liking for spinach, it must be because it is more in accordance with the nature of things.

This latter view is essentially the position taken by Aristotle, who argued that, since reason is what distinguishes man from the brutes, the cultivation of reason necessarily constitutes his highest happiness. The pleasures of sense and the passions man shares with the lower animals. The domain of reason, however, is all his own. It is in this domain that man is man, and not just another animal. Here, then, is where man fulfils his nature as man, which is to say that here is where his true happiness lies. In the language of Newman:

> If, then, the intellect is so excellent a portion of us, and its cultivation so excellent, it is not only beautiful, perfect, admirable, and noble in itself, but in a true and high sense it must be useful to the possessor and to all around him; not useful in any low, mechanical, mercantile sense, but as diffusing good, or as a blessing, or a gift, or power, or a treasure, first to the owner, then through him to the world.[1]

An affirmation of this kind carries with it the implication that the classical ideal is vastly more than the perpetuation of an aristocratic tradition, or that it takes its

[1] Quoted by R. M. Hutchins, *The Higher Learning in America*, p. 63.

content simply from the requirements of a social class. If the latter were the case, then the whole philosophy of conduct would consist in conformity to social convention. Man's distinctive possession — which is referred to by various writers as intellect, reason, or will — is "so excellent a portion of us," so it is argued, precisely because it can rise above the accidents of time and place, by which social convention is created, and set a standard for conduct which is independent of convention. This distinctive possession is something which on occasion

We may agree to call a conscience, since it is independent of social conditioning, and this something, this conscience, sometimes says no in emphatic command. Who is there who, on sincere self-examination, does not find there are a few things he knows with absolute certitude he could never do? No power on earth, no conceivable circumstances, he declares to himself, would make me do thus-and-so. And yet why not do them? There may be no consequences that inspire fear, there may even be strong incentives to take the detested course of action. But something internal says Veto so powerfully that there is no possibility of committing the action. *The action would seem like a betrayal of the species one belongs to* . . . the inner check works in the interests of some essential humanity in us. It seeks to counteract that fluidity of our nature whereby men become beasts or go mad. It warns us when we are about to desert our adult human standards and retrogress to the puerile or infantile or subhuman.[2]

From the standpoint of the writer just quoted, the question whether the classical ideal traces back to an aristocratic tradition may be dismissed as irrelevant. Whatever its historical origin, the ideal stands on its own

[2] G. Munson, *op. cit.,* p. 147. Italics in the original.

feet. There are things one would do under "no conceivable circumstances"; to do them would seem like a "betrayal of the species one belongs to"; there is "some essential humanity" that interposes, regardless of what custom or social convention may say. This "essential humanity" operates in independence of historic or social accident and the person who is rightly attuned to the essential humanity obeys it because it is so "beautiful, perfect, admirable, and noble in itself."

This is a large claim. As it stands, it amounts to the assertion that one part of us is better than another, but with no evidence to support the claim than that it seems so to the observer. Exalting the classical ideal by glorifying our "essential humanity" merely shows that the classicist is the kind of person who likes that kind of thing. A liberal use of eulogistic adjectives does not prove that the classicist is wiser than Omar, with his preference for a book of verses and a jug of wine. To meet this objection, the classical ideal must be shown to be more in accordance with the nature of things; and being thus in accordance means more than merely giving preference to one part of our nature rather than to another. The accordance must be with reality as it extends beyond the limits of the individual self.

Which reality is that? On this point it is obviously useless to consult science, which, according to the accepted tradition, is limited to the multitudinous shufflings and reshufflings of material atoms. Science, so conceived, can tell us nothing about spiritual values. It recognizes only one test, which is the test of survival; and by that test Omar Khayyám is likely to make as good a showing as the classicist. In fact Omar may come out ahead. At any rate, T. H. Huxley, the famous evolutionist, more than hints that moral and spiritual values do not fit into the scheme of evolution any too well, that morality is a handicap in the struggle for existence.[3] Matthew Arnold appears to lean toward the same view:

> Man must begin, know this, where nature ends;
> Nature and man can never be fast friends.
> Fool, if thou canst not pass her, rest her slave! [4]

In the main the classicists seem to be in substantial accord with the view that their ideal signifies a better adjustment between the individual and the "reality of things." However much they may stress the ideal of self-perfection or harmonious development, there is generally this assumption in the background. Here again the Greeks led the way. For Plato the ideal of self-cultivation was very far from being simply a desirable social pattern. In his philosophy human concepts were supposed to be partial reflections or adumbrations of eternal existences, which were called *Ideas*, presumably to indicate their peculiar character as nonmaterial, nonpersonal realities. Truth, goodness, and beauty were regarded as *real*, in the sense of having nontemporal and nonspacial existence, which is about what is meant by transcendentalism.

This breath-taking flight of fancy has won for Plato a permanent place in the history of thought. An aristocrat to the end, he refused to entertain the idea that our values might have their source in the possibilities for the progressive improvement of our common life. Such a lowly, mundane source would never do. So he took the only alternative, which was to enter a claim that the con-

[3] T. H. Huxley, *Evolution and Ethics.*

[4] M. Arnold, in the poem "In Harmony with Nature." Cf. also his poem "Morality."

ception of a good life which he favored was "beautiful, perfect, admirable, and noble," not in any "low, mechanical, mercantile sense," but in the sense that a life lived after his pattern is a continuous striving to reflect, or reproduce, or copy reality as it really is. The claim that there is "some essential humanity" in us, which speaks with authority when there are decisions to be made, may be taken to mean that there is higher, overarching reality that speaks within us. In religious language, this essential humanity within us is sustained by the Everlasting Arms.

Taken as a system of thought, Plato's philosophy is at present chiefly of historical interest. His device of placing our human concepts in the skies as eternal *Ideas* is too simple an interpretation of reality to suit our more sophisticated age. The general notion, however, that the classical ideal, in some way or other, is fashioned in the image of reality, is still popular with the classicists. Thus, Irving Babbitt, after insisting that "humanism is not to be identified with this or that body of traditional precepts," goes on to say that "the law of measure on which it [humanism] depends becomes meaningless unless it can be shown to be one of the 'laws unwritten in the heavens,' of which Antigone had the immediate perception, laws that are not of today or yesterday; that transcend in short the temporal process. The final appeal of the humanist is not to any historical convention but to intuition." [5] More recently Dr. R. M. Hutchins quotes approvingly a writer who assures us that "the good, the true, and the beautiful are something real and ascertainable," and that "these eternal ideals re-embody

[5] In "Humanism: An Essay at Definition," from *Humanism and America*, p. 27. Edited by Norman Foerster.

themselves from age to age essentially the same in the imaginative visions of supreme genius and in the persistent rationality and sanity of the world's best books." [6]

These best books are " books which have through the centuries attained to the dimensions of classics. Many such books, I am afraid, are in the ancient and medieval period. But even these are contemporary. A classic is a book that is contemporary in every age. That is why it is a classic. The conversations of Socrates raise questions that are as urgent today as they were when Plato wrote. In fact they are more so, because the society in which Plato lived did not need to have them raised as much as we do. We have forgotten how important they are." [7]

By this time we have come a long way from the idea that self-perfection can be achieved by following a purely internal principle such as harmonious development. The latter principle, taken by itself, is unworkable; the question now is whether this doctrine of reality can be made intelligible. What does it mean to say that the good, the true, and the beautiful are eternal; that they are " real " and ascertainable?

Believers in revelation make short work of this question. They hold that the good, the true, and the beautiful are gathered up in an infinite personality called God, and that this infinite personality reveals itself to man in some specified way, which is to say that the road to self-perfection lies in surrender to the divine will. The classicist may share the faith in the existence of such a personality, but he cannot make revelation the basis for his philosophy of conduct without ceasing to be a classicist.

[6] R. M. Hutchins, *The Higher Learning in America*, p. 65.
[7] *Ibid.*, p. 78.

Revelation stresses conformity and obedience, whereas classicism relies on personal insight. The principle of harmonious development, for example, does not rest on revelation, but is an insight which the individual must achieve for himself on the basis of self-knowledge. When the classicist undertakes to supplement this principle by having recourse to a transcendental reality, he continues to rely on individual insight. He makes his obeisance to our "essential humanity" because it is so "beautiful, perfect, admirable, and noble in itself"; and he would not for a moment admit that he considers our essential humanity to embody such overpowering excellence simply because someone told him so. He knows of a certainty and from his own insight that our essential humanity ties up with the "law unwritten in the heavens" and is on this account entitled to his unswerving allegiance.

This shift from harmonious development to the comprehension or knowledge of a transcendental reality has its repercussions on the conception of learning. How does this kind of learning take place? Babbitt appeals to "intuition," which is essentially another name for mysticism. The mystic claims that his knowledge is totally different from ordinary knowledge. This alleged knowledge is completely independent of either sense perception or reasoning. It is an immediate envisaging or grasping of truth, which means that there is no room for either doubt or argument. If you possess this intuition you are one of the elect; if you do not, there is nothing that can be done about it. The aristocrat of culture carries his credentials in his own bosom; he requires no further assurance and he can afford to ignore all critics who do not possess his kind of knowledge and so do not speak his language.

Most classicists, however, decline to rest their case on intuition or mysticism, presumably because the history of mysticism is anything but reassuring. Intuition can be invoked to prove almost anything. Like Babbitt they hold to the doctrine that the good, the true, and the beautiful are eternal and real and ascertainable, but they grant that we must rely on ordinary knowing or learning to show that the doctrine is true. Unfortunately no one has ever succeeded in making the doctrine intelligible, let alone succeeded in proving it, despite all the labor expended on transcendental philosophies throughout the centuries. In terms of strategy, Babbitt's expedient of appealing to intuition has much to commend it. If we make an appeal of this kind, we do not need to explain what we mean and no one can prove that we are wrong.

While the doctrine itself is hard to understand, there is no great difficulty in understanding why the classicists take kindly to it. They do so because they have to. Let us remind ourselves again that the approach to classicism is provided by the dualism of mind and matter. Since the natural sciences deal only with the nature and the operations of matter, we know in advance that they can tell us nothing about spiritual values. These must be looked for in the domain of mind. The mind can create values, because it can operate in relative independence of the body. According to one of these writers, our will can operate without assistance from anything outside of itself. "Will must occur in the absence of incentive. Will would persist in working in a given direction *after* the motive had ceased. Will is that which overcomes indifference." [8]

It may be remarked in passing that this *sounds* like a good definition of obstinacy or plain contrariness. The

[8] G. Munson, *op. cit.*, p. 277.

point is, of course, that *if* matter and mind are such complete opposites, then it becomes vitally necessary to protect the thesis that the mind can act independently. Moreover, if we grant that some reality outside the mind is necessary in order to make these spiritual values mean something more than the chance whim of the individual, it follows that this external reality cannot be the world of dead matter, which is indifferent to all values. We have no choice, therefore, but to postulate a beautiful isle of somewhere, in some other world, in order to provide a home for the good, the true, and the beautiful, where they can abide as real and eternal existences. We must assume all this, even if it means that we speak a language which no man can understand.

Being obliged to have recourse to a transcendental reality is a stiff price to pay, and unfortunately we do not get our money's worth. The irony of the situation is that this transcendental reality refuses to help us out, even after we have sacrificed intelligibility in order to secure its cooperation. We may say, if we like, that " the good, the true, and the beautiful are something real and ascertainable " and that " these eternal ideals re-embody themselves from age to age essentially the same in the imaginative visions of supreme genius and in the persistent rationality and sanity of the world's best books." But what have we gained by saying this? Does it mean that we need only read these best books in order to learn about these eternal ideals? It is not quite as simple as that. The " imaginative visions of supreme genius " may have encompassed these transcendental realities, but we can scarcely deny that their vision was sometimes askew. Plato, for example, believed in a certain " nationalizing " of women; and Aristotle saw no objection to the enslavement of persons of inferior intellectual endowment. How are we to decide what is real and eternal and what is unreal and mortal error? These eternal truths, unfortunately, bear no labels by which we can pick them out. Having brought the gods down from the clouds with so much trouble, we now find that they refuse to reveal their identities.

We have, as yet, no official authority that decides which books are to be canonized as classics. The longer the list, however, the more evident the contradictions in their teachings are bound to become. If we include in the list such documents, for example, as the Bible and the writings of Jean Jacques Rousseau, there is some difficulty in reconciling these with the Greek classics; just as the theology of Milton does not harmonize any too well with that of Emerson or Matthew Arnold. The eternal ideals which are alleged to " re-embody themselves from age to age essentially the same " are so much mixed up with other things that there appears to be no way of sorting them out unless we institute some authoritative Supreme Council to do the job, in somewhat the same fashion as is done by the revelationist.

It is not surprising, therefore, to find that the classicists disagree extensively among themselves, both as to the content of these eternal ideals and as to the channels through which these ideals become known to us. With respect to content, some are conservative in religious beliefs, while others are the reverse; some are conservative, not to say reactionary, in economic and political matters, while others lean towards liberalism; some stress the importance of the eternal ideals, while others are apparently indifferent and even mildly sceptical. With respect to the mode of knowing these ideals, some rely on intuition while others stress reason and will. The moral is that people who are tempted to betake themselves to classicism as an escape from the confusions of the present are simply swapping one set of troubles for another.

The source of the difficulty is not hard to locate. The classical tradition has no common creed or doctrine, however much it may talk about eternal ideals. What it has as a common element is admiration for the Greek type of aristocracy, with its emphasis on poise, refinement of taste and manners, personal dignity, and the like. Back of the proposal to rely chiefly on the classics as a source of standards and as material for instruction lies this preference for the Greek ideal as over against the democratic ideal, which replaces both the individualism of aristocracy and the eternal ideals with the ideal of self-fulfilment through participation in a common life. Greek civilization undoubtedly produced an admirable product of its kind. Moreover, its inherent individualism — as expressed, for example, in its indifference to practical affairs — is supported by the age-long habits engendered by the practices of a stratified social order and by the suggestion contained in the soul-substance theory that self-cultivation is the appropriate aim of life. Classicism naturally does not like to admit that it is the posthumous child of a defunct aristocracy, and it is learning to become distrustful of self-cultivation in terms of harmonious development. Consequently it has recourse, whenever necessary, to a world beyond space and time.

If the eternal ideals are to serve any purpose at all, they must be construed in terms of content, i.e., they must furnish the standards or principles which are the distinctive marks of classicism. But this is precisely the difficulty. If we assume, nevertheless, that there are such eternal ideals, how are they arrived at? To say, with Babbitt, that we get at them through " intuition " is to say that we know them in a way that is different from ordinary knowing; it is a way that neither requires nor permits of argument or proof. In other words, we appeal to mysticism. Mysticism, however, has demonstrated its inadequacy all too often in the history of thought. More recently Hutchins has suggested another approach which has the merit of simplicity. Apparently picking out the eternal ideals is much the same kind of thing as picking precious stones out of a heap of pebbles. All that it requires is a trained eye. According to Hutchins, the training that is needed is training in reading. Let a student learn to *read* and all will be well. If a person cannot pick out the right things from the classics, it is because he has not learned to " read." The ability to read can be increased by an intelligent study of grammar, rhetoric, and logic. If we add mathematics, we may consider ourselves pretty well equipped, since mathematics develops the power of reasoning.[9] Here the appeal is not to intuition, since it does not appear that intuition needs to be attuned to eternal truth by a study of grammar, rhetoric, logic, and mathematics. Presumably the appeal is to something called " Reason." At any rate, if there is any trouble about the interpretation of the classics, the trouble lies in the fact that we have not learned to read. The truth is right there on the printed page, if we but have eyes to see. It is all very simple.

How far does this explanation take us if applied to a book like the Bible, which presumably is entitled to rate as a classic? The divergencies in interpretation here are a source of endless wonder to anyone who is interested

---

[9] R. M. Hutchins, *op. cit.*, pp. 82-85.

in such things. Doubtless this can be explained in part by the fact that so many cannot " read." No one has ever been able to show, however, even in this age of statistics, that there is any significant correlation between unanimity of interpretation and proficiency in grammar, rhetoric, and logic, not to mention mathematics. The meaning that the Bible, or any other good book, may have for us is not just a matter of separating the true from the false through the application of grammar, rhetoric, and logic, as a scientist in his laboratory may determine the composition of an object by the use of reagents. The " truth " contained for us in a good book has to do with the help it affords in making our experiences more meaningful; it is not something waiting to be picked up. In other words, truth relates to the organization of experience and is tested by the adequacy of this organization. The person who would profit richly by the experience of others must, indeed, have recourse to reading, but to say that education is simply a process of learning to read is about as helpful as to say that violin-playing is merely a matter of scraping horsehair on catgut.

The implication involved in this emphasis on " reading " has already been indicated, viz., that there are certain basic and eternal truths or principles in the classics which can be discovered if we only know how to look, i.e., to read. We may grant that the great writers of the past said many things which are as applicable now as they were then. The fact, however, that they were shrewd observers and interpreters of their surroundings hardly warrants the inference that they must have had a special pipe-line to a transcendental reality beyond the world of our experience. For the Greeks something of this kind was, indeed, a necessity. Being so largely shut off from practical affairs, they were compelled, in a sense, to postulate a transcendental world as a means of validating their values, and to stress the cultivation of the intellect, both because it means self-perfection and because it gives access to this transcendental world.

We moderns are under no such compulsion. We have open to us the alternative of turning to a genuinely democratic way of life, which seeks to realize itself in the world of practical affairs and which does not need to lean on a transcendental reality. If we insist nevertheless on making the classics the heart of the educational program, it is because we have decided the issue in advance. We then emphasize reading, because our concern is to have the students absorb the classical point of view, instead of giving them a reasonable opportunity to make their own choice. The emphasis on the cultivation of the intellect becomes camouflage to conceal the fact that the basic " frame of reference " for the guidance of thought and conduct is decided for the students, without leaving them a voice in the matter. If we admit that the students are entitled to make an independent decision, the restriction of the curriculum becomes indefensible. In other words, classicism is a program of indoctrination.

In brief, the classical tradition is a child that has repudiated its own parent. As an ideal for a gentleman in an aristocratic society it has a reasonably definite meaning. When taken out of this context, it needs some other validation. If harmonious development is not adequate, recourse is had to the cosmic structure of things, which is supposed to underwrite the ideal. As long as it is not clearly seen that this manoeuvre is ineffective, it becomes possible to perpetuate the aristocratic tradition and yet deny that aristocracy has anything to do with it. It is no accident that the classicists are generally fond of pointing to Socrates and Erasmus, but fail to show a similar enthusiasm for such historic figures as Jesus of Nazareth and Abraham Lincoln.

In the end the whole trouble traces back to the assumption of the dualism of mind and matter. On the basis of this assumption the problem of a good life becomes insoluble. Starting with this assumption we find it impossible to justify or protect " spiritual " values, even if we bring in a transcendental reality to prop them up. The case of dualism looks still worse when it appears that the concept of matter is likewise unable to stand on its own feet. At the outset this concept seemed clear and simple. Matter was supposed to consist of indivisible particles, each of these particles having just a few attributes or qualities, such as shape, size, solidity, and mobility. These atoms were supposed to operate on the principle of push and pull; and the task which the scientist set himself was to explain the whole range of material reality in terms of these atoms. As he proceeded, however, the explanation became more and more complicated. He found it necessary to introduce an unmanageable ether, to dissolve the atom, to flirt with an abstraction called energy, and even to question the whole idea of causation. The nature of matter, which seemed so simple and clear at the outset, became shrouded in mystery. In the language of a recent writer who is both a scientist and a classicist, we are led into a mass of " unbridled hypotheses ":

We have created fictitious ethers, atoms, and electrons which bear no resemblance to sensible bodies; light is alternately a stream of corpuscles, or waves, or quanta of energy, or even a mathematical symbol; space is declared to be impenetrable except along certain curves; and time is confused with space . . . [Our scientists] have pictured a phantasmagoria, instead of a world, as nonsensical as the hallucinations of the medieval monk driven mad by the fevers of asceticism.[10]

If recent developments in the physical sciences mean anything at all, they mean that the concept of mechanism has been found to be inadequate. If this is the case, it seems to follow that we should try to make a different start by revising the concepts of both matter and mind, since these two concepts were developed in relation to each other. Revising the concept of mind, however, would entail a revision of the whole superstructure of classicism. Hence a different course is recommended. It is argued that " the mechanistic method can, at best, only picture an objective world as it seems to us, not as it is." [11] In other words, science must know its place. It must not pretend to know the nature of matter at all. As another writer assures us, science is merely " knowledge of phenomenal relationships " and is " totally unconcerned with substances and causes." [12]

In the light of historical development this is a curious conclusion. We start with the assumption that the nature of matter is simple and quite comprehensible; and it is on the basis of this assumption that we develop the concept of mind. This latter concept is so framed as to take care of those experiential facts which cannot be accounted for in terms of matter. Then, when we find that this does not work out, we decide to retain this concept of mind anyhow, because we have made this concept the basis for a set of values to which we have become at-

[10] L. T. More, in " The Pretensions of Science," from *Humanism and America*, pp. 15, 16. Edited by Norman Foerster.
[11] L. T. More, *ibid.*, p. 23.
[12] Mortimer Adler, *The Social Frontier* (Feb., 1939), p. 142.

tached. When classicism insists that science must limit itself to " knowledge of phenomenal relationships " and be " totally unconcerned with substances and causes," it is sawing off the limb that it is sitting on.

Time was when people were quite unaware that air had weight; and so, in order to explain certain phenomena, they introduced the principle that " nature abhors a vacuum." Fortunately, this principle did not become entangled with their sentiments and loyalties, which made it easy to surrender this principle when further discoveries cast a doubt on the assumption that air has no weight. If, however, the principle of " abhorrence " that was threatened by these discoveries had perchance been a cherished spiritual value, there would doubtless have been a struggle. Making a new start by revising our concept of air would then have been resisted, since the principle of abhorrence depends on the assumption that air has no weight. A way out would be to tell science to mind its own business; said business being to report on " phenomenal relationships " and keep its hands off substances and causes altogether.

To sum up, the classical tradition traces back to an aristocratic origin. It sets for itself the aim of self-perfection. At times the test for self-perfection appears to be an inner principle of harmonious development. At other times there is a frank appeal to transcendental reality in order to validate the ideal. In neither case is it made clear how the content of the ideal is derived. The divergencies among the classicists themselves indicate that the content is bootlegged in from other sources, particularly from the literary and aristocratic pattern set by the Renaissance.[13] Finally, instead of admitting that

13 G. Munson, *op. cit.*, Chap. 10.

there may be something wrong with the dualistic premise, they tend to take a superior attitude towards science
and say to it, in effect, that it had better leave matters
pertaining to spiritual values and ultimate truth to persons who are competent to deal with such things.

Throughout this discussion there have been occasional
references to the powers or capacities or faculties of the
mind. Classicism, as contrasted with Rousseauism, emphasizes discipline. The powers of the mind must undergo systematic development or cultivation. This is
true whether we stress the need of harmonious development or the need of grasping eternal truth. In brief,
classicism tends to insist, both that our capacities or faculties must be cultivated and that they must be cultivated according to a certain pattern. "An intellect
properly disciplined, an intellect properly habituated, is
an intellect able to operate well in all fields." [14]

This general attitude led in the course of time to the
doctrine of Formal Discipline, which will next require
our attention. This doctrine, in its simplest form, neg-
lects the problem of patterns altogether and insists that
" self-development " or self-perfection can be secured
by the simple process of " exercising " the powers or faculties of the mind. Our powers or capacities grow
through effort; what is important is not primarily the nature or quality of the educational material, but the work
that we put in on it. This theory of learning, which is
known as formal discipline, once held a dominating position in our schools, and is still influential in educational
procedures.

[14] R. M. Hutchins, *op. cit.*, p. 63.

## Bibliography

FOERSTER, N., *The American State University*, Chap. VII. University of North Carolina Press.

GIDEONSE, H. G., *The Higher Learning in a Democracy*. Farrar and Rinehart.

HUTCHINS, R. M., *The Higher Learning in America*, Chaps. III, IV. Yale University Press.

HUXLEY, T. H., *Evolution and Ethics* (Romanes Lecture). Appleton.

MORE, L. T., *Humanism and America*, Chap. I. Edited by N. Foerster. Farrar and Rinehart.

MUNSON, G., *The Dilemma of the Liberated*, Chap. VII. Coward-McCann.

# CHAPTER VII

# The Doctrine of Formal Discipline

ACCORDING to the classical tradition a good education must meet a twofold requirement. It requires both the development of the "powers" or "faculties" of the mind and initiation into a certain cultural pattern. This process of initiation is at the same time a process through which the powers of the mind are disciplined or strengthened. It would, therefore, be more accurate to say that the classical tradition aims at the development of capacity, not in any wholesale fashion, but in a specific way. It seeks that particular kind of development which results from the process of becoming initiated into the pattern of classicism.

Even so, however, the predominant emphasis of the classical tradition has always been on self-development. The appeal to truth, goodness, and beauty as eternal existences in a realm beyond the skies was in the nature of emergency legislation, whenever the inner principle of harmonious development proved to be inadequate. The whole idea of patterns being somewhat nebulous, it is not surprising that the schools gave major emphasis to the idea of developing the powers or capacities of the mind, without much reference to patterns.

What are these powers or capacities? As an initial proposition we may say that all learning represents some activity on the part of the mind. But this is only a point of departure. When we inquire into the nature of this activity, we find that it varies according to circumstances. The activity of the mind expresses itself through the use of the sense organs and through the exercise of memory, imagination, and reflective thinking; which is to say that the mind can operate in a variety of ways, or that it has a number of distinct powers or functions. These powers are known as faculties, such as the faculty of observation, of memory, of volition, and the like.

This doctrine of faculties has achieved a conspicuous place in the history of human thought. The type of psychology which is based on the belief in the existence of such faculties has become known as faculty psychology. The time was when this was the prevailing psychology. According to this point of view,

Mental activity is, strictly speaking, one and indivisible. The mind is not a complex substance, composed of parts, but single and one. Its activity may, however, be exercised in various ways, and upon widely different classes of objects; and as these modes of action vary, we may assign them different names, and treat of them in distinction from each other. So distinguished and named, they present themselves to us as so many distinct powers or faculties of the mind. But when this is done, and we make out, for purposes of science, our complete list and classification of these powers, we are not to forget that it is, after all, one and the same indivisible spiritual principle that is putting forth its activity under these diverse forms, one and the same force exerting itself — whether as thinking, feeling, or acting — whether as remembering, imagining, judging, perceiving, reasoning, loving, fearing, hating, desiring, choosing. And while we may designate these as so many faculties of the mind, we are not to conceive of them as so many constituent parts of a complex whole, which, taken together, compose this mysterious entity called the mind, as the different limbs and organs of the physical frame compose the structure called the body. Such is not the nature of the mind, nor of its faculties.[1]

With this conception of the nature of the mind and of its faculties as a starting point, how are we to proceed in the business of education? The answer is simple. Education is effective in proportion as these faculties are trained to function properly. The pupil must learn to observe and remember, to use his power of imagination and of critical, reflective thinking. In other words, all education must be centered on the training of the faculties. There is just one way in which this can be done.

No means are known whereby the faculties of the mind can be developed but by exercising them. By the potent spell of the magic word Exercise, is evoked all human power.

The proof of this proposition is found in multitudes of facts. The senses grow more acute by using them. The memory is improved by remembering, the reason by reasoning, the imagination by imagining. All these powers, too, become weak if not used. These facts may be learned from each person's own experience, or from observation upon others. The law inferred from them is fixed and universal.[2]

People frequently say that children are sent to school in order that they may " learn something." The schools do, in fact, spend much time in imparting information. Moreover, the examinations which are given from time to time are usually tests of information. But if this present point of view is correct, this emphasis on information is misplaced. The important thing in education is not information but the strengthening of the faculties, so that

[1] J. Haven, *Mental Philosophy*, p. 29.
[2] J. P. Wickersham, *Methods of Instruction*, p. 38.

they can meet new situations more effectively than before.

The view that information is of secondary importance in education has considerable plausibility. It is true that a certain fund of information is necessary for the conduct of the affairs of life. But people do not differ in efficiency in strict proportion to their knowledge of facts. Some people, as James says, have an unusual *desultory* memory; they "retain names, dates and addresses, anecdotes, gossip, poetry, quotations, and all sorts of miscellaneous facts, without an effort." It sometimes happens that imbeciles have an extraordinary memory of this kind. "The mere organic retentiveness of a man," as James says, "need bear no definite relation to his other mental powers." As evidence he quotes from the report of another psychologist regarding the case of a young man whose general mentality was so poor that he "had with difficulty been taught to read and speak." But in spite of this mental inferiority, "if two or three minutes were allowed him to peruse an octavo page, he could then spell the single words out from his memory as well as if the book lay open before him. . . . That there was no deception I could test by means of a new Latin law-dissertation which had just come into my hands, which he never could have seen and of which both subject and language were unknown to him. He read off [mentally] many lines . . . [and] remembered his pages a long time." [3]

It appears, then, that learning in the sense of sheer memorizing is not necessarily equivalent to securing a worth-while education. This conclusion is strengthened if we remind ourselves that the bulk of what we

[3] W. James, *Principles of Psychology*, Vol. I, p. 660, note.

learn in school is forgotten within a relatively short time. If retentiveness were our sole test for the value of education, we should be obliged to conclude that a great deal of educational effort is a dead loss.  On the other hand, if we believe in a substantive mind and in faculty psychology, it is possible to justify education, in spite of the fact that so much of what is learned is soon forgotten. Learning may serve an important purpose even if it is forgotten afterwards.  The primary value of knowledge, from the point of view of education, is that it constitutes the material and evidence of exercise or training.  Even though the particular items of fact fade from memory, they leave behind an effect which is permanent, and which is more valuable than a mere knowledge of facts. There is at least an element of truth in the saying that education is what you have left after you have forgotten all that you have learned.

What we call " education " is something different from the sum total of information that we are able to muster at any given moment.  Perhaps an illustration will help to make this clear.  People who go in for athletics have certain things happen to them.  In various ways their physical structure and functions are permanently altered.  There is a permanent change, for example, in their respiratory system, in their circulatory system, in the development of their muscles, in the coordination between eye and hand, etc.  They are never quite the same as they were before.  This change is significant for two reasons.  In the first place, it is easier for them to regain some of their old skill in the sport in which they were originally trained, and secondly, they find it easier to cultivate skills in new forms of sport.  They have acquired a permanent aptitude for athletic performances in general; or at any rate they find themselves more proficient in certain other forms of sport in which they were never trained at all.

This analogy, according to the doctrine of a substantive mind, is applicable to the training of the mind as well as to the training of the body. The things that we learn in school constitute, first of all, material for the exercise of the mind. When pupils are required to memorize, to reason, to exercise the imagination, to cultivate observation, to obey instructions and the like, this training leaves a permanent effect on the mind just as physical training leaves a permanent effect on the body. It is quite true that we may forget very rapidly the particular things that we have learned. There is, however, an effect of such training that abides. And immediately there comes to mind the half-forgotten truth that the value of forgotten knowledge is very great.

It is true, of course, that the mind has no muscles or lungs which take into themselves the effects of the training, but it has an equivalent for these muscles in its faculties. The mind, like the body, acts in a variety of ways. We label these various kinds of activities with such names as perceiving, thinking, willing, remembering, imagining, etc. Each of these names designates a distinctive power or faculty of the mind. That is, the mind has a variety of faculties just as the body has a variety of muscles. These different powers can be trained in relative independence of one another, as in the case of the muscles of the body.

By physical exercise the organs of the bodily frame are invigorated and developed, and by no other conceivable means. By the exercise of its several faculties, likewise, does the mind reach its power to use them. No faculty can interchange with any other in this matter, though it sometimes seems to be thought so. The faculty of language is developed by speaking; of observation by observing; of imagination by imagining; and of reason by reasoning; if we exercise but one, we shall educate but one; if we overexercise one, the excess does not blow over to the benefit of another. We may develop the observation and the imagination, while we leave the judgment weak; whilst no labor which we bestow on the exercise of the reason will ever teach the pupil how to observe.[4]

Perhaps this is an overstatement of the case. If the analogy of the body can be trusted, we are not entitled to say that the faculties operate in complete independence of one another. It has been found, for example, that if the muscles of the right arm are developed by exercise, the muscles of the left arm undergo some development as a result of the exercise, even though the exercise itself is confined to the right arm. Similarly it is quite possible, since the faculties all pertain to the same mind, that the exercise of a given faculty may have some influence on other faculties. The advocates of formal discipline are not in agreement among themselves on this point. As one of them points out, " Since the mind is a unit and the faculties are simply phases or manifestations of its activity, whatever strengthens one faculty indirectly strengthens all the others." [5]

This question of the relation of the faculties to one another, however, need not disturb the main bearing of the argument. If we wish to develop a faculty, the proper procedure is to exercise it directly. Such exercise makes a lasting difference in the faculty concerned. The things

[4] James Currie, *Common School Education*, p. 6.
[5] R. N. Roark, *Methods in Education*, p. 27, quoted by E. L. Thorndike, *Educational Psychology* (Briefer Course), p. 269.

learned may indeed be forgotten, just as a football player may be unable after a time to execute a particular play in which he has been trained, but the effect of the training is built into the texture of the faculties so as to make them permanently different.

According to this theory, the chief benefit of training lies in the development of power and not in the training of specific abilities. Moreover, this development of power can be secured with a variety of materials. A muscle can be developed in various ways, and so can a faculty. It does not matter so much what we exercise our faculties on; the important thing is to exercise them. In fact it would not matter at all, except that some material serves the purpose of training better than others, just as some physical exercises develop the muscles more efficiently than others. Moreover, it is a fact that we do remember some things, even if the amount of what we remember is disappointingly small. Consequently, it is better to memorize useful facts than to exercise the memory on nonsense syllables. The choice of material, therefore, is not a matter of absolute indifference, but it seems fair to say that the choice of material is of secondary importance.

This doctrine has become known as the doctrine of formal discipline. The meaning of the doctrine is indicated by the name. In the first place, the important thing in education is discipline or training. Secondly, the value of this training does not reside in the *content* of what is studied, but in the *form* — that is, in the fact that the faculties are being exercised. Given proper exercise, the faculties are developed or strengthened so that they can meet other situations more efficiently. A person who has exercised his memory on nonsense syllables

will have a better memory for dealing with business affairs, a better memory for names and faces, a better
memory for anything that calls for remembering.

This doctrine, then, gives an explanation of how education prepares for life outside the school.  Formal discipline is frequently identified with transfer of training.
In the interests of clearness, however, it is worth while
to point out that transfer may be explained in more than
one way.  From the standpoint of formal discipline
transfer of training means that training in a subject like
Latin will help in some other quite unrelated field, such
as physics or banking.  The transfer is achieved, not
through the application to the new subject matter of anything that is learned in Latin, but through the increase
in power that has been gained.  It is antecedently possible, however, to account for transfer of training in a different way.  The study of a given subject may make for
greater efficiency in some other field through the adaptation of content or method and not through increase in
the powers of the faculties.  There appears to be no sufficient reason why this should not be called transfer of
training too.  In fact, a number of writers announce that
they believe in transfer of training, although they reject
the theory of formal discipline.  According to this standpoint, transfer of training means the application of previous experience to new situations.  It does not mean
formal discipline, since formal discipline is simply one
particular explanation of how transfer takes place.  It
seems more expedient at the present time to make this distinction.  If we do so, the rejection of formal discipline
simply opens the way for other theories to account for
transfer of training.

The doctrine of formal discipline has an obvious bearing on the construction of curricula. If the choice of subject matter is relatively unimportant, then there is no sufficient justification for the great variety of subjects and differentiation of courses which characterize modern education. In fact all this expansion of the curriculum may easily interfere with the ends of education. Pupils remember a smattering of many things but they do not get the discipline or training which is the really important thing in education. Moreover, much of this new material is less well adapted to the purpose of providing training than the older subjects are. Mathematics, for example, is much better adapted for the purpose of training in thinking than subjects like stenography and typewriting or community civics. Education could be carried on more economically and more effectively by making the course of study consist of relatively few but well-organized subjects. We should have a more effective curriculum if we selected subjects with reference primarily to their value for the development of the various faculties.

An approach from this angle to the problem of the construction of curricula would provide a subject like mathematics for training in reasoning, a subject like literature for training in appreciation, courses in some one of the sciences for training in observation, etc. A curriculum so organized would be relatively small in content and would be adapted to the needs of all pupils, in spite of the fact that it offered little or no opportunity for election. It does not follow at all that the things in which pupils are interested are things which they ought to study. The doctrine of interest has led us astray. Education has been made both expensive and futile because we do not appreciate properly the need of training the faculties and have gone wandering off after false gods.

It might have been expected, perhaps, that when formal discipline became an accepted belief it would have the effect of weakening the influence of the classical curriculum. If the important thing in education is the exercise of the faculties, there would seem to be no particular occasion for limiting the selection of subject matter to the old curriculum. But tradition is stronger than logic. The classical tradition survived despite logic and despite the fact that all too often it had lost its soul. The classics maintained a central position in the curriculum, not because they exemplified an attitude or outlook on life that was touched by a true nobility of spirit, but because they were supposed to furnish the best possible material for the training of the mind. Presumably the schoolmasters of that day were unwilling to change their ways and so they rationalized what they were doing. Thus formal discipline, strangely enough, became an ally of classical education. This arrangement had the incidental advantage that the teacher could mechanize the business of teaching without qualms of conscience. "The student's attention was centered upon the niceties of construction and upon the task of memorizing rules of grammar and a vocabulary, all stuffed into his head in the most artificial manner conceivable." [6] This was considered to be good training for his mind, and was identified with culture; and so the great purpose or end of education was being fulfilled.

In proportion as the idea of culture became dissociated from the spirit of the classical tradition, a vague notion developed that culture was something which inhered in the classical studies, as contrasted with other studies, and which was automatically imbibed by the student. The classics were made a vehicle for whatever ideas the

[6] E. D. Martin, *op. cit.*, p. 253.

teacher chose to inculcate. The ideal of the "free spirit" tended to be supplanted by that of the "Christian gentleman," by which was meant a person who was far too much of a gentleman to even think of being a nonconformist.

In its actual result, therefore, the doctrine of formal discipline became an instrumentality for perpetuating traditional beliefs and attitudes. For a long time the sciences and the social changes growing out of them found no recognition in the curriculum, and educational values were predominantly of a literary sort. The business of education, apart from teaching the utilities, as represented by the three R's, was to mold pupils to a standard pattern.

In justice to formal discipline, however, it must be emphasized that its case does not necessarily stand and fall with that of the classics. Perhaps the alliance was a mistake. In any case, the doctrine warrants the inferences that a comparatively simple curriculum will serve all the essential purposes of education, and that, with regard to method of teaching, there is justification for giving scant attention to individual differences, since all minds are fundamentally alike. The faculty of reasoning or memory, for example, is absolutely the same in everybody. A faculty may differ considerably in strength in different individuals, but the essential nature of the faculty is the same everywhere. Consequently, the same treatment applies to all. The teacher must indeed gauge the difficulty of the work to the capacity of the student, but this is about all that he needs to know concerning educational method.

Modern education emphasizes the doctrine of interest. From the point of view of formal discipline interest is a matter of secondary importance. It may be granted indeed that interest is a desirable thing. A pupil who takes an interest in his study works more steadily and efficiently, but interest is far from being an indispensable condition. A boy may acquire excellent physical development through a regime of training, whether he happens to like the training or not. If a boy is compelled to do hard work, his muscles and other bodily organs are undergoing development, regardless of how he feels about the work. Similarly a boy who takes a course in mental development will have his faculties strengthened whether the work interests him or not. Moreover, distaste for the work has the advantage of strengthening the will. Hence the important thing is to see that the work is done. The big stick may be a very effective substitute for interest.

To put it differently, formal discipline simplifies the business of education with respect to both curriculum and method. Having determined which faculties are to be developed, we can easily select appropriate subject matter in each case and thus dispose of the whole problem of curriculum-making. Mathematics, for example, is excellent material for the development of reasoning; certain kinds of literature are serviceable for cultivating the imagination; names and dates in history or case-endings and conjugations train memory; while almost any kind of distasteful task will help to strengthen the will. With respect to method, little is needed except a certain amount of horse sense in fitting the material to the intellectual level of the pupil, together with adequate firmness in making him carry out his assignments.

The inference that training a faculty, such as reasoning, through courses in mathematics will strengthen it in

other areas, such as salesmanship, or politics, or court-
ship, is based on the belief in a substantive mind and the
existence of faculties.  Does this inference tally with the
facts?  As Thorndike states the case,

The problem of how far the particular responses made
day by day by pupils improve their mental powers in general is called the problem of disciplinary value or disciplinary
effect of studies, or more briefly the problem of formal discipline.  How far, for instance, does learning to be accurate
with numbers make one more accurate in keeping his accounts, in weighing, measuring, in telling anecdotes, in judging the character of his friends?  How far does learning to
reason out rather than guess at or learning by heart a problem
in geometry make one more thoughtful and logical in following political arguments, in choosing a religious creed, or
deciding whether it is best for him to get married?  How far
does the habit of obedience to a teacher in school generate
the habit of obedience to parents, laws, and the voice of
conscience? [7]

These are difficult questions, but formal discipline was
so firmly entrenched in our educational theory and practice that a great deal of dissatisfaction had to be engendered before it was openly attacked.  Occasionally a
voice was raised against it, but that was all.  When the
day of reckoning finally came, however, the doctrine of
formal discipline appeared to be in a sad state.  The argument against it may be conveniently arranged under
three heads.  These are: first, the evidence from observation and experiment; second, the argument from the
facts of physiology; and third, the argument from theory.
With regard to the evidence from observation and ex-

[7] E. L. Thorndike, *Principles of Teaching*, p. 235.

periment, it may be said that when a person once begins to entertain doubts about formal discipline, he is not likely to have much trouble in finding facts which give support to these doubts. One form of evidence against formal discipline, for example, may be found in the " sucker lists " which swindling stock promoters are said to use in their business. These " sucker lists," so we are told, are made up of the names of people who are " easy marks " for promoters of worthless stock, because in business matters they have the gullibility of children. It is said that the names of teachers and physicians rank highest on these lists; in other words, a smooth-spoken salesman can sell them anything, from a hole in the ground to a rubber plantation in Timbuctoo. That is to say, teachers and physicians, in spite of their intellectual training, do not have good judgment in buying stocks, which is the direct opposite of what we are led to expect by the theory of formal discipline.

To take another illustration, it is said of a gambler who played with marked cards that the marks by which he recognized particular cards were so faint as to be almost undiscernible to others, even when these marks were pointed out to them. The man had wonderful eyesight and was highly trained in this particular form of observation. Yet it was found that this same man had failed completely to notice that there were several species of sparrows under the eaves of the roof of the house in which he lived. He was a living illustration of the fact that observation in one field does not necessarily transfer to another.

Such examples seem fairly numerous. The sailor whose power of observation has been trained so as to detect signs of weather that are not noticeable to other people is not necessarily able to report minutely on the fashions in the gowns worn by women at a reception. When Napoleon appointed the famous mathematician, La Place, as his minister of finance, he soon found out that intellectual ability in one field does not necessarily guarantee intellectual ability in another field. La Place, we are told, held the position only twelve months; then Napoleon dismissed him with the contemptuous remark that La Place was capable only of solving problems dealing with the infinitely little.

Observations of this sort are suggestive, but they are too random and uncontrolled to be conclusive. Serious experimental work was a long time in getting under way. Among the pioneers was William James, who made experiments in memorizing for the purpose of determining whether exercise has the effect of strengthening memory. One of these experiments is reported as follows:

During eight successive days I learned 158 lines of Victor Hugo's " Satyr." The total number of minutes required for this was 131⅚ — it should be said that I had learned nothing by heart for many years. I then, working for twenty-odd minutes daily, learned the entire first book of " Paradise Lost," occupying 38 days in the process. After this training I went back to Victor Hugo's poem, and found that 158 additional lines (divided exactly as on the former occasion) took me 151½ minutes. In other words, I committed my Victor Hugo to memory before the training at the rate of a line in 50 seconds, after the training at the rate of a line in 57 seconds, just the opposite result from that which the popular view would lead one to expect.[8]

The experiment was not convincing, because James himself tells us that during the second attempt he was

[8] W. James, *Principles of Psychology*, Vol. I, p. 667, note.

suffering from fatigue due to overwork, a fact which, as Colvin says, "invalidates the whole experiment." James's conclusion, however, that our native retentiveness is unchangeable and that improvements in memorizing are due to improvements in methods of memorizing, was significant in that it raised doubts regarding formal discipline and pointed to a different approach to the problem of transfer of training.

The attack on the problem that really started the revolution was made by the investigations of Messrs. Thorndike and Woodworth in 1901. These investigations were more carefully controlled than James's experiment in memorizing, and in their effects they were like a bombshell dropped into the camp of orthodox complacency. It was shown that the old theory of faculty psychology had mistaken names for things. For example, a person may be quick to detect misspelled words; and if we are lazy or blinded by preconceptions we are tempted to explain this trait by saying that such a person has a faculty of "quickness." But such quickness, it was found, did not guarantee quickness in other respects, such as arithmetical processes. It does not follow that because we apply the word "quickness" to both operations, they are therefore the same thing and due to a faculty of quickness. We might as well say that the rattle of a fender in an automobile is identical with every other rattle in the car, and that an old car makes so much noise because by virtue of exercise it has acquired a highly developed faculty of rattling.

It is sufficient for present purposes merely to indicate the results of these early experiments. In these experiments the persons acting as subjects were trained in such operations as judging the areas of paper cards, judging weights, and striking out certain letters, such as *e* and *s*, wherever they were found on a printed page. After a certain period of such training had been undergone and the amount of improvement had been recorded, the subjects were set to work on different but related tasks in order to determine the effect of the previous training. For example, after the subject had acquired greater facility in striking out the letters *e* and *s*, he was required to strike out certain other letters, such as *a* and *n*. On the basis of faculty psychology one would expect that the improvement acquired by practice on *e* and *s* would carry over practically undiminished to an operation so similar as the striking out of *a* and *n*. But this expectation is not borne out by the facts.

Training in perceiving words containing *e* and *s* gave a certain amount of improvement in speed and accuracy in that special ability. In the ability to perceive words containing *i* and *t*, *s* and *p*, *c* and *a*, *e* and *r*, *a* and *n*, *l* and *o*, misspelled words and *A*'s, there was an improvement in speed of only 39 per cent as much as in the ability specially trained, and in accuracy of only 25 per cent as much. Training in perceiving English verbs gave a reduction in time of nearly 21 per cent and in omissions of 70 per cent. The ability to perceive other parts of speech showed a reduction in time of 3 per cent, but an increase of omissions of over 100 per cent.[9]

Results of this kind look bad for faculty psychology and formal discipline. If there is so much falling off of transfer in training when the shift is so slight, there is clearly no warrant for the assumption that training in a subject like mathematics is good preparation for reason-

9 E. L. Thorndike, *Educational Psychology*, p. 90, quoted by W. C. Bagley, *The Educative Process*, p. 206.

ing in an unrelated field, like politics or real estate. The " spread " of improvement due to training is altogether too narrow to fit in with the traditional notion of formal discipline.

The work of other investigators corroborates this view.

It seems probable that certain functions which are of importance in school work, such as quickness in arithmetic, accuracy in spelling, attention to forms, etc., are highly specialized and not secondary results of some general function. That just as there is no such thing as general memory, so there is no such thing as general quickness or accuracy or observation . . . Accuracy in spelling is independent of accuracy in multiplication, and quickness in arithmetic is not found with quickness in marking misspelled words; ability to pick out the word " boy " on a printed page is no guarantee that the child will be able to pick out a geometrical form with as great ease and accuracy.[10]

An experiment by Bagley and Squire to test the value of training in neatness and accuracy in terms of transfer has been frequently cited and is of considerable interest for our discussion. The pupils in a third grade were told, in connection with their arithmetic work, that the papers must be written with neatness and accuracy, but no mention was made of these qualities in their other schoolwork. After three weeks of drill in the preparation of neat and accurate papers in arithmetic a noticeable improvement was observed. In the language and spelling papers, however, there was not only no gain in neatness and accuracy, but an actual decrease. The decrease in ac-

[10] N. Norsworthy, *Formal Training* (New York Teachers' Monographs, 1902), Vol. IV, pp. 96–99, quoted by W. C. Bagley, *The Educative Process*, p. 207.

curacy was almost as great as the increase that had been gained in arithmetic; and in neatness it was nearly half as great. This result proved so disconcerting to the investigators that " in view of the marked deterioration, it was thought best to stop the test." [11]

A second line of attack on faculty psychology and formal discipline grew out of the development of " physiological psychology." The older psychology, which based itself on the conception of a substantive mind, did not concern itself greatly with physiology. But whatever view we may take regarding the nature of the mind, it is an undoubted fact that our mental life is conditioned by the body.

If the brain be injured, consciousness is abolished or altered, even though every other organ in the body be ready to play its normal part. A blow on the head, a sudden subtraction of blood, the pressure of an apoplectic hemorrhage, may have the first effect; whilst a very few ounces of alcohol or grains of opium or hasheesh, or a whiff of chloroform or nitrous oxide gas, are sure to have the second. The delirium of fever, the altered self of insanity, are all due to foreign matters circulating through the brain, or to pathological changes in that organ's substance. The fact that the brain is the one immediate bodily condition of the mental operations is indeed so universally admitted nowadays that I need spend no more time in illustrating it.[12]

This recognition of the dependence of the mind upon the body resulted, about a century ago, in the development of phrenology. The doctrine of phrenology is of

[11] W. C. Bagley, *Educational Values*, p. 189. The literature on experiments in transfer of training has grown to extensive proportions. The results are so conflicting as to prove only that something is wrong somewhere.

[12] W. James, *Principles of Psychology*, Vol. I, p. 4.

interest here because it represents a combination of faculty psychology and physiology. There is considerable evidence to show that the different areas of the brain represent different functions. Hence physiologists speak of the visual area, the auditory area, the motor area, and the like, and the whole topic is referred to as the localization of function. The suggestion advanced by the phrenologists was that the different faculties of the mind had their "seat" in certain specific parts of the brain, and that if a given trait or faculty was highly developed, this fact would show itself in the prominences or the "bumps" of the skull. Consequently, it was possible to know a great deal about an individual's mental characteristics by the simple process of examining his head.

In order to make this scheme work, the whole set of faculties was largely made over. Instead of determining the faculties of the mind by such abstract qualities as reasoning, imagining, perceiving, etc., the phrenologists studied individuals for the purpose of noting outstanding traits of behavior, such as amativeness, pugnacity, conscientiousness, and the like. These traits were classed as faculties, and the attempt was made to correlate them with the configurations of the skull. Thus according to Gall's system of phrenology, " the brain is supposed to contain more than thirty separate and individual organs which are the seat of the most complex psychic capacities, or internal senses, such as combativeness, the fear-of-God, a sense-of-fact, the impulse-of-self-preservation, philoprogenitiveness, and the sense of language." [13]

In the end, however, the development of physiological psychology proved inimical to phrenology and to faculty psychology in general. In the first place, it is evi-

[13] S. S. Colvin, *The Learning Process*, p. 211.

dent that the exercise of a faculty, such as memory, will not avail a great deal unless the exercise at the same time improves the functioning of the brain.  As James says, some brains, " like a jelly, vibrate to every touch, but under usual conditions retain no permanent mark." [14]  Persons laboring under such a handicap may devise a scheme for fixing particular facts in the memory, but it is difficult to see how the power of memory in general can be improved.  The retentiveness of the brain is a physiological property, and it is probably true that our native retentiveness is an unchangeable thing.

Physiological psychology, then, warrants a doubt of the efficacy of sheer exercise for the strengthening of a faculty.  More than that, however, it calls into question the very existence of the faculties.  For example, there is no such thing as a center for memory.  On the contrary, the facts indicate that the various acts of remembering involve all sorts of " centers."  At one time the memory has to do with color, at another time with sound, or again with taste, or smell, or shape, or form, in endless diversity.  Moreover, a person may have a good memory for things seen, but a poor memory for sounds, or vice versa.  If we choose to talk in terms of centers, we seem compelled to infer that specific acts of remembering are processes which combine a variety of centers and that these centers differ according to the nature of remembering.  In other words, remembering has to do not with an existential but with a *functional* unity.  In a particular case of remembering, a variety of things, such as colors, sounds, places, emotional qualities, etc., are brought together to constitute the total picture, and the physiological correlates of these constituents are not con-

[14] W. James, *Principles of Psychology*, Vol. I, p. 660.

centrated in one area of the brain, but involve the whole brain in a particular way. Consequently it is a waste of time to examine the skull for bumps in order to determine the presence of memory.

From the point of view of physiology, then, acts of memory are only an instance of adaptive behavior, which means that a variety of constituent acts are unified in accordance with the needs of the moment. Each thing remembered has its own distinctive physiological basis. We have no memory, but only memories. An act of memory is in principle like any other act of adaptive behavior, in which the eye and the hand and the foot are co-ordinated in accordance with the exigencies of the situation. To explain remembering by reference to a faculty of memory is like explaining the acts of an automobile mechanic by saying that they are due to a faculty of " construction." Such explanation is objectionable, because it mistakes naming for explanation. Not only so, but it withdraws attention from the fact that the total act being adaptive, is both a complex and a shifting unity in accordance with the character of the situation in which it occurs. We never remember twice in exactly the same way.

The foregoing considerations may be summed up by saying that the weight of the evidence is all against the formal discipline of tradition. The experimental evidence is against the idea that the " powers " of the mind can be trained like muscles, so that the strengthening of these powers will automatically insure a high degree of efficiency in new and unrelated material. The facts of physiology indicate that acts like perceiving, remembering, willing, reasoning, etc., are only responses in which the whole nervous system is directed towards a particular situation, with such shiftings and permutations as the circumstances of the moment may require. The case against faculty psychology and formal discipline is strengthened still further when we examine the theoretical considerations that are involved. The theoretical argument, which will be presented in the next chapter, shows that the old cônception of mind, while historically inevitable, has become wholly untenable, and that it is necessary to move on to a new conception in order to explain the facts of mental life and to secure a working principle for the guidance of educational practice.

## Bibliography

BAGLEY, W. C., *Educational Values*, Chap. XII. Macmillan Co.

BAGLEY, W. C., *The Educative Process*, Chap. XIII. Macmillan Co.

CURRIE, J., *Common School Education*, Chaps. VI, VII, VIII. R. Clarke and Co.

JAMES, W., *Principles of Psychology*, Vol. I, pp. 653–676. Henry Holt & Co.

KELLY, W. A. and M. R., *Introductory Child Psychology*, Chap. IV. Bruce Publishing Co.

ORATA, P. T., *The Theory of Identical Elements*. Ohio State University Press.

THORNDIKE, E. L., *Educational Psychology* (Briefer Course), Chap. XVIII. Teachers College, Columbia University.

THORNDIKE, E. L., *Principles of Teaching*, Chap. XV. Seiler.

WICKERSHAM, J. P., *Methods of Instruction*, pp. 37–45. Lippincott.

# CHAPTER VIII

# The Inadequacy of the Mind-Substance Theory

THERE is a Scriptural saying to the effect that a thing is known by its fruits. The fruit of the mind-substance theory is the doctrine that education is a process of inner development or self-development. As to the nature of this process there are conflicting views. Rousseauism, the classical tradition, and formal discipline disagree widely among themselves, but they all stem from a common stock. They all rest on the assumption of the contrast between mind and matter — a contrast which is of such a nature that education *can* have no task other than the development or cultivation of the immaterial, non-spacial entity which we commonly designate as mind or soul.

The difficulties which we have encountered in connection with the aforementioned theories of education suggest the possibility that there is something wrong with this contrast between mind and matter. The most direct and logical procedure for us to adopt, therefore, would be to re-examine the concepts of both mind and matter, since these concepts stand and fall together. Historical development, however, took a different form. There was little disposition to challenge the conception of classical physics with respect to the nature of matter. This unwillingness to meet physics head on may have been due to the inability to think of matter in any terms other than mechanism and atomism, or it may have been an expression of deference to the tremendous prestige which was gradually acquired by the natural sciences. At any rate, the critics who suspected that something was wrong in the setup were generally inclined to re-examine and revise the concept of mind without going all the way and re-examining also the concept of matter, of which the concept of mind was a product.

The fact that the mind is conceived as an existence which exists somehow without existing anywhere in space at once introduces an element of mystery. Many people have difficulty in thinking of a substance which is not located anywhere. But the quality of mystery does not end here. Within the domain of mind we presently come upon the distinction between the mind as something permanent and the mind as perpetually changing. Our momentary experiences are as fleeting as the snapshots which collectively make up a moving picture show. This relatively permanent element is what we ordinarily call the self. A person is supposed to be the same self throughout all the variety of changing experiences. Is this just a supposition, or are we entitled to say that the self, the permanent element, is experienced just as directly as the aches and pains, the colors and sounds, which make up the transitory experiences?

Many battles have been fought over this question. The average person does not worry about it because he does not distinguish rigorously between the permanent and the changing. He has experiences, and so he is easily convinced that he has a firsthand knowledge of his own existence as a self. But the self with which we are concerned is not just a name for a string of experiences. It is something else. It has permanence, it is a source of energy, it exercises choice, it is indivisible, and so on. If we bear in mind that this is the kind of self we are looking for, can we claim that its presence is given with the same directness and assurance as a toothache?

Let us hear what the philosophers have to say on the point. As usual, they disagree among themselves. Some are very sure that the self, or the ego, is given in immediate experience, and that we need only look in order to find it there. To quote from Sir William Hamilton:

We are immediately conscious in perception of an ego and a non-ego, known together and known in contrast to each other. This is the fact of the Duality of Consciousness. It is clear and manifest. When I concentrate my attention in the simplest act of perception, I return from my observation with the most irresistible conviction of two facts, or rather two branches of the same fact; — that I am, — and that something different from me exists. In this act I am conscious of myself as the perceiving subject, and of an external reality as the object perceived; and I am conscious of both existences in the same indivisible moment of intuition. The knowledge of the subject does not precede, nor follow, the knowledge of the object; — neither determines, neither is determined by, the other.[1]

The testimony on this point is abundant. "All consciousness, properly so called, involves the idea of self or the subjective element. To know that I have a sensation is virtually to know myself as having it."[2] "The soul, the subject of past experiences, abides within me, and possesses the power to reproduce and recognize many of those past experiences, forever alive to its own identity in successive thoughts."[3] "I do not see that entity I call

[1] Francis Bowen, *Hamilton's Metaphysics*, p. 195.
[2] Joseph Haven, *Mental Philosophy*, p. 49.
[3] O. A. Hill, *Psychology and Natural Theology*, p. 57.

'myself,' but I am conscious that I exist, and that, in a way, is to know and see self, and knowledge of any thing, more absolutely certain, man cannot possess. I know that it is the ego that thinks, wills, and feels, and that in such action the senses take no part." [4]  In the language of John Locke:

As for our own existence, we perceive it so plainly and so certainly, that it neither needs nor is capable of any proof. For nothing can be more evident to us than our own existence: I think, I reason, I feel pleasure and pain: can any of these be more evident to me than my own existence?  If I doubt of all other things, that very doubt makes me perceive my own existence, and will not suffer me to doubt of that. For if I know I feel pain, it is evident I have as certain perception of the existence of the thing doubting as of that thought which I call doubt.  Experience then convinces us that we have an intuitive knowledge of our own existence, and an internal infallible perception that we are.  In every act of sensation, reasoning, or thinking, we are conscious to ourselves of our own being: and, in this matter, come not short of the highest degree of certainty. [5]

Assertions of this kind, with all sorts of elaborations, occur over and over again in the literature of the subject. So much energy is expended in arguing the existence of the self as a self-evident fact, that a reader may be pardoned for wondering what the fuss is all about.  If the existence of the self is a matter in which we " come not short of the highest degree of certainty," why all the bother?  The lady doth protest too much.

If all observers reported the same findings with respect to the self, there would obviously be no need for

[4] H. H. Moore, *Matter, Life, Mind*, p. 135.
[5] John Locke, *Essay on the Human Understanding*, Book IV, Chap. 9.

insisting so strenuously that the self is present in experience for anyone who has eyes to see. As a matter of fact, the dissenting reports have become so numerous as to be nearly unanimous. Present-day psychology has become exceedingly sceptical about the possibility of making the self an object of direct observation. The prevailing view appears to be in substantial accord with what was said by David Hume long ago when he wrote:

For my part, when I enter most intimately into what I call myself, I always stumble on some particular perception or other, of heat or cold, light or shade, love or hatred, pain or pleasure. I never can catch myself at any time without a perception, and never can observe any thing but the perception. When my perceptions are removed for any time, as by sound sleep, so long am I insensible of myself, and may truly be said not to exist. And were all my perceptions remov'd by death, and cou'd I neither think, nor feel, nor see, nor love, nor hate after the dissolution of my body, I shou'd be entirely anhihilated, nor do I conceive what is farther requisite to make me a perfect non-entity. If any one upon serious and unprejudic'd reflexion, thinks he has a different notion of himself, I must confess I can reason no longer with him. All I can allow him is, that he may be in the right as well as I, and that we are essentially different in this particular. He may, perhaps, perceive something simple and continu'd, which he calls himself; tho' I am certain there is no such principle in me.[6]

Hume's view of the matter appears to be sound. But if we join in the denial that the mind or self, as distinguished from the momentary experience, is ever an object of direct observation, it follows that the only remaining basis for the belief in a substantive mind is that a mind

[6] D. Hume, *Treatise on Human Nature*, p. 252. Selby-Bigge edition.

is needed in order to explain our experiences. It may be argued that there is more " to " a person than is revealed at any given time in his consciousness. In order to explain our transitory, evanescent experiences we must assume something which is radically different from them and which is abiding and essentially unchanging. Although the mind is never an experienced object, it is nevertheless something in the existence of which we are compelled to believe. The gist of the arguments previously set forth is essentially that the facts of experience cannot be understood except in terms of a substantive mind. The mind may be inaccessible to direct experience, but it does not therefore forfeit its title to a place in the world of fact.

To put it differently, we may be compelled to assume the existence of the mind as an entity, even if it is never an object of immediate experience, in much the same way as we assume that the moon has a " back " side as well as a " front " side, although the back of the moon is never an object of direct perception. Whether it is necessary to make such an assumption depends on another question. Can we account for the facts of experience without bringing in a substance or entity such as the mind? In some sense or other, there is undoubtedly a self. If we can account for the self in some other way, then there is, of course, no necessity for introducing a mysterious mind-substance.

There is reason to think that such an explanation can be provided. To give an account of the self in experiential terms, we may begin with certain tendencies which are the common heritage of childhood. Winking, crying, walking, smiling, clutching, and the like are clearly inborn tendencies. Practically all children delight in such activities as wading through water or mud, rolling a ball or hoop, building with blocks, walking on the coping of a low wall, and playing in the sand.  There are, however, certain observable differences in children, which are likewise due to native endowment.  Some children have a passion for teasing the cat, for working with tools, or for taking to pieces every bit of mechanism that they can lay their hands on; while others show the same predilection for playing with dolls or toy soldiers, for music, or for drawing and painting.  The original tendencies vary with different individuals, and they also vary with the same individual, with growth and opportunity.  As the child grows into the adult, new interests appear, such as debating, writing poetry, earning money, or engaging in politics.[7]  These interests are built on native endowments.  The child is father to the man.

All this provides the raw material for that distinctive form of experience which we call ideals.  What has just been said of the child might also be said, with certain reservations, of the lower animals.  Dogs too, for example, exhibit certain inborn traits or tendencies, such as barking, burying bones, and chasing cats.  Moreover, dogs may display marked individuality.  A dog may show a strong liking for hunting and an equally strong aversion to strangers; he may be friendly or surly, timid or venturesome.  So far, then, there seems to be no outstanding difference.  Such a difference appears, however, when we note the fact that human beings can reflect upon their behavior and desires, can analyze and abstract.  A dog may chase every cat that comes within his field of vision, but he does not seem to spend any time in thinking it over; he does not abstract the common

[7] Cf. Riley's poem, "A Life Lesson."

quality from his various experiences and set up " cat-chasing " as his ideal.  Yet this is precisely the sort of thing that is done by human beings.  We form concepts and then we use these concepts as instruments with which to analyze situations so as to discover their possi-bilities, and we convert concepts into ideals for the guid-ance of conduct.

These ideals represent values or interests which we seek to realize or to maintain and with which we identify ourselves.  The development of ideals is, in fact, the same thing as the development of the self.  The content of the self is furnished by the ideals or interests that we cherish.  This is easily verified by observing the way in which we ordinarily refer to the self.  Very often, it is true, the self is identified with the body, but this is by no means always the case.  If a man says, " He struck me," the " me " in question is clearly the body.  But if he says, " He ruined me " (financially), the " me " is identified with certain economic interests; if he says, " He attacked me " (in the newspapers), the " me " is presumably his reputation; if he says, " He supported me " (in a political campaign), the " me " is the political aim to which he aspires.

It is evident from this account that the self is not one but many.  A man may be one kind of man at home, an-other in his office, a third at his club.  In each case he lives up to different standards, maintains a different set of interests.  The number of selves which it is possible to recognize in connection with any given individual is in-definitely large.  Ordinarily some of these interests dom-inate others, in the sense that when a conflict occurs they have the right of way.  The lesser is then sacrificed to the greater.  But the dominant interest is not the same in all individuals.  With some it is, perhaps, " wine, women, and song "; in the case of John Knox it was indicated by his prayer, " Lord, give me Scotland or I die "; others again may agree with Arthur H. Clough in the sentiment:

> It fortifies my soul to know
> That though I perish, truth is so.

Every individual, then, normally possesses a variety of selves. As James remarks, the average man would fain be " handsome and fat and well-dressed and a great athlete, and make a million a year, be a wit, a *bon-vivant*, and a lady-killer, as well as a philosopher; a philanthropist, statesman, warrior, and African explorer, as well as a ' tone-poet ' and a saint." [8] In a sense he is more of a tenement house of desires than a unitary personality. Yet there is an underlying unity in that these different interests or selves constantly require adjustment and harmonization. We sometimes say that a man's " real " self is revealed wherever there is a crisis or conflict, which is to say that we identify the real self with that ideal or interest which dominates the others. A man's passion for first editions, or for automobiles, may be limited by the condition of his purse or by the opinion of his family or community. He then has to decide how far he is willing to go. As long as the decision is not made, he does not know clearly what he wants; which is just another way of saying that his selfhood is in process of growth and change. All of the conflicting interests may undergo modification as a result of the adjustment. In other words, the self is not a fixed quantity or static thing; it is not an inherited possession, but an achievement. It expands in one direction and contracts in another; it is in the making all the while.

[8] W. James, *Principles of Psychology*, Vol. I, p. 309.

The purpose of this discussion of selfhood is to indicate that the meaning of this concept may be ascertained without making an appeal to a substantive entity, such as the mind, which stands back of experience, so to speak, and never shows its face at all. The psychologist dislikes to make such an appeal, for two reasons: first, it is unnecessary, and second, it does not further our understanding. If we do bring in a substantive mind, what have we gained? Since this mind is not experienced directly, how does it come about that we have an experience of selfhood? What is the content of this experience? In what sense is the self a permanent fact, and in what sense does it change? We get no light on any of these questions. All that we get is the claim that there is a mind-substance which accounts for everything.

A similar situation meets us when we consider the question of free will. It is assumed that the sense of being free comes to us directly from the mind-substance, and further, that if we assume such a mind-substance then the whole question of free will is satisfactorily explained. There is considerable ground for thinking that this theory is wrong on both counts.

To many persons the fact that we have an immediate sense of putting forth effort, of determining both the amount and direction of effort, is a strong argument for the existence of a substantive mind. It is not denied that we do have an immediate sense of activity and of freedom. The question at issue, however, is what inference may be drawn from this fact. Are we entitled to conclude that this sense of activity has its source in a substantive mind?

Such a conclusion can scarcely claim to be self-evident. Most psychologists would hold differently. This sense of activity or effort, so they maintain, has its origin, not in a substantive mind, but in the muscles of the body. Says James,

When we look or listen, we accommodate our eyes and ears involuntarily, and turn our head and body as well; when we taste or smell we adjust the tongue, lips and respiration to the object; in feeling a surface we move the palpatory organ in a suitable way; in all these acts, besides making involuntary muscular contractions of a positive sort, we inhibit others which might interfere with the result — we close the eyes in tasting, suspend the respiration in listening, etc. The result is a more or less massive organic feeling that attention is going on. This organic feeling comes . . . to be contrasted with that of the objects which it accompanies, and regarded as peculiarly ours, whilst the objects form the not-me. We treat it as a sense of our *own activity*, although it comes in to us from our organs after they are accommodated, just as the feeling of any object does. Any object, if *immediately* exciting, causes a reflex accommodation of the sense-organ, and this has two results — first, the object's increase in clearness; and second, the feeling of activity in question. Both are sensations of an " afferent " sort.[9]

One important reason why these bodily feelings are mistaken for a direct apprehension of a substantive mind or self is that many of our reactions are so subtle and complex that they commonly pass unnoticed. Hence they give an impression that there is a pure spiritual activity over and above the grosser bodily activities. This feeling of the self, to quote again from James, " when carefully examined is found to consist mainly of the collection of these peculiar motions in the head or between the head and throat . . . our entire feeling of spiritual activity, or what commonly passes by that name, is re-

[9] W. James, *Principles of Psychology*, Vol. I, p. 435.

ally a feeling of bodily activities whose exact nature is by most men overlooked." [10] Testimony of this kind indicates that the alleged immediate awareness of a substantive self must be viewed with caution. It seems undeniable that bodily feelings constitute at least a part of what passes as the feeling of selfhood; and if so it is quite possible that they constitute the whole of it. Consequently the existence of this feeling is no longer an immediate warrant for the inference to a substantive mind.

Our conclusion, so far, is that the support given by the facts of experience to this inference is of a dubious nature. Further consideration of the matter inevitably raises the question whether the inference is worth making anyhow. Does it explain anything that we wish to understand? Since the reason for accepting the doctrine of a substantive mind lies in the assumption that it explains what would otherwise remain obscure, the doctrine in question must give us a better insight or we have gained nothing in the end. There is reason to suspect that, so far as insight or understanding is concerned, the acceptance of this doctrine leaves us no better off than we were before. Names do not constitute explanations.

In the background of our thinking there is usually a lingering idea that the belief in a substantive mind is bound up with the belief in free will. This idea, when examined, loses much of its plausibility. If we assume that human beings exercise freedom in some sense, it can hardly be said that the existence of a substantive mind sheds any light on the nature of this freedom. In moments of regret we are likely to feel that we could have acted differently. The mind could have made a different decision; it could have guided our actions to a different

[10] W. James, *Principles of Psychology*, Vol. I, p. 301.

end. Perhaps so, but how does the mind reach the decisions which it actually makes? Is it guided by reasons suggested by the environment? If so, would not the environment suggest precisely the same reasons if any given situation were repeated? Or does the mind create its own reasons? In that case, this alleged freedom becomes not only an exceedingly dangerous, but a wholly mysterious and fearful thing. Suppose a man is haled into court for the offense of an unprovoked attack on an innocent policeman. In one sense the attack was an ideally free act. It was not promoted by any outside suggestion or provocation. Why then was the act committed at all? The only answer can be that the offender acted as he did because he saw fit to act that way. This is about as far as we can get. To answer the why is to adduce reasons, and then we seem to be on the road to showing how the act was determined and could not have been anything different. Yet if reasons do not count, free will becomes a synonym for irrationality. The substantive mind does not serve to explain anything, but to shunt off inquiry. A man acts as he does, on this basis of reasoning, because his mind so decided. This is not to explain but to give an official sanction to ignorance.

The purpose of this discussion is not in the least to take sides on the question of free will. The point is simply that the inference to a substantive mind neither has a clear warrant in the facts of activity and freedom nor gives us any insight into the nature of activity and freedom. It merely substitutes a name for an explanation. The "mind" which is supposed to explain turns out to be even more mysterious than the things to be explained.

The case is precisely the same with respect to all other concepts. To grant that a concept cannot be derived from a mechanistic system of inert matter is not the same as saying that it must be the product of a substantive mind.  If, for example, we attribute the concept of right and wrong to such a mind, we find that we are no better off than we were before.  We still have to go to experience to ascertain what it is that makes a thing right or wrong.  Matthew Arnold recognizes this fact by implication in his appeal to the principle of harmonious development.  What constitutes harmonious development can be determined only by reference to specific situations. Arnold was right, not in the sense that harmonious development is a workable principle, but in the sense that our guiding principle, whatever it may be, must come from experience.  If we concede that specific experiences must provide the content of our concepts, then we are warranted in saying that the concepts themselves are derived, not from a substantive mind, but as generalizations of these experiences.

The point may be illustrated further by reference to a concept such as " perfection."  The meaning or content of this concept must come from experience, which is to say that it is relative in character.  Relative perfection means that a given thing is perfect with reference to the purpose in hand.  My watch may serve perfectly to get me home for dinner, although it would not serve the purpose of timing a foot race.  An automobile may be perfect for the process of getting me to a certain place on time; a book may serve perfectly as a paper weight; a nail may serve perfectly as a substitute for a screw to hold a board in place.  Experience furnishes us with endless illustrations of this kind and tends to show that there is ample material in everyday experience for the development of a concept such as a concept of perfection.

The concept of infinity is perhaps more obscure. But when we say that space, for example, is infinite, what do we mean? In practical terms we mean that we can take any given point in space and from this point move in any direction we may choose. This is true of all the points in space. This quality of space comes within our experience and it expresses essentially what is meant by spacial infinity. Similarly the number series is infinite in the sense that any given number, however great, can have another unit added to it. The concept of infinite as applied to space, time, or number does not mean an " infinite number " of units. The notion of " infinite number " is like the notion of round-square; it means " numberless number." The infinite here is rather a rule of procedure. It means simply that we can always add to any assigned number. Any object of experience which is of such a nature as to permit this is called an infinite. It does not appear at all necessary or relevant to introduce a substantive mind in order to explain such objects or facts.

Primitive man, as has been seen, " explained " things by converting them into agencies. Thus a landslide was explained by saying that the mountain did it. Explanation in terms of a substantive mind is essentially a hang-over from this earlier tendency. We can understand, therefore, why the modern psychologist has discarded the conception of a substantive mind. He has a deep-seated conviction that explanations in terms of such a mind are not explanations at all, but the surrender of explanation. The procedure in such " explanation " is to explain what we do know in terms of what we do not know, which is subversive of all scientific method. Instead of explanation, the doctrine of a substantive mind really furnishes nothing but names. It is like explaining opiates by saying that they have a soporific virtue, or like explaining stones by reference to the principle of "lapidity." While the belief in a substantive mind is still widespread, the subject in modern scientific psychology has become one chiefly of historical interest.

The discussion of mind-substance would not be complete, however, without recognition of the fact that to very many persons the belief in a mind-substance is determined primarily, not by argument or even by habits of thinking, but rather by the emotional reactions which have to do with the belief in a life after death. If immortality is accepted as a fact, then the theory of a substantive mind becomes a convenient way of explaining this fact. Moreover, the rejection of this theory may seem to be equivalent to a rejection of the faith in immortality. How can there be a life after death, unless we assume the existence of a mind-substance, which continues its existence after separation from the body?

The answer is simple. We need not assume that the existence of a mind-substance is an indispensable condition for the belief in immortality. The suggestion has been made, for example, that the basis of the connection between the present life and the life after death may be of a physical nature and need not necessarily involve a substantive mind at all.[11] It is true that the suggestion does not amount to more than a vague speculation, yet the fact that a different explanation of immortality is antecedently possible is sufficient to show that we must not be too ready to assume a necessary connection between the belief in immortality and the belief in a substantive mind.

[11] F. C. S. Schiller, *The Riddles of the Sphinx*, Chap. XI.

If the discreet naturalist were asked how he could conceive the survival of intelligence to be affected after the machinery by which it had apparently been engendered had disappeared, his answer might be somewhat as follows: He would first call attention to the fact that in the process of reproduction all the experience of the antecedent life is passed on from generation to generation over what we may term a molecular bridge. Thus, in the case of man, a tiny mass of protoplasm imponderably small, carries on from parents to child the body, the mind, all indeed that the predecessors in tens of thousands of specific forms and unimaginable millions of individuals have won of enduring profit from their experience. Therefore, even within the narrow limits of the known, there is evidence that the seed from which an individual intelligence may be evolved can be effectively guarded and nurtured in the keeping of an exceedingly small body of matter. In a word, the facts of generation show that under certain conditions life as complicated potentially as that which passes away from the body at death may reside and be cradled in states of matter which are, as compared with the mature body, very simple.[12]

By way of summary and conclusion it may be pointed out that the foregoing discussion does not raise any doubts about the dualism between mind and matter with which we started. Our concern has been rather to show, first, that if we assume a substantive mind, then education becomes a matter of developing this mind in some form or other. The alternatives that are open to us in that case are, respectively, Rousseauism, the classical tradition, and formal discipline. Next, it was pointed out that each of these alternatives has its difficulties. Lastly, it was argued that the notion of a substantive mind is, in

[12] N. S. Shaler, *The Individual*, p. 304.

fact, both useless and a serious obstacle to insight. If this last proposition is tenable, it follows that we must move on to a theory of experience in which the substantive mind has no place. In thus moving on to a different theory we are simply following the trail of historical development. Our next task, then, is to examine the concept of mind which grew out of the older concept and to trace its implications for educational practice.

## Bibliography

HUME, D., *Treatise of Human Nature*, Book I, Part 4, Section 6. Oxford University Press.

JAMES, W., *Principles of Psychology*, Vol. I, pp. 291–325. Henry Holt & Co.

OTTO, M. C., *Things and Ideals*, Chap. X. Henry Holt & Co.

SCHILLER, F. C. S., *The Riddles of the Sphinx*, Chap. XI. Macmillan Co.

SHALER, N. S., *The Individual*, p. 304. Appleton Co.

CHAPTER IX

## *The Theory of Mental States*

As was shown in the preceding chapters, the doctrine of a substantive mind, which operates through its "faculties," is beset with numerous and serious difficulties. The passage of time has not served to minimize these difficulties. Psychologists everywhere have rejected the doctrine, not only because it is unverified and unverifiable, but because it is essentially unintelligible. The persistence of the doctrine in popular thinking, albeit in a hazy and confused form, despite the fact that among psychologists it has been generally discarded, is perhaps not surprising when we consider the power of tradition and the tendency of the imagination to convert processes into entities. Yet a new and more adequate theory of mind became a necessity.

The development of a new theory to replace the old was a process that extended over a long period of time. The first step in this process was to emphasize the distinction between the mind-substance and its experiences or "states." In the philosophy of John Locke, for example, this distinction takes on a certain prominence. While Locke was not always consistent, he insisted that the materials which make up experience are " conveyed in " to the mind by the senses. The mind, in his language, is as " white paper," upon which the external world leaves imprints or records, which are designated by such terms as " sensations," " impressions " or " men-

tal states." The term habitually used by Locke himself is
" ideas."

Locke's explanation suggested that our experiences are
made up of various units, which are contributed by different senses. In the course of time this suggestion was
elaborated in considerable detail. The perception of a
tree, for example, came to be explained as made up of
visual impressions, of sound-images derived from earlier
experiences in which the leaves rustled in the wind, of
touch-images which trace back to actual experiences
with the tree, and the like. The stage was thus set for a
new theory of experience. Drop the egregious mind-
substance and what is left is an aggregate of different experiences, each of which is made up of various units that
somehow cluster together. This conception of mind as
an aggregate is frequently called the theory of mental
states. The chief ingredients of these mental states are
sense-impressions and copies of previous sense-impressions, together with " affective " elements of pleasure and
pain. Copies of earlier impressions are commonly designated as images. Sense-impressions, images, and affective elements run together or " integrate " to form experiences.

When experience is approached in this way it is soon
discovered that our mental life or experience is far more
complex than we ordinarily realize. The number of elements which were listed runs into the thousands, and
their various blendings and amalgamations, which were
sometimes referred to as " mental chemistry," were studied with great care. The chief business of the psychologist, from this standpoint, is with the analysis of mental
compounds, and the method upon which he places his
chief reliance is the method of introspection or self-ob-

servation. "We 'look into the mind,' each for himself; or we observe ourselves . . . in order to find out what processes are going on at the time, and how they are influencing one another."[1]

This explanation of experience takes account of certain facts which are usually overlooked by the untrained observer. We commonly say, for example, that the water in the river *looks* cold in the winter, that the rock *looks* hard or solid, that the knife *looks* sharp. A moment's reflection will show us, however, that coldness, hardness, and sharpness are not visual qualities at all. They have neither form nor color; they are not directly seen but are suggested by what is presented to the eye. To put it differently, the total experience is a compound, which is made up in part by what is directly given through sight and in part by associations due to previous experience. If we analyze the total experience into its parts or elements, we discover that it contains, first, sensory elements or sensations, due to the direct stimulation of the sense organ concerned; second, images, which are copies or revivals of former sensations and which are brought in by association; and third, "affective elements," consisting of pleasure or pain. These elements together form a compound, in much the same way that hydrogen and oxygen combine to form water, and the experience as a whole is called a perception. The elements in question are discovered by a process of self-observation, which is called the method of introspection.

According to this point of view, the primary business of psychology is to determine the structure of the mind or consciousness by analyzing it into its elements; consequently this psychology is sometimes known as struc-

[1] E. B. Titchener, *Outline of Psychology*, p. 32.

tural psychology or the psychology of structuralism. This psychology takes as its point of departure the proposition that the objects of our experience have a structure which escapes ordinary notice. The experiences which engage our attention are compounds, although we are not, as a rule, aware of the fact. Furthermore, this analytical approach opens up another perspective which is of considerable interest and significance. The objects or experiences towards which attention is directed are never the whole of what is actually present, but always appear within a larger context or " field." This is sometimes expressed by saying that every experience has both a foreground and a background. In the foreground is the object with which our attention is occupied; in the background is a great variety of material that is perceived at best but dimly and obscurely. When we once begin to make a study of this background, we find that it contains a surprising amount of content. Let the attention but wander, say to the soles of our feet, to the tips of the elbows, to the small of the back, or to the end of the nose, and we at once discover sensations which, until the spotlight of attention was turned on them, were concealed in the shadows of the background. These sensations were present all the while, but we did not happen to attend to them before.

The suggestion may be made that these sensations which we discover when we attend to them were not present all the while, but came into being at the moment when they became objects of attention. But this hardly squares with the facts. For example, a person sitting in a room engrossed in some work suddenly becomes aware that the clock has stopped. The peculiarity of such an experience lies in the fact that previous to this moment the person concerned may not have been aware of the clock at all. He was not conscious of the ticking; yet when the clock stopped he immediately took note of the fact. Such an occurrence is full of mystery, unless we assume that in some way he was conscious of the ticking all the while. His attention was directed toward something else, to be sure, but dimly or marginally his consciousness took note of the clock. If we make an assumption of this sort, we can explain readily why it is that the stopping of the clock should be reported to his attention. He was " keeping tab " on the clock all the while, in spite of the fact that he was not aware of doing so.

According to the psychology of structuralism, the field of consciousness is divided into a " focus " and a " margin." The focus is the point of greatest clearness. It is occupied by that to which we attend directly. But besides this focal consciousness there are all degrees of marginal consciousness shading off from the point of greatest clearness to complete obscurity.

It is customary among psychologists to speak of consciousness as á " field " having a sort of central illumination surrounded by an area of less illumination, which becomes darker in proportion to the distance from the center. In the case of a visual field the point of greatest clearness is the point on which the eyes are focused. The more outlying objects, however, are noted in indirect vision, which becomes progressively more obscure as the distance from the center increases. In listening to a lecturer our immediate attention is given to his words and facial expression. We pay no heed to the lights or windows or the other people in the room; yet our attention is aroused if a cloud momentarily obscures the sunlight, if a curtain flaps, or if someone moves about in the room within the range of our indirect vision. The words and the face of the speaker do not occupy the whole of our consciousness, but are presented in a context which is present, yet not present. In other words, we experience this context in a peculiar way, which is indicated by saying that we have a dim or marginal awareness of it.

The difference between focus and margin is most conveniently expressed in terms of distance from a center. When so expressed it applies quite directly to visual experiences. When we turn to other experiences, however, such as hearing, talking, and smelling, the spacial character of the metaphor becomes more apparent. The contrast between focus and margin obtains in many situations from which the spacial relations are absent. Thus a man eating his dinner may experience elation or depression as a result of business affairs, the details of which linger on in his mind, even if there be no focal awareness of it. An appointment with the dentist may cast a shadow over the hours which precede it, even when the appointment is temporarily forgotten. Similarly a joyful anticipation will cast a rosy hue over all the incidents of the day, in spite of the fact that our attention is not turned in that direction all the time. These illustrations show that the " marginal " consciousness is really diffused over the whole field. Nevertheless, the spacial metaphor is a convenient device. The difference between focus and margin may be expressed in terms of the distance between center and margin in a conscious " field," as we have expressed it just now, or it may be expressed by the symbol of a wave as is done by William James. The crest of the wave represents the focus, from which point it tapers off to the margin. The advantage of this latter symbolism is that the degree of focalization can be represented by the height of the wave. In moments of daydreaming or woolgathering the crest is low; in moments of extreme concentration it is high.

As James points out, the facts of experience conform readily to this distinction. We may have trouble in describing the outlying regions of consciousness, but it is not easy to deny their presence.

What is the strange difference between an experience tasted for the first time and the same experience recognized as familiar, as having been enjoyed before, though we cannot name it or say where or when? A tune, an odor, a flavor sometimes carry this inarticulate feeling of their familiarity so deep into our consciousness that we are fairly shaken by its mysterious emotional power. But strong and characteristic as this psychosis is — it probably is due to the submaximal excitement of wide-spreading associational brain-tracts — the only name we have for all its shadings is " sense of familiarity." [2]

It is evident that the inclusion of the " margin " adds enormously to what is called the content of consciousness. Just how much is added it is difficult to say, since the boundary of the margin is indeterminate. But however obscure the content may be, the margin is nevertheless there.

It lies around us like a " magnetic field," inside of which our centre of energy turns like a compass-needle, as the present phase of consciousness alters into its successor. Our whole past store of memories floats beyond this margin, ready at a touch to come in; and the entire mass of residual powers, impulses, and knowledges that constitute our empirical self stretches continuously beyond it. So vaguely

[2] W. James, *Principles of Psychology*, Vol. I, p. 252.

drawn are the outlines between what is actual and what is only potential at any moment of our conscious life, that it is always hard to say of certain mental elements whether we are conscious of them or not.[3]

Even this, however, does not tell the whole story. Besides the marginal field there is, according to some writers, still another area, which James calls the extramarginal. In James's opinion psychology must take account not only of

. . . the consciousness of the ordinary field, with its usual centre and margin, but an addition thereto in the shape of a set of memories, thoughts, and feeling which are extra-marginal and outside of the primary consciousness altogether, but yet must be classed as conscious facts of some sort, able to reveal their presence by unmistakable signs. I call this the most important step forward because, unlike the other advances which psychology has made, this discovery has revealed to us an entirely unsuspected peculiarity in the constitution of human nature. No other step forward which psychology has made can proffer any such claim as this.[4]

This extramarginal field is a territory from which various ideas or impulses may erupt into everyday consciousness. It offers a convenient way of explaining such phenomena as alterations of personality and post-hypnotic suggestion. To cite a simple illustration, a person who is in a hypnotic state may be told that at three o'clock in the afternoon he is to do a certain thing, such as poking the fire, raising the window shade, or pulling off his coat. When the person comes out of the hypnotic state he knows nothing of this instruction; yet when three o'clock comes, he will experience a tendency or disposi-

[3] W. James, *Varieties of Religious Experience*, p. 232.
[4] *Ibid.*, p. 233.

tion to do the thing that he has been told to do. He will make some trivial excuse to poke the fire or raise the curtain, being unconscious all the while of the real reason for the act. If we assume an extramarginal territory of consciousness, the act is very easily explained. In some way or other this extramarginal territory keeps track of the passage of time, and at the right moment the idea emerges into full consciousness and prompts the act.

In all this discourse about mental states it is taken for granted that the origin of all our experiences traces back eventually to the stimulation of the sense organs by external objects. But now an extraordinary situation presents itself. We assume these external objects in order to explain how mental states occur; but after the mental states make their appearance, it becomes difficult to justify this assumption, because we cannot get outside of these mental states in order to find out what these external material objects are like or even whether they exist at all.

Let us see how this comes about. Starting with the dualism of common sense, psychology is disposed to take for granted that the mind is a sort of observer which takes note of things outside the body. But presently certain problems arise. Let us suppose that two observers, one of whom is color blind, are looking at an object. Let us suppose further that one of the observers sees the object as red while the other sees it as gray. Now if the object is " really " red, we say that the gray is an illusion, a subjective thing. The red is in the object, but the gray is not. What then is to be done about the gray? Where is the gray?

This becomes a formidable question. The gray is not in the object, for by hypothesis the object is red and not gray. We are tempted to say perhaps that it is in the ether-waves, but this will do no better. If the gray were in the ether-waves then the whole distance intervening between the object and the observer would be gray. The ether-waves have no color at all. They have motion, which produces color in the mind of the observer, but they themselves are without color. Apparently, therefore, the only alternative left is to say that the gray is in the mind of the observer.

Perhaps this has a mysterious sound. But let us consider for a moment what takes place in dreams. In the dream-experience we see colors, in much the same way as in waking moments, but there are no objects and no ether-waves impinging on the eye. The colors are just "dream colors"; they are nowhere in space. They are not to the right or to the left of any physical objects; they exist in a world of their own, and although we see them in the dream as occupying space, they do not occupy any real space. It is almost as if they existed in a fourth dimension, without any contact with the space of physical objects. Consequently we say that they are not really in space at all. Neither have they any physical properties. They are mental or "in the mind."

Now let us return to the original illustration. The gray seen by one of the observers is labelled a subjective thing; it is "in the mind." But what shall we say of the red that is seen by the other observer? We are tempted to treat this color differently. It is not in the mind but in the object. But here, too, we presently come upon difficulties. The red is an effect of ether-waves quite as much as the gray. We say that the two observers see different colors because of differences in the retinas of their eyes, but apart from this the process of seeing is the same in the two cases. If one of the colors is in the mind,

why not the other as well? Here again the dream-experi-
ences furnish a convenient illustration. In dreams everything that is experienced is supposed to be in the mind.
But this is equally true in our waking moments. The
physical object does not move bodily into the mind when
we look at it. It is *represented* in the mind by a picture
or photograph of itself, just as objects are mirrored in
the pupil of the eye. To speak generally, all experiences
are at most representatives or pictures of external objects;
the object itself is not in the mind but is represented in
the mind by a picture or symbol. Thus we emerge
with the conclusion that what we immediately experience
is something nonspacial or mental; and this is what is
known as the doctrine of consciousness or mental states.

This conclusion, it will be observed, discriminates
strongly against physical objects. The latter are no
longer on an equal footing with mind. They have been
crowded out of immediate experience altogether. We
do not see objects directly at all, but only pictures or du-
plicates, from which we infer the existence of physical
objects. To use an illustration, we are told that the moon
always keeps the same side turned towards us. We never
see the back side of the moon at all. We might say, then,
that the back side of the moon gets into our experience
only by means of a representative, viz., the front side.
When we see the front of the moon, we infer the existence of the other side; and in the same way the pictures
in the mind lead us to infer the existence of physical
objects.

This result is unexpected and perhaps not altogether
convincing. Is any other conclusion possible? Suppose
we start all over again and assume once more a mind and
a body both of which are directly experienced. We call

in once more our two observers. To the one who reports that the object observed is gray we say that he is in
error. The object is not really gray. But the one who
reports that the object is red is likewise in error. The
object is no more red than it is gray. If we want to know
what the object is like we call in the physicist, who explains to us that the object has no color at all. It consists
of atoms or electrons, and the colors that we see are not
pictures, any more than the pain of an aching tooth is a
picture of a jumping nerve. All these experiences are
just by-products, so to speak; the real things are the
things that science tells us about. As Huxley puts it:
" The nervous system stands between consciousness and
the assumed external world, as an interpreter who can
talk with his fingers stands between a hidden speaker and
a man who is stone deaf." [5]

Common sense is usually quite unaware that there is
any problem at this point. It assumes that objects are
known directly. In order to know an object, all that is
necessary, in any case, is just to look at it. The eye
" takes in " the object and that is all there is to it. If we
listen to what science has to say about it, however, we
soon find that it is not quite so simple. First there must
be light-waves or something of the kind to stimulate the
retina. Then there must be certain processes in the optic
nerve, followed by certain other processes in the cerebral
cortex. It is not until after all this has taken place that
the act of perception occurs. In other words, the object
is at one end of this complicated apparatus which is involved in seeing and the perception or mental state is at
the other end. If we look at a very distant object, such

[5] T. H. Huxley, *Science and Culture, and Other Essays*, chapter
"On the Hypothesis that Animals Are Automata," p. 216.

as a star, there are vast intervening stretches of space and also vast intervening stretches of time.  Astronomers tell us that the star which we see may have ceased to exist years before we were born.  What we experience directly, therefore, is not the object at all, but a mental state.  How then do we get to the object?  It would hardly do to say that the mental state somehow reaches across the intervening distance and lays ghostly hands upon the object.  The only alternative is to say that we get over to the object by inference, i.e., by guessing that it is there.

This guessing soon turns out to be a hazardous business.  There is evidence to show that what we experience is determined by the sense organ as much as by the object which is supposed to provide the stimulus.  Any stimulus applied to the organ of vision, no matter what its character, is translated into visual qualities; and the same applies to the other sense organs.  We do not experience any object directly, but a translation of the stimulus into certain qualities; and the translation may be as different from the object supplying the stimulus as it is possible to imagine.

Whether we press the retina, or prick, cut, pinch, or galvanize the living optic nerve, the subject always feels flashes of light, since the ultimate result of our operations is to stimulate the cortex of his occipital region.  Our habitual ways of feeling outer things thus depend on which convolutions happen to be connected with the particular end-organs which those things impress.  We *see* the sunshine and the fire, simply because the only peripheral end-organ susceptible of taking up the ether-waves which these objects radiate excites those particular fibres which run to the centers of sight.  If we could interchange the inward connections, we should feel the world in altogether new ways.  If, for instance, we could splice the outer extremity of our optic nerves to our ears, and that of our auditory nerves to our eyes, we should hear the lightning and see the thunder, see the symphony and hear the conductor's movements. Such hypotheses as these form good training for neophytes in the idealistic philosophy! [6]

But the full story has not yet been told. Before long we come upon certain facts that have to do with what is sometimes called the " relativity of sense perception." If we look at an object such as a piece of chalk, we see a smooth surface. Both the eye and the hand report that the chalk is smooth. If we apply a microscope, however, we get a different report. We then find that the surface of the chalk is not smooth at all but exceedingly rough, the degree of roughness depending upon the strength of the microscope. The fact suggests a disparity between the report of the senses and the physical fact. We can imagine a microscopic bug crawling over the surface of the chalk, falling down the crevices and climbing up the slopes, and in general having an experience very much like that of the early pioneers who crossed the Rocky Mountains on their way to the Pacific Coast. From the point of view of the bug, certainly, the chalk is anything but smooth. If, now, we ask how rough the surface of the chalk really is, it seems impossible to furnish an adequate answer. The smoothness or roughness which we actually experience is determined by various factors such as the structure of the retina and the power of the microscope that is employed.

To make matters still worse, the reports furnished by our senses are frequently in conflict with one another. " The interior of one's mouth cavity feels larger when

[6] W. James, *Psychology* (Briefer Course), p. 12.

explored by the tongue than when looked at.  The crater of a newly-extracted tooth, and the movements of a loose tooth in its socket, feel quite monstrous. ̦ A midge buzzing against the drum of the ear will often feel as big as a butterfly." [7]  Again, " Apply the blunt end of a pencil to the forehead, to the lips, to the back of the hand, to the tip of a finger, to the drum of the ear.  The resulting tactual sensations vary conspicuously in extent, though the areas of the skin affected are throughout equal and the surface with which they are brought in contact remains constant in size.  None of the tactual sensations has any better logical claim than the others to be identified with the real extent either of the skin stimulated or of the surface applied to it; and their rival claims are mutually destructive.  Skin sensibility is also variable in this respect from one individual to another; it is different in the child and the adult; it is affected by disease of the brain, and by the use of drugs such as narcotics." [8]

These considerations involve a curious and startling reversal of the situation with which we started.  At the outset men seem to have had no awareness at all of a distinct existence such as we now refer to as mind or mental states.  While the concept of something called mind has gradually developed to the point where it is now accepted by practically everybody, it has never reached a definiteness, with most persons, which is at all comparable with the definiteness of our concept of matter.  Most of us can discourse with considerable fluency about material objects, but we hesitate and stumble when we undertake to talk about mind.  The quality of immaterial-

[7] W. James, *Principles of Psychology*, Vol. II, p. 139.
[8] G. F. Stout, *Proceedings of the Aristotelian Society* (1903-4), p. 15.

ity and nonspaciality presents a formidable obstacle in this connection. But now the shoe is suddenly on the other foot. If we take our clue from the theory of mental states, we seem to have no especial difficulty about our experiences themselves, but we become immersed in overwhelming difficulties with respect to the material objects to which these experiences seem to refer. Matter goes into retreat behind these experiences and becomes apparently inaccessible.

It is not surprising, therefore, that men have become agnostic and have asserted that the nature of reality must remain forever unknowable, or that they have even denied the existence of matter altogether. To Bishop Berkeley, of whom mention was made previously, it seemed altogether self-evident that it was folly to talk of matter at all. If we start with the proposition that matter and mind are altogether different, and then discover that our experiences are limited entirely to what is mental, what other conclusion can we draw? No one would argue seriously that a toothache could have a duplicate in the realm of pure matter. A toothache is quite obviously a *mental* fact; it is a " creation " of " mind." But so, it appears, is everything else that we experience. Every experience is something that is " felt," though not necessarily felt in the same way as a toothache. And so Berkeley enunciated his celebrated dictum: " An idea [i.e., a mental state] can be like nothing but an idea."

Whenever men get into a jam in their thinking, there is often a temptation to seek a solution in a realm beyond ordinary experience. An instance of this was encountered previously, in our discussion of the classical tradition in education. When a better foundation for faith in beauty, goodness, and truth was needed than they were able to derive from experience, the classicists took their case to a higher court.  They asserted that these values, as they conceived them, were founded on the external and immutable structure of the universe.  Something similar happens, on occasion, in connection with the problem of experience and external reality.  If we can know only our experiences, which are mental and not material, then perhaps external reality is likewise a form of mind — not limited or finite mind, such as our minds, but an infinite, overarching, transcendental Mind. This idea recurs again and again, not merely in our philosophies but in literature as well.  It is some such conception that is expressed in Tennyson's poem " The Higher Pantheism ":

The sun, the moon, the stars, the seas, the hills and the
    plains —
Are not these, O soul, the Vision of Him who reigns?

Is not the Vision He? tho' He be not that which He seems?
Dreams are true while they last, and do we not live in
    dreams?

For our purposes it is not necessary to follow these speculations further.  Perhaps the truth lies in the direction indicated by them; on the other hand, the moral of the tale may be that the original dualism of matter and mind is a treacherous and untenable view.  The history of thought makes it clear that this dualism is an unstable thing.  Matter and mind have difficulty in maintaining a serene equilibrium.  At one time it is mind and at another time it is matter that tries to dominate the other member of the dualism.  At the present point in our discussion matter is the under dog and very much on the defensive.  At a later time we shall return to the perennial struggle between these two. First of all, however, we must consider the implications contained in the theory of mental states for education.

## Bibliography

BERKELEY, G., *Principles of Human Knowledge*. Paragraphs 1–24. Open Court Publishing Co.

BODE, B. H., *Outline of Logic*, Chap. XVI. Henry Holt & Co.

HUME, D., *Treatise of Human Nature*, Chap. I. Oxford University Press.

JAMES, W., *Psychology* (Briefer Course), Chap. I. Henry Holt & Co.

JAMES, W., *Varieties of Religious Experience*, pp. 230–236. Longmans, Green and Co.

JUDD, C. H., *Psychology*, Chap. I. Ginn and Co.

PEARSON, K., *Grammar of Science*, Chap. II. E. P. Dutton and Co.

# CHAPTER X

# Apperception and Teaching

THE psychologists who have devoted themselves to the analysis of mental states have told us much about experience which ordinarily escapes our notice. They have told us that our experiences are compounds of various elements, such as sensations, images, and affective qualities; they have called our attention to the distinction between focus and margin; they have even brought in an extramarginal domain, called the subconscious, which is connected in some way with ordinary experience but which keeps out of the way of direct vision.

All this may be summed up by saying that whenever we have new experiences there is a background provided for them. These new experiences do not come into an empty mind, but find a kind of reception committee awaiting them. Former experiences do not simply drop out when they pass from the focus of attention but abide in some manner. This conclusion is based on the fact that former experiences modify or color the later experiences as they arrive. It has, therefore, been found convenient to suppose that these former experiences stay with us in the domain of the marginal or the extramarginal. On the basis of this supposition, we cannot be sure that any experience is ever completely lost. At any rate, we normally have on hand a considerable body of previous experiences, which join up with new sensory impressions so as to form the complete unit which we call a mental state.

We may go a step further and say that the subconscious, as this "underground experience" is sometimes called, constitutes by far the greater part of what we ordinarily designate as the mind. The mind is like an iceberg in that most of it is submerged. If we assume that experiences after they have occurred remain somehow in the possession of the individual, we can understand that they may have considerable influence in determining the character of subsequent experiences. They constitute what we call our memories; and these memories enable us to interpret the experience of the moment. A timid person who finds himself near a cemetery on a dark night stands an excellent chance of seeing ghosts, for the reason that any casual object which meets his eye is immediately clothed with a set of qualities which are suggested by past experience. A football scout who is observing the play of a team reads into the various manoeuvres all sorts of tactics or plans which are suggested by his previous experience. It is notoriously difficult in reading proof to catch all the misprints, because the mind supplies what is lacking to the eye by converting an *h* into a *b*, a *3* into an *8*, or a *c* into an *o*. As Ruskin remarks, most of our seeing is done behind the eye. Without a background of experience the eye would report almost nothing at all. This background is known in technical jargon as the "apperceptive mass." A background of this sort is involved in all ordinary experience. All perception is apperception.

To illustrate further, let us construct a figure of three lines, one straight and perpendicular, one broken and oblique, and one curved, thus:

Sight gives us the figure as it stands, but the apprehension that we get at first view is unsatisfactory.

We have perhaps had experience enough with lines to enable us to relate each one to its appropriate class, but we see no idea, no purpose in the whole. Remembering, now, however, that a painter once boasted that he could, by means of three lines, represent a soldier and his dog entering an inn, we can at once associate the hitherto meaningless marks with a system of ideas, and when this is done, the process of apperception may be said to be complete.[1]

As a matter of convenience, this account of apperception has taken for granted the existence of both a marginal and an extramarginal field of consciousness. For present purposes, however, it makes no difference whether or not we believe that our experiences persist indefinitely. We may, if we like, reject the extramarginal altogether and hold to the view that former experiences recur, not because they have been waiting all the while for their turn before the footlights, but because they are called into being anew by the activity of the cerebral cortex. In either case we are obliged to recognize the fact that our experiences, when they come, are a compound of new and old. We experience things as we do because old experiences come in and blend with the present fact. The old experiences provide a background and give to the new experience its actual character.

This leads directly to a new theory of learning. We can no longer say that learning is a matter of developing or training the " mind," since there is no such mind to be developed. Learning has to do with the formation of apperceptive masses, i.e., it is a process of organizing experiences so as to give depth of meaning to new facts. The task of education is to make present experiences combine with an appropriate background. By doing

[1] C. De Garmo, *Essentials of Method*, p. 25.

this, education gives a person a new world to live in.  Education in architecture, for example, enables a man walking along the street to recognize and classify various types of architecture as Colonial, or Greek, or Gothic; education in medicine enables a physician to interpret symptoms; education in languages enables us to detect grammatical errors and incorrectness of sentence construction; education in literature enables us to recognize and appreciate literary excellence, etc.  The problem of education, therefore, is to select the right material to form these backgrounds or " apperceptive masses " and to devise a technique for developing them.

The term " apperception " was contributed by Herbart, and the theory of learning which was constructed on the concept of apperception has become closely associated with his name in the history of education.  This concept indicates an entirely different approach to the problem of learning.  Instead of centering our attention on the training of faculties, whether for the sake of " harmonious development " or for some other end, we turn to the task of building up " apperceptive masses " in the mind of the pupil.  To do this, we must start with the experience which the pupil already has, for the purpose of enlarging and enriching this experience.  All learning, therefore, becomes in a real sense an extension of present experience; it changes the quality of present experience, instead of being information that is merely added to what is already there.  Real learning is based on the principle of the " continuity of experience "; and, by the same token, effective teaching requires what is sometimes called the psychological approach or the psychological organization of subject matter.

When this approach is neglected, peculiar results may

occur. Dewey makes mention somewhere of a pupil who was studying, in class, the geography of the Mississippi Valley. She learned her lessons dutifully, but she did not happen to discover that the river flowing past her home town was the Mississippi River. A psychological approach would have started with facts already familiar to the pupils, such as the near-by river and the contour of the neighborhood as a valley. This knowledge would then have been extended so that, in the end, the familiar environment of the home town would have become part and parcel of what is called the Mississippi Valley. In this process the familiar facts would have taken on new meanings; the river would have become a symbol of many things; and the larger perspective would have shown, perhaps, why the town was built where it was or why it was built at all, how its fortunes were linked up with river transportation, what changes were wrought by the building of railroads, and the like. The entire "apperceptive mass" of the pupils, with respect to the home town, would have been transformed. Instead of that the pupils studied and learned a set of facts which were presented without any particular reference to their own personal experiential background. When subject matter is handled in this way, the tendency is to deal with the information as something to be learned, and not as material for making over the "apperceptive mass" of the pupils. This particular educational vice is sometimes called rote learning. Whether the material thus learned will connect up with the experience of the pupil is left more or less to chance.

·The moral is that there is an order of learning which the teacher must take into account. This fact has led to some interesting theorizing. Some educators have argued that, since the experience of the pupil must be our point of orientation, history should begin with the present and work backwards. Similarly geography should begin with the pupil's particular locality and work outwards. We are advised to consider " replacing the description of our globe and the proofs that it is a globe by simple geographical studies of the schoolroom, yard, and neighborhood." [2]

One effect of this emphasis on apperception was to give impetus to the movement to enrich the curriculum. As long as we think of education chiefly in terms of the development of faculties, a meagre curriculum is likely to be deemed sufficient. If we stress the need of building up apperceptive masses, however, we at once create a demand for appropriate subject matter. Since Herbart's day there has been an astonishing enrichment of the curriculum.

Our immediate concern, however, is with what was called a moment ago the " order of learning." There is undoubtedly an order of learning in the sense that learning must relate to experiential background, which means that the way a pupil learns is conditioned by his " apperceptive mass." Can this order of learning be formulated into a series of successive steps, so that the teacher will know at every point just what to do next? This would obviously be a great help. Herbart and his followers thought this could be done, and so they devised the famous Five Steps of the Herbartian method.

These Five Steps are called, respectively, Preparation, Presentation, Comparison and Abstraction, Generalization, and Application. First, the teacher must remind the pupils of certain facts or experiences with which they

2 E. L. Thorndike, *Education*, p. 146.

are already acquainted.  This is called the step of Preparation; it teaches nothing new, but simply stirs up the apperceptive mass which is to be enlarged and enriched.  Then comes the next step, which is Presentation, in which certain new facts are added to the old.  In the third step, Comparison and Abstraction, the new and the old are welded together by showing that they relate to a common principle or fact.  The formulation of this common element is the fourth step, Generalization.  Then comes the final step, Application, in which this common principle or element is applied or used to explain further facts.  The whole process is one of extending or transforming the apperceptive background with which we started.  According to Herbartianism, effective teaching requires that these steps be followed in a fixed order, and it is held that this should be done regardless of diversities in subject matter.

An excellent illustration of this procedure is provided by Dr. W. C. Bagley.[3]  The theme of the lesson to be taught in this illustration is that vapor is condensed through the lowering of temperature.  The first step — Preparation — consists in reminding the pupils of certain familiar facts, such as the steam from a teakettle, dew, hoarfrost, and frost on the window in wintertime.  Next comes Presentation, in which new facts are introduced.  The teacher brings in a pitcher of ice water and pours it into another pitcher or a tumbler (thus lowering the temperature of the new container, which causes it to "sweat").  Or he may breathe successively on a cold and a hot surface of glass, to show that in one case a film of vapor appears, while in the other case it does not.  This leads naturally to the third step, Comparison and

[3] *The Educative Process,* Chap. XIX.

Abstraction, in which the underlying principle, viz., that vapor is caused by the lowering of temperature, is brought to light. The formulation of this principle is the fourth step, Generalization, after which comes the last step, Application, in which this generalization is used to explain certain further facts, such as the formation of clouds, the dampness at cave entrances, and similar phenomena.

For further illustrations we may summarize briefly two examples given in McMurry's *The Method of the Recitation*. Let us suppose that the aim of the recitation is to present the subject of " The Irrigation of Arid Lands." [4] The first step is a discussion of rainfall and a survey of previously acquired geographical knowledge pertaining to the arid regions. This step is supposed to be limited to a consideration of facts with which the pupil is already acquainted. In the second step, a detailed study is made of some irrigation system, which introduces new knowledge. In the third step, this irrigation system, including the topography, rivers, and towns which are important in irrigation, is compared with other irrigation systems, for the purpose of drawing conclusions about the significance of mountains, plains, cities, size of streams, etc., in irrigation. This leads into the fourth step, which consists in specifying the common features of these areas relative to irrigation. The pupils discover, for example, that the areas compared are all arid, that adjacent rivers furnish the possibility of irrigation, that the areas contain large towns which furnish a market for agricultural supplies, etc. The fifth step, Application, would consist in locating other arid regions,

[4] F. and C. McMurry, *The Method of the Recitation*, pp. 257-269.

discovering the rivers that could be used for irrigation, and the like.

The second illustration [5] consists in a study of the battle of King's Mountain during the Revolutionary War, for the purpose of showing the energy and patriotism of the common people. The step of Preparation is a survey of previous classroom work, in which maps and books are used, so as to get the geographical and military situation in which this battle occurred. The next step, Presentation, tells the story of the battle in detail, beginning with the sending out of a detachment of 1200 troops by Cornwallis for foraging purposes. In the step of Comparison and Abstraction this battle is compared with the battle of Bennington in Burgoyne's invasion. In the step of Generalization it is brought out that relatively small battles may have a great influence on the fortunes of a campaign and that the spirit of the common people in the two battles was largely the same. The step of Application consists in making comparisons with other battles, such as Bunker Hill, Stony Point, and Saratoga.

As a matter of historical interest, a word may be added about Herbart's theory of mind. His doctrine of apperception makes it clear that, for him, the important thing about mind is not that it is a substance, but that there are mental states which can be built up and made over in all manner of ways. Consequently, Herbart was an avowed opponent of the doctrine of formal discipline. Yet for some strange reason, he insists on leaving a place in his theory for a substantive mind. He offers a complicated theory of this mind, the point of which is that for practical purposes it may be disregarded. Appar-

[5] F. and C. McMurry, *ibid.*, pp. 270–281.

ently Herbart was not quite ready to break completely with tradition, and so the substantive mind is retained, but is honorably retired on a pension. Or, to change the figure of speech, the mind in Herbart's scheme occupies a status very much like that of a hereditary monarch in a country that is run by a system of popular government. Its position is one of considerable dignity but little power. As Herbart himself says, "The simple nature of the soul is totally unknown and forever remains so; it is as little a subject for speculative as for empirical psychology." Everything is explained in terms of various alliances or groups that are established among the mental states or "ideas" that arise in the soul. "The soul is regarded as little else than the battle ground of contending ideas." [6]

At the time that Herbart wrote, psychologists were beginning to turn their attention to the problem of determining the principles by which the flow of experience is controlled. To explain this flow, they introduced such principles as association by similarity, by contrast, and by contiguity. Herbart is more mysterious. According to Herbart, every experience has a certain quality which gives it an affinity for certain other experiences and makes it "allergic," so to speak, to others. The experience of "horse," for example, fits in readily with our subconscious experiences of "circus," and so these experiences amalgamate readily. On the other hand, the experience of "horse" has no affinity for "League of Nations" or "North Pole," and so it fights against annexation. Hence the mind is a "battleground of contending ideas." The perception of a horse brings forward its appropriate associates and at the same time it

[6] John Adams, *The Herbartian Psychology in Its Educational Applications*, p. 50.

struggles to keep other elements from appearing upon the scene. These affinities and oppositions are connected by Herbart with the concept of " interest "; and so Herbart became a precursor of the doctrine of interest, which is so prominent at the present time.

From a twentieth-century point of view such an explanation of what takes place is pure fancy. It is of interest to us primarily as an indication of the extent to which mental states were treated as independent existences, which grow and change according to laws or principles of their own. Since mental states are endowed with so high a degree of independence, it is understandable why Herbart should have believed that the teaching process is reducible to a fixed order of steps. The learning situation is so set up that the environment can spring no surprises. In the step of Presentation the environment is, indeed, the source of new material, but, apart from that, learning is a process of organizing our mental states, with little reference to the outside world. There is no apparent reason why this organization should not be achieved in accordance with a fixed procedure. Teaching accordingly takes on a certain analogy with the drilling of recruits in the army. The experiences are lined up and made to go through various combinations and rearrangements, with the teacher functioning as drill-sergeant and relying upon the Five Steps as his manual of arms.

Much of Herbart's psychology has been repudiated, but his doctrine of learning and teaching was widely adopted by teacher-training institutions and is still influential. Prospective teachers are taught that there is a fixed order of steps; they are required to write lesson plans in which the material to be taught is arranged according to these steps, and they are expected to follow these steps in the classroom. It is highly pertinent, therefore, to inquire whether these steps give a correct picture of how learning goes on.

On this point there is room for serious doubt. The doctrine of evolution has made us familiar with the notion that life is a process of continuous adjustment; and the concept of adjustment is prominent in all present-day psychology. If we take our cue from this idea, the whole perspective changes. Learning as a process of adjustment means that there is a problem of some kind to be solved; or, in other words, that the environment makes a demand which must be met. This is very different from organizing a set of hypothetical mental states, since it has yet to be shown that problems can be solved in accordance with any prearranged order of steps. The experience of inventors and research men is all to the effect that the solution of problems is a matter of catch-as-catch-can. If learning is related to problem-solving, then pupils are in precisely the same position as inventors and research men; and these " lesson plans " become an obstacle to education. It is worth noting that Herbart makes no mention of problems, although it is precisely the reference to a problem that gives unity to his method, from the standpoint of the pupil.

By way of illustration, let us take another look at the lesson plan for teaching that condensation is related to the lowering of temperature. The step of Preparation, which consists of calling attention to steaming teakettles, dew, frost on windows, etc., becomes a hodgepodge, bordering on mind-wandering, unless there is a sense that these phenomena, in spite of their diversities, have some kind of relevance, i.e., unless there is a sense of a problem.

Without this sense, the step of Presentation is just so much more irrelevance. On the other hand, if the sense of a problem is present, the pupil is expected to be on the alert for the detection of the underlying principle. But this is the same as saying that comparison and discrimination (Step III) should go on simultaneously with Step I. Perhaps some bright pupil will suggest that temperature is the important factor, and he may mention the fact that sweaty horses give off " steam " in the winter (which is Step V, Application). All this may happen before we are through with Step I.

This is but part of the story. It may happen that the class reacts slowly, so that when Step III, Comparison and Discrimination, is reached, it is found expedient to return to Step I, Preparation, for further data. Or, again, wrong suggestions may be offered, which must be tested and found inadequate before we can proceed. In brief, the steps may occur simultaneously and they may occur in practically any order — all of which indicates that the Herbartian Lesson Plan gives a false picture of how learning takes place.

It follows that the conscientious teacher who tries to take the steps in order is bound to go wrong. The aforementioned bright pupil, for example, would have to be given to understand that the right moment or " step " for his suggestion had not yet been reached. The deductions which he makes from his suggestion would likewise be ruled out. Wrong suggestions would have to be got rid of as regrettable obstructions to the teacher's plan. The whole procedure becomes rigid and artificial. It loses all resemblance to the way in which learning goes on outside of school. All genuine learning, whether in or out of school, is much more like the process by which an

inventor finally arrives at his goal. The inventor clearly
has no sequence of steps for solving his problem. He
tries one thing after another, he makes detours, he mixes
up the steps in all conceivable ways. He has to do this
in order to be " creative." To the pupil a lesson that is
well learned has an element of " creativeness " in it, no
matter how familiar the thing learned may be to others.
It is as preposterous to concoct a recipe for learning as
for invention.

This is not to say that the lesson plan does not have its
uses as a guide in preparing the materials to be used later
in teaching. The step of Preparation directs attention
to the experiential background of the pupils and thus
gives clues to pupil interest, and at the same time mini-
mizes the danger of assuming more background than the
pupils actually possess, which leads to the error of " talking over their heads." In the next step, Presentation, the
suitability of the new material that is introduced — experiments, maps, pictures, or what not — is conditioned
by the way in which this material fits in with the background. The material thus selected must pave the way
for Comparison and Discrimination, and for Generalization. Lastly, the step of Application requires the teacher
to have on hand an adequate amount of illustrative material, so that the basic principle may be illuminated and
extended. The lesson plan may thus help the teacher to
get the " feel " of the pupil's mind, to focus his attention
on the central purpose of the lesson, and to make him
sense the need of being equipped with appropriate illustrative material. We may concede that the lesson plan
has its merits, provided we do not use it, i.e., provided we
do not follow it as a plan of campaign in the classroom.

When the prospective teacher is required to follow the
successive steps and perhaps even — save the mark — to

set down beforehand in his lesson plan the answers that are to be elicited from the class, then spontaneous and effective learning gives way to dreary, soul-destroying pedagogy. Moreover, the whole scheme then becomes a device for indoctrination. The conclusion to be reached is determined in advance, and the successive steps are so arranged as to culminate in this conclusion. The method makes indoctrination the normal aim of teaching.

Let us have recourse once more to illustration. We may suppose that the theme of the lesson is communism and that the teacher aims to show the evils of this doctrine. The step of Preparation then might consist of reminding the pupils how dogs fight for a bone and how thieves steal from honest people. The step of Presentation might consist of narratives relating the distress and general demoralization that result in situations where property is insecure. Then in the third step, Comparison and Discrimination, the inference would be drawn that respect for property rights is necessary for happiness and prosperity. The inference would be formulated into a generalization, and finally application would be made, say to Russia or to the experiments in communism that have been made by local communities in this country in the past.

All this would be formally correct, and the final conclusion would be logical on the data as presented. It is evident, however, that the steps could be so arranged as to lead to a diametrically opposite conclusion. The step of Preparation might consist of reference to family life as a beautiful example of holding things in common on the principle of all for each and each for all. To this might be added the example of the post office or the fire department, neither of which is private property. Then, in Presentation, the pupils might be told of the extension

of governmental agencies, such as reforestation, soil con-
servation, dam-building etc., together with some lurid
stories of the slave trade or of industrial exploitation, to
show what men will do for profit, and how civilization
has found it necessary to eliminate, or at least to restrain,
the possibilities of profit. This would set the stage in the
third step, Comparison and Discrimination, in which
the inference would be drawn that happiness and prosperity require community of property and the final elim-
ination of the profit motive. This conclusion would
then be made into a Generalization, and finally would
come Application, consisting, let us say, of reference to
Russia, to the municipal ownership of power plants and
water systems, and the like. Whether the purpose be to
prove or to disprove communism, the result is a foregone
conclusion, if the teacher sticks resolutely to his lesson
plan.

The point of all this is that the teacher who follows this
method is committed to a program of indoctrination, in
the sense that he determines in advance what it is that the
pupil is to believe. Since the teacher's chief concern is
with the organization of mental states, some guiding prin-
cipal or pattern or " frame of reference " is necessary,
and no adequate provision is made for this need. In the
case of the soul-substance theory the quest for a guiding
principle led to such principles as harmonious development, eternal ideals, and formal discipline, each of which
turned out to be a device for imposing upon the student
the beliefs of the teacher. In the case of the mental-states
theory the difficulty is even more acute, since we cannot
appeal to a mind-substance nor to faculties; and so there
appears to be nothing to fall back upon except the beliefs
or prejudices of the teacher or the community.

We may cheerfully admit that Herbartianism has made important contributions to education. It rendered valuable service in its repudiation of the barren doctrine of formal discipline, in emphasizing the importance of the psychological approach, in calling for an enriched curriculum, in directing attention to the significance of interest, and in making the preparation of teachers an important business. On the debit side of the ledger is the fact that the doctrine of mental states, upon which Herbartianism rests, separates the mental states so completely from the external world as to make a knowledge of it impossible, and likewise that this separation leads to a false account of the learning process and makes teaching virtually synonymous with indoctrination.

This reopens the entire question of mind and education. If the mind-substance doctrine proved to be too easy a solution for psychological and educational problems, the same may be said of the theory of mental states. We do not learn in the way that Herbartianism says we do. How then do we learn? A more adequate theory of mind is necessary as a basis for educational theory and practice.

## Bibliography

ADAMS, J., *The Herbartian Psychology in Its Educational Applications*, Chap. III. D. C. Heath and Co.

BAGLEY, W. C., *The Educative Process*, Chap. XIX. Macmillan Co.

DE GARMO, C., *Essentials of Method*, Chap. II. D. C. Heath and Co.

DEWEY, J., *How We Think* (Revised Edition), Chap. XVIII. D. C. Heath and Co.

McMURRY, F. C., *The Method of the Recitation*, Chap. II. Macmillan Co.

# CHAPTER XI

# The Rise of Behaviorism

THE history of mind is a record both of logical development and of temporal sequence. At the outset a substantive mind was set over against substantive matter, and each of these two substances was assumed to operate with a certain degree of independence. This view of mind led to a distinction within the mind between the mind-substance and its "states." The analysis of these states revealed an unsuspected degree of complexity in the make-up of these states, and at the same time it tended to make the notion of a substantive mind a superfluity. Psychologists embarked on the task of explaining the states in terms of certain principles of association, such as similarity, contrast, and contiguity. The mind-substance was permitted to fade out of the picture, and so the doctrine of mind-substance was replaced by the theory of mental states.

Our next concern is to trace the process by which the psychology of mental states led on to a different point of view. As mental states replaced the mind-substance doctrine, they fell heir to a portion of the independence, or capacity of spontaneous action, which was originally an endowment of the mind-substance. The mental states organized themselves in various ways on their own initiative, so to speak. According to Herbart, they constantly struggle among themselves, because of their inherent affinities and antipathies. The principles of association, such as the principle of similarity, were assumed to express an inherent tendency of mental states to act in certain ways. The disposition to deal with mental states in this fashion was presumably due, at least in part, to the fact that the development of modern physiology and neurology is a comparatively recent affair.

The identification of mind with mental states resulted in casting a shadow on the status of matter. If these mental states are all that we know at first hand, how can we ever know the nature of matter or even be sure of its existence? By a strange development, however, the theory of mental states, which created so grave a threat against the concept of matter, eventually became the means of giving matter the opportunity of taking the offensive and endangering the status of mind.

This development started simply and innocently enough. Psychologists learned as they went along that they could discover the constituents of mental states better if they took account of the physiological factors involved. The average person, for example, is unaware that his ordinary visual perceptions contain an element of eyestrain. The psychologist probably would not discover this either, if he confined his attention to immediate introspection. The knowledge, however, that all looking involves a focussing of the eyes gives him a clue as to what to look for.

When we are looking at an object that is a considerable distance away, the eyes converge but little and the strain remains unnoticed. In proportion as the object comes closer the convergence increases. If we try to look at an object like the end of a lead pencil, when it is held halfway between the eyes and a few inches from the face, the convergence becomes so great as to produce an unpleasant strain in the muscles of the eyes. It is when the strain reaches a certain degree of intensity that we become aware of it. But there are sensations of strain even when we do not notice them, and it would be no easy matter to locate these sensations if the physiological processes did not point the way. Experimental evidence has been adduced to show that these unnoticed sensations of strain are a factor in determining judgments of distance. The same applies to estimates of visual magnitude or extent.

There is good reason for thinking that our estimation of visual extent is originally made by the help of the intensity of strain sensations. Each eye is slung in its socket upon six separate muscles. When we compare two lines, the natural thing to do is to " run the eyes along them "; and this movement of the eyes calls forth sensations of muscular contraction or tendinous strain. A longer line occasions a more severe (stronger) strain, and a shorter line occasions a less severe strain. We estimate extent in terms of intensity.[1]

But a further and more potent reason for studying physiological processes lies in the fact that physiology furnishes an opportunity to explain what is going on. Analysis can tell us of what constituents or parts a given compound is made up, but it does not shed much light on causal connections; i.e., it does not seek to ascertain the conditions under which events take place. If the mind is dependent on the body, it is evident that knowledge of causal connections must be secured through the study of physiological processes.

In the matter of causal connections the older psychology left much to be desired. Faculty psychology was usually content to say that our experiences were due to

[1] E. B. Titchener, *An Outline of Psychology*, p. 83.

the activity of the mind.  But, as James points out, it is
no explanation of memory to say that we remember because we have a faculty of memory.  This is not explanation, but naming, since it adds no new insight, no new
understanding of the relations between the remembered
fact and other facts.

Why should this absolute godgiven Faculty retain so
much better the events of yesterday than those of last year,
and, best of all, those of an hour ago?  Why, again, in old
age should its grasp of childhood's events seem firmest?
Why should illness and exhaustion enfeeble it?  Why should
repeating an experience strengthen our recollection of it?
Why should drugs, fevers, asphyxia, and excitement resusci-
tate things long since forgotten? . . . Evidently, then, the
faculty does not exist absolutely, but works under conditions; and the quest of the conditions becomes the psychologist's most interesting task.[2]

When the belief in a substantive mind was finally given
up, psychology attempted to explain everything in terms
of association.  Thus the rumble of distant thunder suggests lightning, because these things have been associated
together previously in our experience; or the clouds in
the sky suggest a snowbank, because the two have a certain resemblance.  This is good enough, as far as it goes,
but it does not go very far.  As James insists, it " does not
explain the effects of fever, exhaustion, hypnotism, old
age, and the like."  Here again we are forced to the conclusion that association works under conditions: and
these conditions are of a physiological kind.  The functioning of remembering varies with the condition of the
cerebral cortex.  To explain remembering by reference
to associations is not to say the last word, for the sufficient

[2] W. James, *Principles of Psychology*, Vol. I, pp. 2, 3.

reason that association in turn depends upon processes that take place in the brain.

It is not surprising, therefore, that psychology in its later development should go hand-in-hand with the study of physiology. The study of physiological psychology, however, had not gone very far before it began to appear that the interdependence of mind and body was much more extensive and intimate than had first been supposed. The earlier notion of a " mind " — whether the term mind be understood to mean a substantive entity or a collection of discrete states — which was capable of acting quite independently of the body, was found to be a myth. The effects of stimulants, brain disease, narcotics, exhaustion, weather, old age, and the like all tend to show that " consciousness is inseparably bound up with the brain process, and cannot take place in its absence." [3]

There is no space here to review the evidence in detail. In general, however, we may say that all consciousness appears to involve movement of some kind; which disposes of the notion that the mind may act in complete independence of the body. Thus experiments have shown that if a person thinks of his feet or of his home, or of any other objects to which his thought assigns a more or less definite place, the muscles of his body respond in such a way as to indicate the direction of that place.[4] What is ordinarily called mind-reading is just a case of muscle-reading. The old joke to the effect that some city apartments are so small as to make it necessary for

[3] C. A. Strong, *Why the Mind Has a Body*, p. 37.

[4] Some of the earlier experiments in this field are recorded by Jastrow, *Fact and Fable in Psychology*, in the chapter entitled " A Study of Involuntary Movements." Cf. also W. James, *Principles of Psychology*, Vol. II, Chap. XXIII.

an occupant to go out into the hall in order to change his mind is by way of receiving scientific sanction. It is literally necessary to have room for the purpose of changing one's mind. No psychosis without neurosis — no mental change without concomitant bodily change — is the verdict of present-day science.

At first the development of physiological psychology was merely in the nature of expanding and amplifying the work of the earlier psychology. Eventually, however, the results of physiological psychology began to react on the original point of view. One effect of the reference to physiological causes was to cast a doubt on the status of the subconscious. The notion that we carry earlier experiences around with us in a kind of basement, so to speak (the *sub*-conscious), has an unmistakable quality of naïveté. It is perhaps convenient to assume that ideas retire to a subconscious until they are called forth by memory, or that it is the subconscious which notifies us that the clock has stopped. But the assumption is not needed. Memory does not require that ideas be kept on deposit, but is explained quite as well by the theory that certain brain-processes are reinstated. And it may be that such a phenomenon as noting the stopping of the clock can also be explained adequately in terms of physical responses.

We have evidence to show that when we are engaged in reading a book, for example, the ear lends assistance to the eye by shutting out disturbing sounds. Instead of being " set " to hear sounds, we are " set " not to hear them, which is an equally positive reaction. While we are reading, the ear co-operates with the eye by shutting out the stimulation that comes from the ticking of the clock. When this stimulation is suddenly withdrawn, the ear is set to resist an impact which does not arrive. The result is something like what happens when we come downstairs and find that there is one more step than we had expected. That is, we are "set" to step on the solid floor, but step into a vacuum instead, so that there is a hasty readjustment of response to inform us of what has happened.

This is, of course, only a more or less figurative explanation of the phenomenon in question, but it serves to indicate that there is an alternative to the explanation by means of subconscious ideas. Moreover, this alternative type of explanation has the great advantage of being couched in terms of objective fact. We can be reasonably sure that we have a body and that the body makes responses of various kinds. We do not have the same assurance that there are subconscious experiences. In fact the whole notion of the subconscious seems to involve a contradiction. It is of the essence of a pain, for example, that it hurts. If the hurt disappears, the pain is gone, and it would be just plain obscurantism to talk of a subconscious pain. A pain of this kind would be a pain that did not hurt. We may suppose that the nerve of an aching tooth continues to vibrate after a person has fallen asleep, but it is nonsense to say that the pain still continues in the realm of the subconscious. This conclusion can be generalized. We know what it is to have experiences of colors, sounds, and the like, but when we transfer these experiences to the realm of the subconscious we find ourselves talking about unexperienced experience or unconscious consciousness. This is mythology of a peculiarly vicious kind.

In effect, the domain of the subconscious is annexed by physiology, which means that the sphere of free and independent action by the mind or by mental states is greatly curtailed. The subconscious is no longer a realm where "ideas" act more or less independently; it becomes essentially a physiological phenomenon. But the program of conquest does not stop here. Eventually, in connection with what is called the mind-body problem, physiology issued a challenge to the whole idea of mental action. Is there anything at all in human behavior that cannot be accounted for in terms of purely physiological processes?

It is commonly assumed that mental states and the body are related to each other by interaction. This notion, however, presents difficulties when we examine it. The cause of the trouble lies in the fact that mind and body have no common denominator. How then can they interact? We may grant that little enough is known about causation in any case; but, at all events, the interaction of physical objects goes on among objects all of which occupy space. When we try to understand such a process, we aim to trace its course along a line of physical movements. Thus when we set a row of bricks on end in such a way that when the first brick in the row is knocked down all the bricks go down successively, every part in the process is embodied in a form of movement. But when we deal with the relation of mind and body, the situation is different. The mind or consciousness does not occupy space; consequently, if matter acts on mind, the sequence of movements is interrupted. The effect of the antecedent physical process does not show itself in a subsequent movement, but seems to disappear into a fourth dimension. Just what happens we cannot guess, even remotely. Presently the mind does something to the body, which means that a certain amount of force or energy emerges from this fourth dimension and sets up certain movements. Perhaps this is what actually happens, but the whole business looks suspicious enough to give us pause.

The only effect of further study is to deepen the mystery. How can a nonspacial, disembodied " idea " do anything to the brain? Does it exert some sort of push or pull on the molecules in the cortex, and, if so, does it operate from the top or from the bottom or from the side of the brain? Such questions are, of course, nonsense. Since mental states are not in space, we cannot ask in which direction they push or pull. It is a problem without any discoverable head or tail. To understand the action of mental states on brain states is about as difficult as to understand how the square root of minus two can help to lift an automobile out of the ditch. As W. K. Clifford says: " It will be found excellent practice in the mental operations required by this doctrine to imagine a train, the fore part of which is an engine and three carriages linked with iron couplings, and the hind part three other carriages linked with iron couplings; the bond between the two parts being made up out of the sentiments of amity subsisting between the stoker and the guard." [5]

Eventually most psychologists came to the conclusion that the belief in interaction between mind and body must be discarded and adopted instead the theory of parallelism, which holds that the mental series and the physical series go on side by side, but without causal relationship. The mind does not control the body any more than our shadow controls our walking or the speedometer controls the speed of the automobile. We may say that the mental states merely register the bodily hap-

[5] Quoted by W. James, *Principles of Psychology*, Vol. I, p. 132.

penings, except that there is no causal relation of any kind. There must be some kind of relationship, of course, to account for the concomitance, but this was regarded as a question outside the province of psychology; it was a question for philosophy. A conclusion of this kind evidently constitutes a sweeping victory for physiology. It concedes the principle that all human behavior can be explained in terms of physiological processes.[6]

This doctrine of parallelism has the obvious disadvantage that it leads into a disquieting sort of mystery. It asserts that pin-pricks are not the cause of pain, but that the pricks and the pain come and go together. This concomitance is admittedly not just a coincidence, but on the other hand we are forbidden to construe the relation in terms of causation. But if the relation is not a causal relation, what sort of relation is it? The question is not easy to answer. Huxley's doctrine of *conscious automatism*, which may be regarded either as a modified parallelism or as a modified interactionism, is an attempt to escape from the difficulty. According to Huxley, the body can produce experiences or mental states, but these mental states have no power to change the workings of the body. Our experiences simply record the reactions that take place in the body, just as the barometer records changes in air pressure. As Huxley says:

The consciousness of brutes would appear to be related to the mechanism of their body simply as a collateral product of its working, and to be as completely without any power of modifying that working as the steam-whistle which accompanies the work of a locomotive engine is without influ-

[6] For a detailed statement of the different psychological theories regarding the relation between mind and body see C. A. Strong, *Why the Mind Has a Body*, Chaps. IV, V, VI, and VII.

ence upon its machinery. Their volition, if they have any, is an emotion indicative of physical changes, not a cause of such changes. . . . There is no proof that any state of consciousness is the cause of change in the motion of the matter of the organism. If these positions are well based, it follows that our mental conditions are simply the symbols in consciousness of the changes which take place automatically in the organism; and that, to take an extreme illustration, the feeling we call volition is not the cause of a voluntary act, but the symbol of that state of the brain which is the immediate cause of the act. We are conscious automata.[7]

For present purposes it does not matter a great deal whether we hold to parallelism or to conscious automatism. From either point of view we are encouraged to make psychology a study of behavior. More specifically, the situation invites us to try explaining human behavior in terms of bodily processes alone. Why not ignore what we call "mind" altogether and confine ourselves to a description of how the organism behaves? A procedure of this kind has the advantage of being strictly objective, in the sense that different observers can watch the same fact and can verify what they see. This is not true in the same sense in introspection. If a person watches what is taking place in his own inner consciousness, other observers cannot share in the observation, and cannot check in any direct fashion on the report that the introspecting observer may see fit to make.

The tendency to make psychology a study of behavior rather than an introspective analysis of mental states eventually made considerable headway and became known as Behaviorism. At the outset it did not chal-

[7] T. H. Huxley, *Science and Culture*. The two passages here quoted are from the chapter "On the Hypothesis that Animals Are Automata."

lenge outright the existence of consciousness, but raised the question of method. Traditional psychology had depended almost exclusively on introspection, but why continue to do so? When observers disagreed in their findings, there was no way of settling the disagreement. In the analysis of visual perception, for example, different observers made different reports as to the number of shades of color or degrees of brightness that could be detected. Introspection did not prove anything. Moreover, we have at hand a method that is objective and final. In certain experiments with rats it was found that the rats could be trained so as to go to a food box when a green light was displayed and to avoid the box when a red light was shown. The experiment proved beyond peradventure that the rat was capable of distinguishing in some way between green and red. It was quite unnecessary to consult the introspective findings of the rat. All that was necessary was to observe his behavior. Experiments of this sort, can, of course, be made on human beings quite as readily, and they can be refined without assignable limit. We have in this method a procedure that is objective and scientific. Why not abandon the method of introspection altogether and make psychology a real science?

In a plea of this kind it is not necessary to argue that there is no such thing as consciousness, but simply that psychology has no more to do with consciousness than any other science. We may grant that a physicist, for example, has consciousness and that he uses consciousness in making and recording his observations. The physicist may use consciousness, but he does not study it. His business is with the properties and relations of matter. Similarly the psychologist may use consciousness, but he is not called upon to study it. His business is with certain forms of behavior.

Will there be left over in psychology a world of pure psychics, to use Yerkes' term? I confess I do not know. The plans which I most favor for psychology lead practically to the ignoring of consciousness in the sense that the word is used by psychologists today. I have virtually denied that this realm of psychics is open to experimental investigation. I don't wish to go further into the problem at present because it leads inevitably over into metaphysics. If you will grant the behaviorist the right to use consciousness in the same way that other natural scientists employ it — that is, without making consciousness a special object of observation — you have granted all that my thesis requires.[8]

Before long, however, the cloven hoof began to show itself. In proportion as the new method yielded results and seemed adequate for the purposes of the psychologist, the old psychology became more and more artificial and unreal. The behaviorist developed an attitude towards the traditional psychologist akin to that of the trained physician towards a witch-doctor. Why put up any longer with the superstitions of the past? Science leaves no place at all for mind in any form. In proportion as psychology has become scientific, mental states have lost prestige and finally have become a mere shadow hovering over cerebral activities, as useless as the squeak of an ungreased cartwheel. Why not take the final step and abolish them altogether? Natural science furnished excellent precedent for this. It has shown that heat, light, and sound are merely forms of motion, that water is really a compound of oxygen and hydrogen. By the

[8] J. B. Watson, " Psychology as the Behaviorist Views It," *Psychological Review*, XX (1913), 175.

same token a pain, an emotion, a noise, a color are, one and all, merely disturbances in the cerebral cortex. Matter is the only reality. Everything that we call personal experience is reducible to forms of motion. It is a mistake to distinguish between a perceptual quality like blue and the physical conditions on which the perception depends. They are one and the same thing.

Blueness is not something in *addition* to these conditions. If the self-observer could designate all the anatomical and physiological factors that are involved, he would find merely a specific sensori-motor condition that is rather complex but always functions when acted upon by light of the specified frequency. . . . For the behaviorist the quality of blueness indicates the fact that the individual has developed a response that is specific for a spectral blue stimulus.[9]

In a word, the behaviorist applies the same sort of explanation to sense-qualities as that adopted in the physical sciences. If it is correct to say that sound consists of air waves, that water consists of $H_2O$, and that diamonds consist of carbon, why may we not say that the quality blue consists of certain processes or activities? Moreover, this explanation accounts simply and conveniently for illusions and variations in sense perception. These are all reducible to specific reactions. There is no mystery about it. In particular there is no need of introducing a consciousness to explain the facts. It would be just as reasonable for the chemist to bring in a consciousness in order to explain how water can be made up of hydrogen and oxygen. Water is not something over and above the hydrogen and oxygen, and

9 A. P. Weiss, *A Theoretical Basis of Human Behavior*, pp. 272–273.

similarly blue is not something over and above the sum of its conditions.

The same type of explanation obviously applies to images. We can close our eyes and call up scenes of the past or indulge in irresponsible daydreaming. There is no particular problem about this if we keep our eye on the fact that these images and memories consist of activities engaged in by the organism. We make certain responses, we act, and these activities are known as images.

With the reduction of sensations, perceptions, and images to activities or processes the behaviorist succeeds in reducing all the terms of his explanation to a simple common denominator. Everything that we call experience consists of physical reactions. It is not necessary at any point to have recourse to a different kind of reality called "mind" or "consciousness." Such terms as foresight, purpose, motive, desire, have no proper place in a psychological vocabulary. They are literary, not scientific terms. We can explain everything that a human being does in the same terms with which we explain the operations of a machine.[10] "Behaviorism in psychology is merely the name for that type of investigation and theory which assumes that man's educational, vocational, and social activities can be completely described or explained as the result of the same (and no other) forces used in the natural sciences."[11]

Thus matter takes its revenge on mind. After suffering all manner of aspersion, after having even its

[10] A. P. Weiss, *A Theoretical Basis of Human Behavior*, pp. 346–353.
[11] *Ibid.*, p. 7.

existence called into question, matter now turns the tables on its tormentor and repays in kind. In the psychology of Behaviorism matter becomes top dog. The more we look behind the scenes, the clearer it becomes that things are rarely quiet in the household of mind and matter. The attempt to give each member of the household a certain degree of independence ended with the repudiation of the mind-substance theory. The recognition of interdependence did not establish peace but led to a contest for domination. The efforts of "mental states" or "consciousness" to rule the establishment resulted in its being dispossessed of house and home. Matter then took title to all the visible assets in the name of Behaviorism, and in doing so it assumed responsibility for demonstrating that it is able to give an adequate account of human behavior and a satisfactory program for education.

## Bibliography

HEIDBREDER, E., *Seven Psychologies*, Chap. VII. D. Appleton-Century Co.

HUXLEY, T. H., *Science and Culture*, Chap. "On the Hypothesis that Animals Are Automata."

MEYER, MAX, *The Psychology of the Other One*, Chaps. I, II, XIX. The Missouri Book Co.

THORNDIKE, E. L., *Educational Psychology* (Briefer Course), Chaps. II, III. Teachers College, Columbia University.

WATSON, J. B., *Behaviorism*, Chaps. I, V, X, XI. The People's Institute Publishing Co.

WATSON, J. B., *The Ways of Behaviorism*, Chaps. I–V. Harper and Brothers.

WEISS, A. P., *A Theoretical Basis of Human Behavior*, Chap. I. R. G. Adams and Co.

WOODWORTH, R. S., *Contemporary Schools of Psychology*, Chaps. I, III. Henry Holt & Co.

# CHAPTER XII

# Behaviorism and Learning

As we turn to the psychology of Behaviorism, we are relieved, for the time being, of the troublesome question of dualism. Mind is definitely out of the picture. All problems of human behavior must be accounted for in terms of physiological response to stimulus.

As a point of departure, let us consider briefly the equipment with which the newborn infant comes into the world. Even though he is completely lacking in experience, the infant is capable of making responses to its environment. Such responses as breathing, crying, swallowing, sneezing, coughing, winking, and the like, are clearly of such a character that nothing is needed to explain them except the native constitution of the organism. These responses are unlearned and yet they have a definite character. They are commonly called reflexes, by which is meant that they are determined by inborn connections in the nervous system, which makes them independent of learning. A reflex action has no relation to purpose; it is regarded as purely mechanical in character, like the action of a shotgun or of a creeping ivy.

According to Behaviorism, however, no human behavior of any kind is determined by purpose, since purpose has been reduced to physiological activity. How, then, are we to explain what is ordinarily called learning and purposive behavior? To this the answer is simple.

All behavior is reducible to the type of reflex. In other words, learning is a process of building up new reflexes. This is done by coupling up stimuli with new responses so as to make new pairs. A reflex action which is thus built up in the course of experience by joining a stimulus to a new response is called a " conditioned reflex," in contrast with reflexes which are inborn.

To illustrate, let us suppose a child reaches for an object, such as a toy. This act of reaching is an inborn reflex. Now if a sharp noise is made whenever the child reaches for the toy, the reflex action of fear is set up, which causes the hand to be withdrawn. The same reaction may be secured by a slap on the wrist. If this is done a number of times, the child will eventually withdraw the hand when the toy is shown, even if the noise is absent. The toy has then become a stimulus to withdrawal. Or if we say " dinner " every time we hand an infant his bottle, he will presently react for " bottle " whenever the word " dinner " is spoken, even if the bottle is not in sight. The only difference between a conditioned reflex and an inborn reflex is a difference in origin. When a conditioned reflex has once been acquired, it is just like any other reflex. That is to say, all behavior, whether original or acquired, is of the reflex type, which means that it is essentially mechanical in character. We never get off the level of reflex action. There are, of course, all kinds of complications and integrations of the reflexes, but all that is only a matter of detail. Learning of every kind consists ultimately in the building up of conditioned reflexes.[1]

This " conditioning " of the nervous system explains the formation of " complexes," of which the psycho-

[1] J. B. Watson, *The Ways of Behaviorism*, pp. 31, 32.

analysts have made so great a mystery. Watson illustrates by what he calls " nest habits." A child is " spoiled " by having everything done for him by his mother. He must be fed, bathed, and dressed only by his mother; he must have his mother with him at all times, etc. The result is a " nest habit " which makes it almost impossible for the child in later life to break away from these ties. He — or perhaps more frequently she — may marry, but the old ties are too strong, and the marriage turns out a failure, because the life of the young person so brought up continues to center on the mother. The explanation, as Watson insists, is not to be looked for in terms of " subconscious needs " or in " repressions," but in the early conditioning of the nervous system. The child had learned to react in a certain way, and that is all.

The cases just cited represent learning of a very simple kind. This learning is simple because the connection between the stimulus and the new response is rather easily established. In other cases learning may be slower and more involved, but the underlying principle, according to Behaviorism, is the same. Whether simple or complex, learning is a process of " stamping in " a new connection in the nervous system. The connection between Stimulus and Response is designated by Thorndike as an S–R bond. According to Thorndike, the basic laws, known as the laws of learning, which control the formation of an S–R bond are two in number. One is the Law of Exercise, by which is meant that repetition tends to make the bond permanent. The other is the Law of Effect, which means that if the result of an action — such as ringing a bell or rolling a ball — is pleasurable, the connection between the stimulus and the response is strengthened, whereas if it is unpleasant — as in reaching for a hot stove and being burned — the connection is weakened. These two laws, so it is claimed, suffice to explain the entire range of learning operations.

An example of such explanation is provided by the pioneer work done by Thorndike in the field of animal learning. Some of this work consisted in experiments with cats in order to observe how they learned to escape from a box or cage. A cat was placed in a cage after it had been deprived of food for some considerable time. Food was placed outside of the cage, where it could be seen through the bars but at a distance where it could not be reached by the cat. The animal would then struggle in the usual cat fashion to get at the food. It would reach through the bars, try to squeeze through them, and claw around promiscuously. The purpose of these experiments was to find out how long it would take the cat to learn to do a certain thing, such as pulling a string, turning a button, or pressing a lever, which would release it from the cage.

These experiments furnish some interesting results. Since the cat had no knowledge of the mechanism by which the release could be effected, it could at first escape from the cage only by accident. In the course of its struggles the cat would eventually hit by chance upon the thing that had to be done in order to open the door of the cage. For example, it would just happen to pull a string suspended in the cage, which would then open the door so that the cat could get out. What made the experiment interesting was the fact that the cat evidently did not " catch on " to the meaning of the string. This was made clear by what happened in subsequent experiments. When the experiment was repeated, the cat would not go straight to the string, as we should expect a human being to do, but would claw around in a more or less random fashion as before. In other words, the successful outcome was again dependent on accident. With the repetition of the experiment, however, the time necessary for opening the door of the cage was gradually shortened. The number of wrong responses was gradually decreased, which meant that the cat was in process of building up an association between the situation of " being in the cage " and performing the action of pulling a string. In the end the cat was able to do the right thing as soon as it was placed in the box. In ordinary parlance, the cat had learned how to get out of the cage.

The significant feature of this experiment is that we seem to be dealing with a very specific kind of learning. It is learning without the element of " catching on " to the meaning of the string. The learning is just a process of fixing certain reactions, as we do in learning to play tennis or to run a typewriter. According to Thorndike, it is just a process of building up a conditioned reflex. If we consider the manner in which the time interval between being placed in the cage and escaping from the cage is shortened, we find that the facts give some color to this interpretation. " Thus the successive times taken by one cat in a certain box were (in seconds) 160, 30, 90, 60, 15, 28, 20, 30, 22, 11, 15, 20, 12, 10, 14, 8, 5, 10, 8, 6, 6, 7." [2] If we plot a curve for these figures, we find, indeed, considerable irregularity, but we also find a general, unmistakable slope downwards. There

[2] *Psychological Review*, V, 552. Quoted by G. F. Stout, *Manual of Psychology*, p. 262.

is no sudden drop, as might be expected if the animal had discovered, by a flash of insight, that the string was a means of escaping from the cage. The gradual descent of the slope indicates that, for some reason, the wrong responses tend progressively to drop out, until finally the tendency to do just one thing is firmly established in the nervous system of the cat.

It seems reasonable to suppose that if the cat had perceived the causal connection between pulling the string and escaping from the cage, the time expended on the third trial would not have run to ninety seconds. The record indicates that the cat was not "learning" anything, in the sense of gaining an understanding of causal connections. It had no more insight at the end of the process than at the beginning. The final reaction, like the original reflexes, was as devoid of understanding or purpose as the act of withdrawing the hand when it comes into contact with a hot stove. This is Thorndike's doctrine. In his view, this process of learning is merely a matter of establishing a new neural pathway, so that the stimulus eventually produces just one reaction, to the exclusion of all others. The reaction or response which opens the door of the cage has become definitely associated with a particular stimulus.

The explanation to be given of this learning may take either or both of two forms: It may be pointed out, as Watson [3] does, that the cat does the right thing each time that it gets out of the cage; it also does a number of wrong things, but it does not do the same wrong things on each of the different occasions. In other words, the right thing is done oftener than any one of the wrong things; consequently, the Law of Exercise

[3] J. B. Watson, *Behaviorism*, pp. 164–166.

or repetition covers the case. Or we may say, with Thorndike,[4] that doing the right thing results in pleasure or satisfaction, and that acts which result in satisfaction have a tendency, in some obscure way, to gain predominance. They become "stamped in," as a consequence of the resulting pleasure, and so are repeated more easily. This brings in the Law of Effect. The point is that both of these explanations for learning of this kind go back to physiological habit, without recourse to any guidance by "insight," for which there is no room in a behavioristic program. As a result of repetition the wrong movements are gradually eliminated and the right actions are retained. This is the whole story. It means that the right response has been reduced to the type of reflex.

If, now, we turn to learning as it takes place in men, we seem to find a great difference. Whatever we may say of the lower animals, human beings seem to exercise intelligence, and it is not apparent how their behavior is to be explained in terms of simple habit formation, as in the case of cats or other animals. On the surface, at any rate, there is a tremendous difference, and this difference lies in the fact that human beings have the power of abstract thinking. They can analyze a situation and figure out what is important or what needs to be done for the purpose of getting the results that are desired. In other words, they can cut out the random movements and the wearisome repetitions almost entirely, and pick out the right act at once, because they are endowed with understanding or insight. Consequently the learning of human beings seems to be some-

[4] E. L. Thorndike, *Educational Psychology* (Briefer Course), Chap. IV and p. 172.

thing more than mere habit formation of the kind just described. However we may see fit to explain animal learning, it seems clear that human learning is directed by ideas and purposes which raise it far above the level of mechanical habit.

That there is a difference of some kind is recognized by Thorndike when he points out that animal learning of the kind previously discussed

. . . is characterized negatively by the absence of inferential, ratiocinative thinking; and indeed by the absence of effective use of "ideas" of any sort. Were the reader confined in a maze or cage, or left at some distance from home, his responses to those situations would almost certainly include many ideas, judgments or thoughts about the situation; and his acts would probably in large measure be led up to or "mediated" by such sequences of ideas as are commonly called reasoning. Between the annoying situation and the response which relieves the annoyance there might for the reader well intervene an hour of inner consideration, thought, planning and the like. But there is no evidence that any ideas about the maze, the cage, the food, or anything else, were present to determine the acts of the chicks or kittens in question. Their responses were made directly to the situations as sensed, not via ideas suggested by it.[5]

The recognition of this difference between animal and human learning suggests that it is necessary to give only a limited scope to the behavioristic doctrine that all learning is reducible to the type of the conditioned reflex. But if we impose this limitation on our explanation, we seem forced to return to the ancient dualism of mind and matter, to which Thorndike is very much averse. While he has never classed himself as a behaviorist in psychology, he is at one with the behaviorist in his insistence

[5] *Ibid.*, p. 131.

that all conduct, whether animal or human, is fundamentally a matter of acquiring conditioned reflexes. As he says:

If any learned response is made to the situation — if anything is done over and above what man's original nature provides — it is due to the action of use, disuse, satisfaction and discomfort. There is no arbitrary hocus pocus whereby man's nature acts in an unpredictable spasm when he is confronted with a new situation. His habits do not then retire to some convenient distance while some new and mysterious entities direct his behavior. On the contrary, nowhere are the bonds acquired with old situations more surely revealed in action than when a new situation appears. The child in the presence of a new object, the savage with a new implement, manufacturers making steam coaches or motor cars, the school boy beginning algebra, the foreigner pronouncing English — in all such cases old acquisitions are, together with original tendencies, the obvious determiners of response, exemplifying the law stated above.[6]

The import of this view is, apparently, that human reasoning is at bottom simply a more complicated instance of what happens when the cat " learns " to get out of the cage. Human behavior differs in that it involves " such sequences of ideas as are called reasoning." The human being has capacity for " inner consideration, thought, planning, and the like." In Thorndike's view, however, ideas or reasoning present nothing that is essentially new; and so our next task must be to trace the explanation by which ideas and reasoning are reduced to the form of conditioned reflexes.

Our point of departure here lies in the fact that human beings are far superior to the lower animals in the ca-

[6] E. L. Thorndike, *Educational Psychology* (Briefer Course), p. 149.

pacity to respond to the elements of a complex situation separately and in detail.  Analysis is a plant of slow growth.  We tend to deal with situations as gross, undefined wholes and only gradually learn to pick out their salient features.  To the baby, in James's vivid phraseology, the environment presents itself as a great, big, blooming, buzzing confusion; and it is not entirely clear to what extent the lower animals ever escape from this level.  To be sure, they recognize differences among things, just as we may be able to say that the manner of one person is more friendly or more sincere than that of another.  But we may experience the difference without being able to say why or how; each total situation has a unique " feel " or quality which marks it off from others.  In human experience, however, these gross total situations may break up into elements which can be dealt with separately.  This breaking up of situations eventually becomes the source of " ideas " and of those processes which we call reasoning.

Man's intellectual supremacy is due to the fact that he is able to isolate and respond to elements which for the lower animals remain inextricably imbedded in gross total situations.  The furniture, conversation, or behavior which to a dog are an undefined impression (such as the reader would have from looking at an unfamiliar landscape upside down or hearing a babel of Chinese speeches, or being submerged ten feet under water for the first time, or being half awakened in an unfamiliar room by an earthquake), become to man intelligible aggregates of separate " things," " words," or " acts," further defined and constituted by color, number, size, shape, loudness, and the many elements which man analyzes out of the gross total situations of life for individual response.[7]

[7] *Ibid.*, p. 141.

The things which are thus analyzed out of the " gross total situations of life" are of two kinds. Some of them, like articles of furniture, are physical components of certain situations, but are not dependent on those situations for their existence. Furniture can easily be shipped from one place to another. Other elements, however, such as number, size, shape, and loudness, are *abstractions*, by which is meant that they cannot be physically lifted out of one situation and transferred to another. It is quite possible to carry away a chair and leave the room behind; it is not possible to carry away the shape or the size of the chair and leave the chair behind. But we can consider the size or shape of the chair as readily as we can consider the chair itself or the room in which the chair is placed. That is, we can react to those abstract qualities more or less independently of the other qualities. But this is only because we have powers of response which the lower animals apparently do not have. The evidence in the case indicates that animals cannot isolate these qualities as human beings can. In Thorndike's language, " an element which never exists by itself in nature can influence man almost as if it did so exist, bonds being formed with it that act almost or quite irrespective of the gross total situation in which it inheres." [8]

This ability to react to aspects or traits of things is the source of our abstract ideas. The account given of the process by which these ideas are formed is interesting and important. As an instance, let us take the idea of " triangle." The triangular shape is associated with all sorts of things — with lines on the blackboard, harps, wedges, buildings and building lots, and even with the

[8] E. L. Thorndike, *Educational Psychology* (Briefer Course), p. 161.

"eternal triangle" of love affairs. Just because the shape appears in so many different settings or contexts, these latter tend eventually to drop out. This tendency is due to what James calls "dissociation by varying concomitants." Since the shape occurs with so many different concomitants, it is but loosely associated with all of them. The associates get in one another's way, so to speak, whenever the word triangle is mentioned. They gradually drop out, and in the end the reaction to "triangle" functions independently. When this result is achieved, we are said to have the idea of triangle. This process of learning, it will be observed, differs in no essential respect from that by which the cat learns to get out of the cage.

It is true that there is a great apparent difference between the flexibility of thinking and the routine character of habit. This difference, however, is accounted for if we keep our eye on the fact that our responses are not simply to "gross total situations" but to elements of the situation as well. Superficially an achievement like Newton's discovery of the law of gravitation appears, indeed, as a wide departure from the domain of habit. Closer scrutiny, however, shows that it was, in fact, simply an exemplification of the law of habit. According to the familiar story, the falling of an apple suggested to Newton that the moon likewise is a falling body. The path of the moon around the earth, indeed, is circular and not a straight line, like the path of a falling body. A circular motion, however, is analyzed by mathematicians into two components, a centrifugal motion and a centripetal motion. The latter, in the case of the moon, is a straight line towards the earth, exactly like the path of the falling apple. When Newton suspected the moon of being a falling body, he did not react to the " gross total situation," but towards one abstract element of the situation, viz., the centripetal motion of the moon. In doing this, he simply transferred to his perception of the moon a habit which he had formed in connection with falling bodies on the surface of the earth. The application of a habit in this fashion may classify as a stroke of genius, but it is habit all the same.

This explanation has an engaging simplicity. Learning in the case of the lower animals consists in building up a certain response to a certain kind of situation. The right response is retained, while the others gradually drop out, through the operation of mechanical causes. On the human level we seem to be confronted with a different situation, since the human mind can analyze and can distinguish between the important and the unimportant. But this difference between human beings and the lower animals is more apparent than real. When we look more closely, we find that the process in the two cases is essentially the same. Human beings have a much greater capacity for reacting to *elements* in a situation, which is what is called insight, but this introduces nothing that is essentially new. When a man " reasons out " a problem, he is simply reacting to such elements, instead of reacting to " gross total situations." He can deal with new and strange situations, just because he detects elements in them which are not at all new, but old and familiar. Thus a dog that has learned to open a gate by pressing a lever will be completely " stumped " by the substitution of a sliding bolt. A change of this kind would not keep an average human being for more than a few moments from opening the gate. He would de-

tect the essential identity in the two cases, viz., removal
of the bolt or latch from its groove. This ability to
react to abstract qualities is what has given to man his
mastery over the material environment. We can fly in
airplanes because we have discovered that air is a fluid
like water; we can build steam engines because we have
discovered that steam exerts a push. All such discoveries
rest on the ability to react to abstract qualities. "The
insights of a gifted thinker seem marvelous to us because the subtle elements which are prepotent for his
thought elude us." [9]

As the foregoing quotation indicates, Thorndike is
disposed to make free use of the terminology of dualism. He does not hesitate to speak of "insight" and
"thought," or to make reference to "ideas," "satisfaction," "annoyance," etc., without taking pains to
explain just what is meant by such terms. On some
occasions his language creates the impression that he
believes in mental states. Thus he explains that the difference between the reactions of an animal finding its
way out of a maze and the reactions of a child trying
to solve a problem in arithmetic is due to the fact that
the reactions of the child "include ideas as components." [10] This *sounds* like saying that certain physical
responses call forth mental states, which in turn are the
cause of further physical responses, just as is taught by
interactionism. But it is reasonably certain that Thorndike means nothing of this kind. The term "ideas" is
only a convenient, not to say lazy, designation of certain
physical responses. The tenor of Thorndike's whole
doctrine is to the effect that to react to an abstract or

[9] E. L. Thorndike, *Educational Psychology* (Briefer Course), p. 170.
[10] *Ibid.*, p. 140.

" subtle " element in a situation is to have an idea. What we call insight is just a matter of responding to some element in the situation that happens to be important for the particular occasion. "Insight," along with everything else, is reducible to physical response and comes under the general principle of habit formation. Thorndike will have no commerce with dualism, since dualism is a doctrine by which it is " asserted or at least hinted, that ' the will,' ' the voluntary attention,' ' the consciousness of the problem,' and other such entities are endowed with magic power to decide what is the ' right' or ' useful' bond and to kill off the others." [11]

Another reason why the process of " reasoning out " a problem seems so different from the random fumblings of a cat in a box or of a dog trying to get through a gate is that men rely so extensively on verbalization. In thinking our way through a difficulty, we may sit back and appear to be doing nothing at all, as far as physical responses are concerned. The whole procedure seems to be an exercise of pure intelligence. The behaviorist will, of course, have none of this. So he offers an explanation of such behavior, the upshot of which is that thinking is a process in which the responses of " verbalization " take the place of ordinary overt action. Thinking is a mode of behavior, but it happens to be a behavior of a distinctive kind.

The average adult verbalizes nearly everything that he does. He is talking to himself all the time during his waking hours and even in his dreams. Most of this talking is not audible, but takes the form of " implicit response " or " subvocal speech." It consists of muscular contractions in the lips, tongue, throat, and chest.

[11] E. L. Thorndike, *Educational Psychology* (Briefer Course), p. 171.

Much of this verbalization may go on without any awareness on the part of the person concerned. Because of this tendency to verbalize, the things that we do get themselves expressed simultaneously in vocal or subvocal speech. A person reaching for a newspaper or disposing of an umbrella will say " pick up newspaper " or " put umbrella in corner " as the act is performed. Consequently the act which gets itself recorded in the nervous system is made up of both verbal response and other response.

This is going on all the time. Let us suppose that a child copies a bit of verse in his notebook. He sees each word, writes it down, and verbalizes it, all at the same time. Consequently two neural organizations, the manual and the verbal, are built up simultaneously in connection with the visual stimulus. These two organizations are of course in more or less intimate relation with one another, since different processes going on in the nervous system at the same time tend to become interconnected, so that, if one of them recurs, it reinstates its former associates.

If an American were copying Chinese hieroglyphics, the verbalization would naturally proceed less smoothly. We cannot assume that no verbalization occurs, but it would be of a different kind. We should still tend to verbalize the symbols, as for example, " vertical-line-with-three-cross-pieces," or perhaps we should give the symbol some arbitrary name like " telegraph pole," and the like. It is conceivable, however, that a manual process, like copying, might be repeated so often that it could finally be performed " from memory," but without any help from language. We should need only to start the process by copying the first symbol, and the rest would follow, as sheep follow a leader. We get something like this in tennis playing. A good player makes skilful and complicated strokes because his nervous system provides for certain correlations of eye, hand, and muscles. He knows how to make these strokes, but he may be quite unable to tell a novice how to reproduce them. The correlation got itself built up without any concomitant verbal organization.

In a purely manual organization the repetition of the act depends on the power of each step in the process to call up its successor. On the other hand, if a parallel verbal organization has been built up, the proceedings become more complicated. The first step in the process has two associative links, one of these being the next step and the other the name for the first step. Let us suppose that a child starting to write down the alphabet gets a start by writing the letter *a*. This writing is connected with the verbalization *a*, and also with the next act, viz., the writing of *b*. At the same time the verbalization *a* starts off another series. The verbal *a* is connected with the verbal *b* which in turn is connected with the manual act of writing *b*. Consequently the child after copying *a* may proceed to *b* in either of two ways. He may proceed directly through the manual series, from the writing of *a* to the writing of *b*, or he may reach *b* by a roundabout route, viz., through the verbal *a* to the verbal *b* and hence to the manual *b*. In other words the writing of *a* is connected with the verbal *a*, and the verbal *a* then arouses the verbal *b*, which is connected with the writing of *b*. The verbal responses have got themselves built into the total acts so as to become a convenient medium for reinstating these former total acts.

When these verbal responses have thus become a part of the total responses, we can talk about what we have done by rehearsing the various steps. All we need to do is to reinstate the verbal process; this constitutes remembering. Consequently this form of remembering goes back only to events which were accompanied by verbalization. We cannot remember things that happened before we learned to speak.

For some unexplained reason it is easier to repeat an act if we have verbalized it than it is to repeat independently of verbalization. It would be a tremendous job to learn to write the successive letters of the alphabet in correct order without the help of names. It is much easier, apparently, to associate the verbal *a* with the verbal *b* than to associate the manual *a* with the manual *b*. Consequently we tend to get from the manual *a* to the manual *b* through the verbal series. The longest way around is the shortest way home.

The great difference between man and the lower animals, with respect to thinking, lies in this fact of verbalization. It is this power of verbalization that enables men to do things which we admiringly call " creative." In fact, the difference is only a difference of degree. When lower animals are confronted with a difficulty, they fumble around until they hit upon the right reaction, or until they grow tired and stop. Human beings, when confronted with mechanical puzzles, do the same thing, except that a part of the fumbling may be done with verbal organizations, which serve as substitutes for things. The human subject in an experiment of this kind is likely to talk to himself all the while, either audibly or subvocally. The gate is to be opened — " lift it off its hinges," " release the latch," "pry it open with a lever," etc. That is, the situation which requires the opening of the gate sets off all sorts of verbal organizations that have been built up previously. We have built up such organizations for hinges, latches, and the like, and now use them. Thus we have built up verbal responses for hinges, such as oiling, swinging, and lifting off, and the fact that we " think " of " lifting off the hinges " instead of " oiling " in the present situation is determined by physiological laws of association and not by a mysterious something called " intelligence." The fact that one verbal response rather than another comes into play constitutes what we call analyzing the situation. The lower animals by comparison fumble around with the object as an undifferentiated total object. Human beings can attack the problem more in detail, thanks to these verbal organizations. But in either case the solution of the problem consists in combining previous conditioned reflexes or habits into a new pattern.

All learning, in brief, is a matter of habit-formation, and habit-formation is, in turn, a matter of building up certain connections in the nervous system in accordance with the laws of learning. To put it differently, education is a process of " conditioning," which is to say indoctrination. Some authority decides which kind of conditioning is desired, and then the appropriate habits are built up. The school is expected to produce an output according to certain specifications, in much the same way that we expect a machine shop to do so.

The parallel is striking when we consider the way in which appreciations are conditioned. The reactions involved in appreciations are determined in large part, as Watson has explained, by visceral reactions, which are not directly amenable to voluntary control. These reactions can, however, be influenced indirectly. To show how this is done, Watson cites the case of a small child that showed fear of rabbits. To change this reaction, a rabbit was placed at the far end of a long table from which the child was eating. The rabbit was far enough away not to disturb the composure of the child; but day by day the distance between the two was gradually reduced, until they were together at the same end. The fear had disappeared; the reaction had been changed.

The generalization to which this case points is that we can shape up the appreciations of young people pretty much to suit ourselves. Given the right conditions, a child can presumably be made to react with an emotional thrill to any kind of object, such as a lead pencil or a handkerchief, or these objects can be made to arouse feelings of aversion. That is, our appreciations are determined in the main by the accidents of conditioning. Certain forms of art or of literature are labelled " great," and certain social institutions and customs, such as property, monogamy, truth-telling, etc., are held to be desirable and perhaps even sacred, for no better reason than that we were conditioned from early childhood to this end. We talk much about " progress," but we fail to see that progress is a name for whatever we happen to like. The savage, being conditioned differently, has his own standards of progress, and there is no way of proving that he is wrong. The visceral reactions are a law unto themselves. *De gustibus non est disputandum;* or, in more modern phrase, all love is blind.

What actually happens in our educational procedure is that we make pupils conform to the standards of the group. We make them like these standards, but at the same time we create the impression that our standards are intrinsically better than those of others. For example, we not only learn to prefer democracy to autocracy, but we may even engage in war so that the whole world may be made safe for democracy. The incentive toward reform and missionary zeal generally springs from the delusion that there is such a thing as an objective good.

Behaviorism rids us of dualism, but it does so at a price. Terms like purpose, aim, ideal, insight, have become taboo in the vocabulary of the scientific educator. In education the important thing is to build up desirable responses, instead of talking about insight, which brings in the connotation of dualism. Indoctrination comes in, naked and unashamed. Preferences for one value rather than another cease to have any meaning except as symbols of different forms of conditioning. All education becomes a matter of forming connections in the nervous system; it is all reducible to mechanical habit. These conclusions, so it is alleged, have the august sanction of science. Whether this allegation can be sustained will form the theme of the next chapter.

## Bibliography

GATES, A. I., *Psychology for Students of Education*, Chap. X. Macmillan Co.

JORDAN, A. M., *Educational Psychology*, Chap. III. Henry Holt & Co.

THORNDIKE, E. L., *Animal Intelligence*.

THORNDIKE, E. L., *Educational Psychology* (Briefer Course), Chaps. VI, X. Teachers College, Columbia University.

WATSON, J. B., *Psychological Care of Infant and Child*, Chaps. II, III, IV. W. W. Norton and Co.

# CHAPTER XIII

# *The Reaction against Behaviorism*

THE philosophy of materialism, of which Behaviorism is a modern form, has had a long career. It was espoused among the Greeks, and it has been a more or less familiar point of view ever since that time. All forms of materialism share in common the doctrine that mind or purpose is reducible to the action of material atoms or units. Every event in the universe, so it is held, can be explained in terms of a few elementary principles, and these principles are to be found in the sciences of physics and chemistry.

Behaviorism consists in the application of this point of view to the explanation of what is commonly called conscious behavior, and especially the conscious behavior of human beings. In such explanation the nervous system naturally occupies a prominent place. The simplest form of behavior is reflex action, which is explained by the theory that there is a fixed connection in the nervous system, so that when a stimulation occurs, the nervous energy travels along a path that is inborn and discharges into the muscles that provide the response. This notion of reflex action as a direct tie-up between stimulus and response along a fixed path or channel in the nervous system is known as the *reflex-arc concept.*

These reflexes are the units in terms of which all behavior can be explained. The reflexes may occur in sequences; they may be coupled up with various stimulations; they may be combined so as to form complicated responses. These variations do not alter the fact that purpose has nothing to do with behavior. The most brilliant performances of creative genius trace back to the same principles as those by which we explain events in inanimate nature or the operations of a machine.

This, in broad outline, is the theory of Behaviorism. Is it adequate as an account of human behavior? Granted that we are equipped with inborn and " conditioned " reflexes, there is still the problem of combining these in the right way. To the average man purpose in some form is an indispensable condition for giving direction to our acts. Is it really possible to dispense with purpose and foresight altogether?

According to the theory under consideration, it would be theoretically possible to construct an automaton that would enact to perfection the part of a Romeo bent on seeing his Juliet. It would be necessary, indeed — since the course of true love never did run smooth — to provide this automaton with reflexes for scaling walls, opening windows, constructing a rope out of his mantle, moving stealthily, and, in short, for meeting the various exigencies of the situation. This becomes complicated, but perhaps not beyond all reason. A more serious difficulty is encountered when we remind ourselves that all these different reflexes must be so combined as to ensure the success of the undertaking. Our Romeo must not convert his mantle into a rope when a ladder is handy, still less must he be so constructed that the mere sight of a mantle sets off the reaction for cutting it into strips. He must not open the windows in the first house that he comes to on his journey to Juliet, nor must he waste his efforts in trying to open a window that is already open. Moreover, he must be so constructed as to hunt around for something with which to pry open a window that is stuck. In addition to all this, he must be protected against irrelevant stimuli. If a garden seat which he happens to pass on his way to Juliet's abode should release the mechanism for sitting down, the whole adventure would have a disappointingly unromantic ending.

It is difficult to see how our mechanical Romeo could be depended on to act in accordance with the requirements of circumstances, unless he were put together by some power or agency possessing unlimited foresight and skill. Simply to endow our Romeo with plenty of reflexes gives no assurance that he will be able to act appropriately. Unless the reactions can be made to suit the occasion, he will be as ill-adjusted as a bull in a china shop, since what will suit the occasion depends altogether on the occasion itself. Sitting down on the garden seat, for example, may become an appropriate part of the proceedings, if it turns out that a wait is necessary and if the seat is so placed that Romeo can keep an eye on doors and windows without being observed himself. How can we make sure that the right reaction will normally take place? There is something lacking in the explanation. It is necessary to provide some sort of control which will determine the order or the combination in which the reactions of the organism are to be set free. The appropriateness of the present act is determined by reference to a future act or future state of affairs, i.e., appropriateness is dependent on foresight and purpose.

Perhaps the essential point will stand out more clearly if we observe how Romeo proceeds in the presence of unforeseen difficulties. His path is obstructed, let us say, by a garden wall that is too high to be vaulted. So he explores the surrounding territory and returns with a box on which to stand. The wall is still too high. So he takes his knife and cuts niches into the wall for climbing. Next he removes his shoes, so as to make the climbing easier, and throws the shoes over the wall. Perhaps in addition to all this he places the knife between his teeth, so as to have it handy for cutting further niches. Each of these acts taken separately is doubtless based on previous habits. The difficulty lies in explaining how these several acts get combined so as to become means to an end or elements in an inclusive program, which is about what we mean by purposive behavior.

The import of the foregoing discussion is that the reduction of purposive behavior to a combination of reflexes is a bit too simple. The reflexes which together make up a case of purposive behavior are not just placed in a row like beads on a string. Our explanation must provide also for the string which holds the beads together, that is, it must give to the activity as a whole a unity which controls or directs each of the constituent parts. In other words, we must provide some sort of substitute for the purposive control which the older psychology placed in an extraneous " consciousness " or " will."

If the reduction of purposive behavior to reflexes is a case of oversimplification, the same may be said of the manner in which mental states are ejected from the premises. Whatever one may think of the theory of mental states, it is a risky thing to say that all our aches and pains, our hopes and fears, our joys and sorrows, are simply forms of motion. We can easily understand, however, why the behaviorist says so. The "reduction" of mental states is performed in the interests of safety. As long as mental states are given any distinctive status at all, that is, as long as we recognize them as distinct psychic existences, we are in danger of lapsing into the theory of mental states. It is well enough to say that we will ignore them, but if there are such mental states and if they, and not physical objects, are what we immediately experience, they cannot be ignored altogether. Our starting point must necessarily be the immediate facts of experience, and so we easily slip back into the old groove of dualism. This danger is obviated if we make a clean sweep of the whole business and eliminate altogether the pestiferous dualism out of which so many problems sprouted, by reducing the whole of mental life to movements.

This is not only expedient, but it has a certain antecedent plausibility. It is only what science is doing, as far as possible, all along the line. We are assured that science has reduced colors and sounds to movements. There are no colors or sounds in the physical environment. For a long time we have been content to label these qualities as purely " subjective " and to say that they are " in the mind." But the mind has now been abolished. There is no convenient attic or limbo at hand where these troublesome things can be put. If we leave them floating around as something different from physical things, we still have mental states, no matter how much we may try to camouflage the fact. The only way out is to repudiate mental states altogether. Nothing exists but movement.

At this point it becomes necessary to take time out for reflection. Just what is it that we are asked to believe?

Shall we say that we do not see colors or hear sounds? This is a bit too extreme, since it is contradicted every hour of the day. Or does this "reduction" mean that wherever we experience colors and sounds, movements are also present? This is presumably true. The scientist assures us that this is the case, and since he is the expert, he has the last word on this point. But the assertion that colors and sounds are connected with motion is far from saying that colors and sounds do not exist at all. We might as well say that, since there can be no husband unless there is a wife, all husbands are really wives in disguise.

What the behaviorist means to say is apparently that certain things which seem to be quite different from one another are in fact absolutely the same. He does not deny that the eye sees colors and the ear hears sounds. Nor is he content to maintain simply that colors and sounds are accompanied by movements. A person need not be a behaviorist to accept this view. What he means is that color and movement are the same thing; that there is "really" no difference.

What does such a statement mean? If we compare a color with a movement we are not impressed with any likeness between the two. On the contrary it is hard to discover any likeness or identity at all. A color is a color and a movement is a movement. How are we to get any sense out of the assertion that these two things are really one and the same?

If we take an example from the field of physical science, the same difficulty confronts us. The chemist tells us that water consists of two gases, viz., hydrogen and oxygen, the combination of the two being represented by the formula $H_2O$. What does it mean to say that water *is* hydrogen and oxygen? Water is curiously unlike these gases. It has a freezing point of its own, it flows down hill, it quenches thirst, it passes off into steam, etc. In all these particulars it differs from both hydrogen and oxygen. If the expression " water is $H_2O$ " means that hydrogen and oxygen under certain conditions take on new properties, i.e., change into water, or that these new properties can be made to disappear and to be replaced by hydrogen and oxygen, we not only can understand the statement, but we can verify it. Moreover, if we study the chemical processes involved, we discover no warrant for saying anything more than this. To say that hydrogen and oxygen are a cause of water, or that water in turn can become a source of hydrogen and oxygen, is science. To say that water *is* hydrogen and oxygen is not science; it is nonsense. Water is water; hydrogen is hydrogen; and oxygen is oxygen. A thing is what it is; it is not something else. What it can mean to say that water is $H_2O$, or that thought is a movement, is past finding out. Statements of this sort rank with the incantations of the aboriginal medicine man, but with the advantage on the whole in favor of the medicine man, since he does not claim that his verbiage has the sanction of science.

To put it differently, the whole notion of " reduction " rests on a misconception. There is no such thing as reduction anywhere, in the sense that one thing is identical with another, different thing. There is plenty of reduction, if by reduction we mean that one thing is the cause of another thing or changes over into something else by taking on new properties. If we stay within the limits of verifiable fact we cannot say that a color *is* a movement, but that movement is connected with or is a cause of color. To say that a color *is* a movement is like saying that a man is his own grandfather.

It would probably be unnecessary to insist so strenuously upon what ought to be obvious, if the language of the natural sciences were not a source of constant confusion and ambiguity. The physicist is not seriously concerned with the question whether color is a movement or a product of movement, and so he identifies the two. Color is just a movement, *as far as he is concerned;* i.e., he is not interested, as a physicist, beyond the fact of movement. So he brushes everything else aside, which, on the level of physics, is quite legitimate. He is never confronted with the necessity of distinguishing between the proposition that color is a movement and the proposition that color is a product of movement. Consequently, he economizes on his thinking by not bothering himself with a question of this sort. The psychologist, however, is in a different position. It *is* necessary for his purpose to distinguish between the two propositions, because he has a different problem. He claims that he is giving an account of what we have been accustomed to call mental life, and so he is not permitted to beg the question from the beginning by taking advantage of an ambiguity in order to reduce all mental life to movement. To do so in his case is not to economize on thinking but to become a victim of laxness or antecedent prejudice.

It is not difficult to sympathize with the behaviorist in his hostility to mental states. Some of the reasons to justify such hostility have already been given, and more might be added. But it is more difficult to be tolerant with his refusal to recognize or maintain the distinction between identity and causal relation. The behaviorist slips from the one to the other in accordance with the exigencies of the argument; and his failure to understand the difficulty that is troubling persons who do not happen to agree with him is apparently due to the preconception that all criticism of Behaviorism is inspired by the belief in mental states. He foresees that if he makes any concession at all, he will find himself moving back to the theory of mental states, and he is bound to have done with that.

One further difficulty may be mentioned in connection with this tendency towards the reduction of experienced qualities to movements. This process of reduction is applied not only to colors and sounds, but to such qualities as solidity and weight. Things evaporate into movements, and the word " things," as used in this connection, includes the body of the individual as well as the objects that make up his environment. If we follow out the logic of this reasoning to the bitter end, we seem to emerge with the conclusion that all reality consists of movements. Just what this may mean it is difficult to say. Objects in motion are familiar enough as an experience, but when these objects themselves are said to be forms of motion the element of mystery enters. To common sense it means motion with nothing to move except itself. It is no wonder if in the face of such a phenomenon our thoughts stray to Alice in Wonderland and her experience with the Cheshire Cat. This wonderful cat at one time " vanished quite slowly, beginning with the end of the tail and ending with the grin, which remained some time after the rest of it had gone. ' Well! I've often seen a cat without a grin,' thought Alice, ' but a grin without a cat! It's the most curious thing I ever saw in all my life.' " [1]

[1] Quoted by J. Ward, *Naturalism and Agnosticism*, Vol. I., p. 140.

If we assume the validity of the foregoing criticisms, where does this leave us? Having examined and rejected the theory of mental states, we now find that Behaviorism is equally unsatisfactory. In other words, we are unable to arrive at an adequate theory of mind and of learning, whether we take mind and matter together or take either mind or matter separately. The only conclusion to be drawn from this result is that the trouble must lie in the initial assumptions. We get into difficulties because we start with erroneous conceptions regarding the nature of mind and of matter and of the relation between the two. These conceptions must be revised if we are to entertain the hope of ever getting out of the woods.

These initial assumptions are matters of theory. Primitive man found that objects which we have learned to call "inanimate" respond to stimulations of push and pull; and out of this observation there eventually emerged the theory of classical physics that all material phenomena are reducible to relations of push and pull among the constituent atoms. This was a theory; and it proved to be, in many respects, a very useful theory. Experience has shown, however, that a theory may be useful as a means of dealing with facts and guiding anticipations without being entirely adequate. It was long believed, for example, that the earth is flat; and this theory was made the basis of a system of astronomy which proved to be useful for navigation and for predicting eclipses. Moreover, a theory may point the way to experiments as a means of testing the theory. Various illustrations of this are furnished by the studies relating to the transmission of light. Knowledge is thus advanced, whether the results of the test support the theory or are found to be incompatible with it. The mechanistic theory has, in fact, directed observation and experiment, and in so doing it has opened the way to a different and more adequate concept of matter.

The experiments in learning by K. S. Lashley are a case in point. The experiments were designed to test the behavioristic theory that learning is a matter of building up conditioned reflexes. The author states that he " began the study of cerebral function with a definite bias toward such an interpretation of the learning problem. The original program of research looked toward the tracing of conditioned-reflex arcs through the cortex, as the spinal paths of simple reflexes seemed to have been traced through the cord." [2]  If learning means the building up of conditioned-reflex arcs through the cortex, then an injury to the cortex, so as to break up the arc, should mean the destruction of learning. To test this, Lashley taught rats to run a maze, and then, after the learning had been completed, he operated on the rats by cutting or burning a certain portion of the cortex. According to the mechanistic theory, such operations would mean the destruction of learning, provided of course that the brain injury was applied to the region in the cerebral cortex in which the conditioned-reflex arc had been set up.

In order to make sure that the brain injury was inflicted at the right place, Lashley made successive experiments with a considerable number of rats destroying one brain area after another so as to cover the whole surface of the cortex. The results of these experiments were not at all in conformity with the requirements of the mechanistic theory. At no time did he find that the learning

[2] K. S. Lashley, *Brain Mechanisms and Intelligence*, p. 14. For a summary of these experiments see Wheeler and Perkins, *Principles of Mental Development*, p. 62.

could be destroyed simply by cutting a connection in the brain at a particular spot, like cutting a particular electric light wire or telephone connection. Behavior was indeed impaired by the brain injuries, but the degree to which this took place was determined, in general, by the *extent* of the injury, and not by its location. In other words, the brain acts, in some sense, as a unit. It is not just a collection of " paths " or " arcs," bundled together as independent entities, like telephone wires wrapped up in the same cable. If one part of the brain is injured the other parts take over the work, provided the injury is not too extensive. The brain integrates the responses in some way so that the adaptive behavior which is called learning may take place anyhow. This adaptive behavior, or learning, was lost only if a certain maximum of tissue was destroyed; it made little or no difference in which part of the cortex this destruction took place.

It is precisely this " integration " of which mechanism is unable to give an adequate account. This process of integration means that the nervous system somehow organizes itself, not in terms of fixed connections, but with reference to an end or goal. Adaptation is achieved, not by " stamping in " a connection in the nervous system, so that the stimulation will always travel along a fixed path, but in some more complex and more mysterious way. If there is a blocking at any point, a new combination of responses takes place, and this new combination is of such a kind that the job gets done anyhow, and it gets done without the benefit of any fixed connections. We seem forced to conclude that living matter has properties which defy explanation in terms of mechanical habit-formation.

A few illustrations may be cited. One of Lashley's

rats was unable at first, after the brain operation, to walk at all, except in circles.  After some days it managed to walk in a straight line, but could not make a left-hand turn.  When placed in the maze, it solved the problem of making a left-hand turn in a striking manner.  Instead of turning left to make an angle of ninety degrees, which it was unable to do, it pivoted two hundred seventy degrees to the right, which served the same purpose.  This was done three times in the course of the journey from the starting point to the feedbox at the end of the maze. To explain this in terms of mechanical habits would be about as difficult as to explain our Romeo's love-making in such terms.  Behavior of this kind is not reducible to simple and fixed reflexes.  We are obliged to insist that the responses are integrated in a distinctive, nonmechanistic fashion, which is a learned and academic way of saying that we do not know what goes on in the nervous system.

In experiments on chicks and rats and goldfish it was found that after the animals had learned to respond to the brighter of two lights as a sign that there was food to be had, they would continue to select the brighter light, despite changes in the intensity of the lights.  Even if the dimmer light in a new situation was of the same intensity as the brighter light in previous situations, it would still be ignored in favor of the still brighter light. These results show at least that the responses of the animal were not to any fixed stimulus but to a *relationship*, which indicates that the behavior in each case involved a co-ordination of the responses involved in the larger situation.[3]  A monkey whose left arm and hand were temporarily paralyzed learned to open a latch box with its

[3] R. M. Wheeler, *The Science of Psychology*, pp. 122–126.

right hand; after the left arm had recovered, the right arm was paralyzed, and it was observed that the monkey could then open the box with the left hand quite expertly, without any fumbling or random movements, although the left arm had not participated in the training originally given to the right arm. Learning in such a case is evidently something more than the building up of a simple reflex arc. Large-scale co-ordination is involved, for which mechanism offers no adequate explanation. A striking instance of such " large-scale co-ordination " is reported by Lashley, who tells of " a student of piano who, in the stress of a public recital, unknowingly transposed one-half tone upward an entire movement of a Beethoven sonata, a feat which she had never attempted before and could not duplicate afterward even with some practice." [4]

The doctrine of the reflex arc suggests that when a stimulus is applied the action follows in much the same predetermined fashion as in the case of a shotgun, which discharges when the trigger is pulled. Facts such as those just cited lend color to the conclusion that such an explanation is altogether too simple. As Lashley says: " I am coming to doubt the validity of the reflex-arc hypothesis, even as applied to spinal reflexes. There are many indications that the spinal reflexes are no more dependent upon isolated conduction paths than are cerebral functions." [5] He considers it " very doubtful if the same neurons or synapses are involved even in two similar reactions to the same stimulus. Our data seem to prove that the structural elements are relatively unimportant for integration and that the common elements [in similar responses] must be some sort of dynamic patterns, de-

---

[4] K. S. Lashley, *op. cit.*, p. 159.     [5] *Ibid.*, p. 163.

termined by the relations or ratios among the parts of the system and not by the specific neurons activated." [6] The references to "integration" and "dynamic patterns" are intended as a rejection of mechanistic explanation. In some way the nervous system acts as a unit. The principle that controls is organization or co-ordination for some goal or end.

This principle operates even on levels where purpose is presumably absent, thus indicating that living matter is not the kind of thing which mechanism assumes it to be. Experiments on lower forms of life show strikingly the operations of "dynamic patterns." "The frog or salamander begins as a single cell, which divides into two. Usually one of these two produces the right half of the body, the other the left half. But this depends on the relation of the two cells to one another; separate them, and each produces an entire animal instead of half a one." [7] Again, in the developing mass of small cells, "transplant a small piece of prospective skin to the center of the eye-producing region; it now transforms into eye instead of into skin; transplant a prospective ear to another region, and it becomes skin or spinal cord, as its place in the pattern requires. It is proved that any particular cell may become part of any one of these structures, depending on its relation to the other cells." [8] The whole, in such cases, is evidently greater than the sum of its parts.[9]

In the case of what is ordinarily called purposive behavior, the "integration" or "dynamic pattern" is iden-

[6] *Ibid.*, p. 173.
[7] H. S. Jennings, *Prometheus, or Biology and the Advancement of Man*, p. 32.
[8] *Ibid.*, p. 35.
[9] For further illustrations of "dynamic patterns" see W. B. Cannon, *The Wisdom of the Body*, Chap. XIII.

tified with the end in view. The boy trying to get an apple from a tree may use a stick, he may climb on an adjoining shed, he may throw stones to knock it down, he may try to lasso it with a rope. Whichever course he follows, his responses are co-ordinated with reference to an end which is foreseen, but not yet achieved. To explain his behavior in terms of reflex arcs, variously combined, appears to be a hopeless undertaking. The theory of the reflex arc becomes still more dubious when we come upon evidence that living matter has the power of co-ordinating for a given " end " or " goal " without the intervention of purpose. The organism strives to maintain itself; and this striving appears to be a mode of behavior that is not reducible to mechanistic categories. Shoes wear out, but feet get tough and hardened when not protected by shoes. Ropes get thinned and frayed from constant use, but muscles increase in size and strength. An automobile deteriorates from minor collisions, but the jaw of a pugilist becomes increasingly able to " take it " as a result of collisions in the ring. The organism fends off germs, maintains a certain temperature of the blood, heals its wounds, has other parts of the organism take over the function of parts that are incapacitated, and does countless other things to keep itself going. This insistence on keeping itself going is a " dynamic pattern," which defies mechanistic explanation.

But the attack on mechanism does not stop at this point. It is carried over even into the realm of " dead " matter, which has always been the stronghold of mechanism. Modern physics has made much of the " field " concept, which carries with it the implication that the entire concept of mechanism must be revised. The concept of the " field " has long been familiar. A gravitational field, for example, is conceived as a unitary affair; the various bodies in the field do not go into action successively, like the cars in a long freight train when the engine starts to move, but operate simultaneously. The same interpretation is applied to electric and magnetic fields.[10] These all provide analogies to the " integration " and " dynamic patterns " which prevail in living matter.

The illustration of the gravitational field affords opportunity for speculation even to the layman to whom the intricacies of modern physics are unfathomable mysteries. Suppose it were possible to cut off an object from its surrounding environment with a metaphysical knife; what would happen to it? It would evidently lose the property of weight. If all relations were destroyed, it would likewise lose its color, its position, and, presumably, all its other properties. Since weight is an integral part of the object, the dependence of weight upon relationship to other objects seems to imply that the object extends beyond the surface of its " skin " or exterior. The object is literally everywhere!

These speculations find confirmation in the deliverances of our modern physicist. Taking his cue from the field concept he is eventually led to a repudiation of the presuppositions of mechanism. " The recognition of the new concepts grew steadily, until substance was overshadowed by the field. It was realized that something of great importance had happened in physics. A new reality was created, a new concept for which there was no place in the mechanical description. . . . The electromagnetic field is, for the modern physicist, as real as the chair on which he sits." [11]

[10] For illustrations of such fields the reader may be referred to almost any current elementary textbook on physics.

[11] Einstein and Infeld, *The Evolution of Physics*, p. 158.

The reasoning and the experimental evidence involved in this conclusion we can afford to leave to the specialists in the physical sciences. What is of importance for our purposes is the fact that the concepts underlying the traditional dualism of mind and matter are proving their inadequacy. The transformation in the concept of matter is as radical as anything that has happened to the concept of mind. "According to the theory of relativity, there is no essential distinction between mass and energy." [12] Where then is any given object located? If there is "no essential distinction" between mass and energy, the object extends as far as its gravitational field; which is to say that it extends everywhere. The distinction between an object and the surrounding space is a practical distinction. We locate objects at particular places because this is *expedient* if we wish to do anything to or about the objects. [13] There is no real discontinuity between the object and the surrounding space. "Matter is where the concentration of energy is great, field is where the concentration of energy is small. But if this is the case, then the difference between matter and field is a quantitative rather than a qualitative one. There is no sense in regarding matter and field as two qualities quite different from each other. We cannot imagine a definite surface separating distinctly field and matter." [14]

The upshot of it all is that mechanism is being attacked from every direction — as an explanation of purposive behavior, of the behavior of nonpurposive living organisms, and even of the facts that constitute the domain of physics. As a device for the control of everyday expe-

[12] Einstein and Infeld, *The Evolution of Physics*, p. 208.
[13] Cf. J. Dewey, *Philosophy and Civilization*, p. 197 *et seq.*
[14] Einstein and Infeld, *op. cit.*, p. 257.

rience the concept of mechanism is indispensable. As a tool for scientific discovery it has been invaluable. But as a transcript of " cosmic reality " it has proved to be thoroughly unreliable.

We must remind ourselves again that the mechanistic concept of matter was the basis for the historic concept of mind-substance. If we reject this basis, it becomes necessary to reconsider the question of mind in the light of this new approach. The present disorganization in the field of psychology is evidence that our notions of mind require reinterpretation. A more adequate concept of mind is the most urgent need of psychology at the present time.

## Bibliography

CANNON, W. B., The Wisdom of the Body, Chap. XIII. W. W. Norton and Co.

EINSTEIN and INFELD, The Evolution of Physics, pp. 255–260; 310–314.

JENNINGS, H. S., Prometheus, or Biology and the Advancement of Man. E. P. Dutton and Co.

LASHLEY, K. S., Brain Mechanisms and Intelligence, Chaps. I, II, and Summary. University of Chicago Press.

THORNDIKE, E. L., Human Learning, Chap. I. D. Appleton-Century Co.

WHEELER, R. H., The Science of Psychology, Chap. XVII. Thomas Y. Crowell Co.

WOODWORTH, R. S., Contemporary Schools of Psychology, Chaps. III, IV. Henry Holt & Co.

# CHAPTER XIV

# A Pragmatic Theory of Mind

IN THE preceding chapter we skirted the formidable domain of modern physics. It was not to be expected that
the deep mysteries of this domain would fade away before the casual glance of the passer-by, like mists before
the rising sun. The weight of the evidence which impels
the physicist to transform the concept of matter so extensively is not easily appreciated by the layman. The
fact, however, that the day of the self-sufficient, self-
contained atom has passed, or is passing, is fairly clear.
Every atom is located in a " field " and is continuous with
that field, and every field is, in turn, overlapping with
other fields, world without end. The field, and not the
atom, is now being regarded as the unit of action. A
change anywhere is a change in a whole field; it is a
manifestation of a process that is as wide as the field itself.
Thus saith our oracle, modern physics.

This general point of view provides a clue for a different theory of mind. If we follow out this clue, it soon
appears that the concept of mind is, indeed, due for an
extensive overhauling. First of all, we discover that the
term " mind " is a less inclusive term than it has usually
been taken to be. In the theory of mental states, for example, all our sense perceptions, such as colors, sounds,
tastes, and smells, are supposed to be mental. From our
present standpoint they are not mental at all, but just
" natural   occurrences, like rainfall or the budding of a
flower.

In terms of the preceding theories, sense qualities must be either mental states or else forms of motion. If we think in terms of the field concept, however, we are no longer obliged to hold that all qualitative changes are reducible to quantitative changes. Qualitative changes can and do make their appearance, without being reducible to anything else, or without requiring to be labelled "mental." Water is not in the least like hydrogen and oxygen; and common salt is very different from chlorine and sodium. All sense perception involves a field; which is to say that the physiological processes involved in sense perception involve corresponding changes in the field outside the body. In other words, the qualities of color, sound, etc., are in the objects, just as the properties of magnetism are in the material objects. Flaming sunsets or the noises of a busy street are not "subjective" events; they are as truly environmental as anything else in the whole universe. In considering them there is no occasion to refer to a "mind" at all. To account for them we need to assume nothing beyond a physical organism in relation to its "field." Perceptual qualities have an environmental status, which is precisely what has always been taken for granted by common sense. As Dewey says: "The qualities themselves are not sensory; 'sensory' designates an important condition of their occurrence, not a constituent in their nature." [1]

The idea that new and irreducible qualities can appear has nothing against it except the preconceptions of mechanistic thinking. In recent years this idea of emerging qualities has become popular and is sometimes referred to as "emergent evolution." In a field that includes a percipient organism, the conditions are fulfilled for the ap-

[1] J. Dewey, *Philosophy and Civilization*, p. 189.

pearance of "sense qualities." Every such field is somewhat different from every other perceptual field, since
no two organisms are exactly the same. There is room
for endless variations in the perceptual experiences of
different percipients, but these variations provide no warrant for the supposition either that perceptions are just
cerebral disturbances and therefore identifiable with motions or that they are merely "mental states."

Advocates of mental states are much disposed to stress
what is called the "relativity of sense perception" in
support of their theory. If different observers see different colors or shapes when they are looking at the
"same object," it is plausible to maintain that these different observations cannot all be "true." The inference
is correct if we assume that the purpose of observation is
to give us a faithful, photographic report of the object.
In this assumption the dualism of mind and object is taken
for granted. Perception is supposed to be a process by
which the mind seeks to know what the object is like.
But this assumption is precisely what the field concept
rejects. Colors and sounds are just happenings; there is
no more point in saying that they are true or otherwise
than there would be in saying that an earthquake or a
cyclone is "true." There is no one standard, "objective" color or size by which the perceptions of different
observers are to be measured. Every sense quality belongs to a field, and it varies with variations in the field;
in no case is a sense quality located in a mind.

The argument may be carried a step further. The
reference to a field is intended to show that sense qualities may vary, in the case of different observers, without
necessitating the inference that these qualities are located
in a mind. Where then are they located? The simplest

answer is to say that they are located wherever we happen to find them. This answer, however, requires elaboration. If we stick to the field concept we are obliged to say that locating an object is a practical matter and is determined in terms of the responses of the observer. A man walking through a field sees things as far or near, as high or low, as to the right or to the left. The relativity of all this is obvious, but it is a relativity that is tied up with the field concept. Our pedestrian does not first see the objects and *then* respond to them, as the mental-states theory assumed, but he sees them *in terms of* the responses that he makes to them. Similarly a baseball player learns to " judge " a fly ball by learning to see it in terms of the responses that are appropriate to the situation. These responses of running forward or backward, and to the right or to the left determine the seeing. They enable him to " see " where it " really " is and where it is " really " going. We locate things by seeing them with our muscles. To cite an experiment by Dr. George Stratton which bears on the point:

Stratton in this experiment placed before one eye a system of lenses which made things appear upside down and with reversed right and left relations. The other eye was blindfolded. These lenses, of course, caused the eye-muscle coördinations which Stratton had built during his lifetime to function unsuccessfully. That is, at the beginning of the experiment, movements which were performed unthinkingly and automatically ceased to produce the customary results. After two or three days there were brief intervals during which he had no difficulty in making appropriate movements. The best way to describe these intervals is to say that everything looked natural and there were no questions of right or left, or up or down. But as soon as a blunder or hesitation occurred, i.e., as soon as the new habits ceased to function automatically, the scene looked upside down again. In eight days Stratton acquired a new and adequate set of eye-muscle habits. And on the eighth day the scene *looked* as natural, as right-side up, as it did before he began the experiment.[2]

So far so good. But presently we come upon other cases of perception which are less simple. Seeing a rainbow is the same kind of thing as seeing a flying baseball or a distant hill, except that the rainbow cannot be located in the same offhand, practical way. If we walk towards it, the rainbow recedes; we cannot locate it by driving a peg or locating the pot of gold that is alleged to mark the place where the foot of the rainbow touches the earth. The rainbow is a quality in a field which has interacting elements such as sunlight, clouds, and a sentient organism. We locate the rainbow in the heavens by the same kind of responses as those by which we locate an umbrella or a fountain pen. Following out these responses, however, gets no results, since moving towards the rainbow merely repeats the original situation; it recreates the rainbow by bringing in other particles of moisture than those which were involved in the original rainbow. Where then is the rainbow at any given moment?

Since the question cannot be answered by the simple test of reaching and grasping, we might be tempted to locate the rainbow in the skies on the ground that the moisture in the clouds causes the diffraction of light. In other words, we base our decision not on reaching and

[2] C. Rosenow, *Psychological Review*, XXX, 199. Stratton's experiment is recorded in the *Psychological Review*, Vol. IV (1897), 341–360, 463–481.

grasping, but on causation. But this is arbitrary, in a sense, since sunlight and the eye of the observer constitute conditions for the appearance of the rainbow which are just as indispensable as the moisture in the clouds. Why not say that the rainbow is " really " located in the retina of the eye? We must either refer the question as to the location of the rainbow to physics, which merely tells us that the rainbow is a function of a field, or else to the tribunal of practical life, which decides a question of this kind in terms of what is to be done about it. The rainbow is in the sky in the sense that the sky is the place to look if we wish to see it; but it is in the observer's eye in the sense that there is no profit in chasing rainbows.

The mechanistic theory of classical physics had an absolute " position " for everything, and if it came upon such occurrences as rainbows or echoes or reflections in a mirror, which did not fit into this picture, it disposed of them by locating them in a mind or else by alleging that these occurrences were just forms of motion. Modern physics, however, rejects the idea of absolute position, which is incompatible with the field concept. Every object is literally everywhere. It seems, therefore, that the location of a thing is a practical matter; we locate a thing at the point where we may act with reference to it. A desk may be everywhere, but for purposes of working at it or selling it to a secondhand dealer it is in a specific place. An earthquake may be everywhere, but there is a specific place that had better be avoided. In the case of occurrences such as rainbows and echoes and reflections of light, where our ordinary tests do not apply, we provide location in whatever way may best suit our convenience.

If localization is a practical matter, we escape from the

disagreeable alternative of either providing a definite, absolute place for everything or else having recourse to dualism.  We either locate a thing at a place as a matter of convenience or we may not bother to locate it at all. If a man sees a ghost he is likely to locate it where he sees it.  If he dreams of being chased by a bear, the bear is definitely localized, as long as the dream lasts.  If he has a toothache, the pain is located in the jaw, where the remedies need to be applied.  If he thinks of a plan for a vacation, the thought may be located in the head or it may be left without local habitation of any kind, just as we do not bother to locate dreams after we have become awake.  All such experiences involve corresponding "fields," in the same way as rainbows and echoes; they do not in the least mean that there is a separate mental or psychic realm which serves as a haven of refuge for the outcasts of a mechanistic universe.

From this general point of view there is obviously no basis for the theory that our experiences are composites of sensations, images, and feelings.  The "field" concept suggests that the unit of a given experience is not a product of blending or of "mental chemistry" but is rather an aboriginal quality or characteristic of the situation.  The experience is not a composite because the field is not a composite.  The perceived object necessarily appears in some kind of context, and all the elements in the situation modify one another reciprocally.  The insistence that there is a basic unity of this kind in experience — or, as it is sometimes put, that the whole is greater than the sum of its parts — is a cardinal doctrine of what is known as the *Gestalt* psychology, a name which is sometimes translated as the psychology of configuration.  To quote a representative of this point of view:

Membership in a clang alters the phenomenal character of the partial tones. We do not hear the partials as loudly as we would if they were separate and distinct tones. In spite of the identical physical conditions, a sound is less intensive when it is a member of a clang than when it exists independently. A phenomenal *configuration,* such as a clang, is both something more and something different from the sum of its ingredients; for these ingredients are no longer separable entities, but members of a " whole," and being such they must lose some, indeed a great deal, of their individuality.[3]

Up to this point the explanation has proceeded without the hypothesis of a mind. Sense qualities are " sensory," not because a mind is involved but because sense organs are involved. The responses of the perceiving body are essential conditions for the occurrence of these qualities — and the same holds true for dreams, thoughts, memories, and the like. Reference has already been made to the fact that these responses vary with different organisms. Next, account must be taken of the further fact that the responses of the same organism vary at different times. The nervous system is highly modifiable; which means that the responses of yesterday have a carry-over into the responses of today. Not only so, but the carry-over is of a distinctive kind, and so puts us in the way of formulating a correspondingly distinctive theory of mind.

To take a simple illustration, suppose that a very small child sees a lighted match and reaches for it. Just how the match appears to the child it would be difficult to say. The responses of the adult have been changed so extensively, owing to the modifiability of the nervous system, that his experiential world is of necessity vastly different

[3] R. M. Ogden, *Psychology and Education,* p. 150.

from that of the infant. In reaching for the match, however, the infant starts the process of changing his nervous system. His fingers are burned, which means that a different set of responses come upon the scene. The next time the match is seen, the response is very different, because it has been modified by the experience of being burned. The reactions to the burn become incorporated in the reaction of seeing the match. Consequently, the match is seen differently; the match as seen takes on the quality of " bad," or " will burn "; and so, instead of being reached for, it is avoided. In this transformation of the perception we have the meaning of " mind." The perception foreshadows, or symbolizes, or points to, what will happen " if you don't watch out." This peculiar *function* of things in pointing to the future is what is meant by mind. The term mind is a name, not for a substance or a mental state, but for a *function* of the environment.

The change in the perceived object is a change in both its quality and its function. As a consequence of the changes in our responses, things *look* different, and they also provide clues to adaptive behavior. The fire looks hot, the stone looks hard, the ice looks cold, and the knife looks sharp. There is no assignable limit to this transformation. We *see* the lighted firecracker as " going to explode " because the response for " explosion " is already under way and is translated into what we see. We see that the speeding automobile is " going to turn over," that the man is " angry and going to strike," that the couch is soft and comfortable. These things are not " in the mind "; they are as truly " objective " as the shape and size and weight of objects. They are not in the mind because the mind is not a thing — whether a substance or a collection of mental states — but a function. The *function* of pointing or leading is what is meant by mind. This function is not anything separate; it is something that things *do*. Through the medium of our responses future events or possibilities get themselves translated into present fact, and thus they become effective for the control of behavior.

In Dewey's words, mind is " the power to understand things in terms of the use made of them." [4] This conception of mind, with its emphasis on adaptation, is an integral part of pragmatic philosophy. The term " experience " is a name for situations in which this function called mind is in some sense operative. The function of pointing or leading is nature's way of introducing foresight, purpose, intention, into behavior. Materialism tries to explain behavior without reference to purpose. Dualism tries to explain behavior by importing purpose from some other realm and then trying to hitch it on to the body. Men have struggled in vain for centuries to solve the problems that are thus created. The source of all the trouble lies in the basic assumptions. There is little ground for the hope that the problems can ever be solved unless we revise our concepts of both matter and mind.

Mind, then, is a function of symbolizing or forecasting, or, as we sometimes say, of understanding or foreseeing. In order to complete the account it is necessary to indicate how this peculiar and distinctive function operates in the control of behavior. By way of contrast we may refer once more to the explanation of purposive behavior that is commonly offered by the soul-substance theory and the theory of mental states. According to

[4] *Democracy and Education*, p. 39.

these theories there is first a stimulation of some sense organ. This stimulation is transmitted to the cerebral cortex, where it arouses a perception. This perception marks the beginning of conscious experience and is identified as the stimulus. This stimulus directs the discharge of neural excitation from the cortex into the muscles. Everything that comes after the occurrence of the sensory experience which is called forth in the cortex is labelled response. The account given by Behaviorism is essentially the same, except that the sensory experience as a distinctive happening is omitted altogether. The stimulus is the physical process that operates on the sense organ or the cortex and from that point on everything is response.

In terms of the field concept the relation of stimulus and response is less simple. Since the field operates as a unit, we are bound to assume that the whole field, including the body, is active from the start. This is just another way of saying that the reflex-arc concept, in which the activity is a pure sequence, is all wrong. The "stimulus" does not precede the "response" but the two operate simultaneously. And this, in turn, is just a way of saying that both stimulus and response require redefinition.

The pioneer work in this direction was done by John Dewey, who wrote a searching criticism of the conventional notion of stimulus and response and of the reflex-arc concept more than forty years ago. This work is all the more remarkable because it antedates the development of the field concept by modern physics. According to Dewey, the traditional conception of stimulus and response oversimplifies the facts, and, consequently, is thoroughly misleading. Since Behaviorism had not yet appeared as a psychological movement at the time that Dewey wrote, and since the soul-substance theory had already passed out as a live issue in psychology, he confined his attack, in the main, to the explanation of behavior furnished by the theory of mental states. This view, as was stated previously, is, briefly, that the stimulation of the sense organ is first conveyed to the cerebral cortex, where it arouses a sensory experience, and then continues into the efferent nerves which produce the response. In opposition to this view, Dewey argues that such events as seeing and hearing take place because there is already a response going on. This response is necessary if seeing or hearing is to occur; the response is not a consequence of the sensory experience but is an antecedent or condition of it.

There is a certain definite set of the motor apparatus involved in hearing just as much as there is in subsequent running away. The movement and posture of the head, the tension of the ear muscles, are required for the " reception " of the sound. It is just as true to say that the sensation of sound arises from a motor response as that the running away is a response to the sound.[5]

All this is obviously in entire accord with the requirements of the field concept. The perceiving body, as a part of the field, is in action from the start of the perceptual process; and so it is " just as true to say that the sensation of sound arises from a motor response as that the running away is a response to the sound." But if this be so, why speak of stimulus and response at all? In the case of gravitation, for example, these terms seem to have no appropriateness. The moon pulls on the earth and

[5] J. Dewey, *Philosophy and Civilization.* Chapter on " The Unit of Behavior," p. 239.

the earth pulls reciprocally on the moon. Neither moon nor earth can be designated usefully as the stimulus, just as there is no point in describing the action of either as a " response " to the other member of the team. Are the terms " stimulus " and " response " anything more than a hang-over from mechanistic explanations of behavior?

The answer is that these terms do represent something more than that. The fact that inanimate objects and living bodies have in common the circumstance that they all operate in fields of force does not preclude or exclude certain differences in the way they operate. A projectile fired from a gun, for example, functions in a co-ordination of forces, as do living bodies. There is a difference, however, in the way that these forces are reorganized or reco-ordinated if a new factor intervenes. Thus a strong gust of wind will deflect the projectile from its course by that much. It adapts itself to the new circumstance by a change in direction. The projectile does not care where it goes. The case is different with living organisms. To put it metaphorically, the organism is bound to maintain its direction. If there is an obstruction to breathing, the breathing does not simply diminish or stop altogether. An effort is made, which may be convulsive in its proportions, to remove the obstruction. The organism refuses to be deflected from its original course, which is to keep itself going. The show must go on.

All this is just another way of saying that the co-ordinations by which living beings maintain themselves are of a distinctive kind. These co-ordinations constitute a kind of moving equilibrium, which is constantly being reshaped with reference to an end. Reference has already been made to the marvelous adaptations by which the organism maintains itself. (Cf. pp. 211, 212.) In the case of these adaptations there is presumably no foresight of the end towards which these adaptations are directed. In human behavior, on the other hand, there is such foresight. The end is present as an element in the whole situation, and it is for this reason that we continue to make a distinction between " stimulus " and " response."

How this distinction is to be interpreted is perhaps best shown by an illustration. Let us take the case of a pedestrian who is picking his way carefully over a muddy or slippery path. His general aim or purpose is, of course, to get on to his destination. His co-ordinations, however, must be constantly readjusted as he goes along. Every time he moves forward he first looks to see where to place his foot. Perhaps he pauses a moment each time. Stated in terms of stimulus and response, his progress is interrupted at each step because the stimulus for the next step is incomplete. There must be a reorganization of his responses each time before he can go on. The important thing to note in this connection is that this reorganization is just as much a reorganization of the environment as it is a reorganization of the response, in accordance with the requirements of the field concept. The reorganization of the environment takes place in accordance with the requirements of the situation; which is to say that our pedestrian must manage to see the spot where the foot is to be placed and he must see it in terms of the length for the next step, in terms of direction, and in terms of the height to which the foot must be raised — in precisely the same way that a baseball player " judges " a fly ball. The whole process is both a process of shaping up the outward conditions and a process of co-ordinating the responses.

The moral of all this is that the reorganization of both

the responses and the environment goes on as a unitary process. In any situation where the responses are not adequately organized for adaptive purposes, there is a corresponding lack of organization on the side of the environment. We cannot react appropriately to a situation because the situation is not clearly defined. It is "blurred," perhaps, or at all events it has a quality of indefiniteness or incompleteness, which is what makes it a stimulus. On the side of the body there is a corresponding activity which is pressing forward towards a greater completeness, and this activity of the moment is the response.

The categories of stimulus and response, then, still have a meaning, even if we reject mechanistic explanations. They indicate a distinctive way of securing adaptations. Mechanism separates stimulus from response by making the stimulus come first, to be followed by the response in a temporal sequence. This has the virtue of simplicity, but it leads to endless difficulties. According to the present point of view, stimulus and response mark a distinction within a larger co-ordination or "field." The entire field operates as a unit, and so stimulus and response cannot be separated from each other temporally. But they can be contrasted in terms of function. The reason why we speak of a stimulus at all is that the co-ordination or situation is *inadequate;* there is a drive or pressure towards a better co-ordination or adaptation. The stimulus is that phase of the situation which requires to be made more definite or explicit; the response is constituted by the reactions which create the need for a more adequate determination of the conditions for further activity. A stimulus, then, is a stimulus, in a psychological sense, only as long as there is this need of greater definiteness. When this definiteness is achieved, there is no longer any purposiveness at this point; the resultant action becomes an element in the next co-ordination.

All this is rather high-brow, but it has important practical implications for the study of behavior, which constitutes the field of psychology. On the negative side it means a rejection of the notion that psychology should follow the analogy of chemistry by trying to resolve experiences into constituent elements, such as sensations, images, and feelings, or that it should identify these experiences with disturbances in the cerebral cortex. On the positive side it means that the special concern of psychology should be with that basic trait which is distinctive of what is called conscious behavior, viz., the way in which a conscious activity is carried forward to a goal by a process of constantly searching out the conditions for the " next step " all along the way. The fact that conscious behavior is a distinctive way of securing adaptation is what marks off the domain of psychology from that of the other sciences. Psychology is a study of behavior, and it might conveniently be called Behaviorism to distinguish it from the psychology of soul-substance and mental states, were it not that this name has been spoiled by being used as a designation of a mechanistic psychology.

The foregoing discussion has not got very much beyond an insistence that human behavior has a certain kind of distinctiveness. To study this behavior in detail is the proper task of psychology. This distinctiveness is present even in the simplest type of activity, such as reaching for an object. In the act of reaching, the hand and the eye must work together, because the conditions are in principle the same as in the case of the pedestrian who keeps moving by determining the conditions for his successive responses as he proceeds. In more difficult situations this determination of conditions may become a very elaborate affair; it may be necessary, for example, to meet the situation (or determine the conditions) by a process of careful and ingenious thinking. Whether simple or complex, our behavior may involve memory, and emotion, and habit, and imagery, and what not. It is clear that this general point of view involves a distinctive approach to the whole problem of learning. How it relates to learning will be the topic for consideration in the next chapter.

## Bibliography

DEWEY, J., *Philosophy and Civilization*, Chaps. on "A Naturalistic Theory of Sense Perception"; "The Unit of Behavior"; "Body and Mind." Minton, Balch and Co.

JENNINGS, H. S., *Behavior of the Lower Organisms*, Chaps. XVI, XVIII. Columbia University Press.

SYMPOSIUM — *Creative Intelligence*, Chap. on "Consciousness and Psychology." Henry Holt & Co.

THURSTONE, L. L., *The Nature of Intelligence*, Chap. I. Harcourt, Brace and Co.

# CHAPTER XV

# Education from a Pragmatic Point of View

I<small>T</small> <small>IS</small> to be expected that the conception of mind discussed in the preceding chapter will have significant bearing on educational outlook. If mind is a function, there can be no room for a faculty psychology. If this function is a function of a " field," then education cannot be a process of organizing mental states. Lastly, if this function is a process of progressively shaping up the environment so as to bring an ongoing activity to a successful termination, then education cannot be identified with a mechanistic stamping in of S–R bonds.

In approaching the problem of learning, our clue must come from the idea that mind is such a process of " progressively shaping up the environment." This process was illustrated earlier by the example of the pedestrian making his way along a difficult path. He picks and chooses, as we say; which means that a whole field, consisting of environmental relationships and bodily reactions, is in continuous reorganization. This process of reorganization is not, indeed, the same as learning, since no new elements may be involved. The case is different if our pedestrian discovers, as a result of his experience, that clay is slippery, whereas sod or gravel affords a firm footing. He learns about clay, for example, provided that he notes the connection between the appearance of clay and what the clay does to him when he tries to walk on it. To note the connection is to learn something, and the learning takes the form of changing the experience. The clay now *looks* slippery; it has acquired meaning. Such change in an experience whereby it becomes more serviceable for the guidance of behavior is what is meant by learning.

In this illustration learning is an intellectual affair, since it is identified with the perception of significant relationships. This kind of learning naturally occupies a prominent place in formal education. Instruction in golf, for example, is possible because the reason why a beginner " hooks " his drives or fails to get distance can be analyzed out. The significant relationships can be brought to the attention of the learner. Where such analysis is difficult, instruction is correspondingly difficult, as, for example, in teaching a boy how to balance himself on a bicycle, or to wag his ears, or to be at ease in a social gathering. Such accomplishments are also classed as learning, but they are generally acquired by trial and error, and perhaps without any perception of significant relationships. The result may be achieved without any knowledge of how it was done. But, even so, the learning is a process of getting the " feel " of the thing; which is to say that the experience is changed so as to provide better control for behavior.

To what extent relationships are clearly perceived in learning is sometimes open to doubt. If a baby touches a hot stove and thereafter avoids the stove, we are tempted to assume that the baby sees the relationship between " stove " and " hot." It is evident that the experience of being burned changes the infant's response to the stove, and the inference is warranted that there has been a change in his experience of the stove. The precise nature of this change, however, is not so clear. Psychologically there is a vast difference between seeing the stove as " stove-meaning-burn " and seeing it merely as " bad " or " hot." In the former case there is a clear distinction between the object and the thing meant or pointed to; in the latter case the meaning is so completely incorporated that there is no clear distinction. This complete assimilation of the meaning to the thing is exemplified in all cases of simple recognition. Persons seeing a lemon will sometimes " make a face "; they react to the object as sour, but they may not make the distinction which we ordinarily make when we infer that a person broken out with rash has measles or smallpox. That is, we do not distinguish between " thing " and " meaning "; we " recognize " the thing without this internal distinction. Recognition, however, implies a change in the perceived object; a lemon *looks* different after we have had experience with it. Moreover, the lemon thus seen controls behavior in terms of future consequences; we decline, for example, to bite into it. Hence the lemon exercises the function which we have identified with mind. But this is mind in its lowest terms, so to speak; the " sour " is nót definitely marked off as something symbolized, or indicated, or pointed to. The function is performed, but it is not definitely intellectualized.

In the case of the lemon it is easy enough for the average person to distinguish between " lemon " and its meaning, " sour," if there is occasion to do so. There are many situations, however, where we are unable to draw a satisfactory contrast between " thing " and " meaning." An experienced physician, for example, may " sense " that a patient stands no chance, before he has even started to make a diagnosis; a lawyer may

" sense " that there is something crooked about the case that is brought to him, even if it baffles him to find anything wrong. The expert has learned to " size up " situations in advance of tangible evidence. Cases of this kind are not wholly devoid of the contrast between thing and meaning; but they suggest how thing and meaning can run together and blend, and they suggest why we speak of being guided by " intuition." They also suggest the possibility that there are experiences where the *contrast* between " thing " and " meaning " is not present at all. Sometimes the contrast is lacking because it has gradually faded out. The child learns at one stage that the man in uniform *means* letters; later on he simply recognizes the man as the mailman. But there may be other instances when the experience may undergo an adaptive change without the clear intervention of this contrast at any point. The case of the baby and the stove may perhaps be explained either way.

A reference to the learning of the lower animals may serve to emphasize the fact that there are different varieties of learning and that careful interpretation is necessary. There is a story of a cat eating from a dish of codfish under which a mischievous boy had placed a large lighted firecracker. According to the story, that cat would never touch codfish again, no matter in what form it might be offered. Did the cat remember the original experience and relate the codfish specifically to explosions, or did the learning consist in a simple transformation of the experience so that the codfish did not look good any more? Then there is the familiar experiment with the pike, which was placed in a glass tank inside a larger tank, for the purpose of ascertaining whether the pike could learn to keep away from the small fish swimming around outside the glass tank. The pike finally learned, but only after countless collisions with the walls of his glass tank. In this case the learning presumably consisted simply in a change in the appearance of the small fish, so that they no longer looked inviting or appetizing. It is related that the pike did not offer to molest these fish even after the inner glass tank was removed, but that it unhesitatingly pursued other kinds of small fish when these were introduced into the tank. This bears out the supposition that the learning was confined to a change in the appearance of those kinds of fish with which its experience had been unfortunate. There was no evidence of anything resembling what, on the human level, is called analysis and generalization.

By contrast the experiments of Koehler with apes do provide evidence of this kind. These experiments were so devised as to require a comprehension or "insight" into relationships, if the apes were to solve their problem, which consisted in each case in adapting ways and means for securing tempting fruit. The situations were so arranged that the ape would at least stand a chance to "figure out" the solution. That is, the difficulty was, from a human standpoint, relatively simple, yet it required some kind of new adaptation of means to ends, such as fetching a box for the purpose of standing on it so as to reach an object overhead.

The experiment provides a situation in which the direct way to a goal is barred, but in which an indirect way is left open. The animal is introduced into this situation, which has been so planned that it is fully comprehensible. The animal is then left to indicate by its behavior whether or not it can solve the problem by the indirect means that have been provided.[1]

It is not necessary for our purpose to do more than to make brief mention of some of these experiments. In one experiment, fruit was placed beyond reach outside the cage, but a string was attached to it which was in easy reach; in another there was no string, but a stick was placed inside the cage with which the fruit could be reached. One variation of this experiment consisted in placing in the cage, not a stick, but a part of a dead tree from which a branch could be broken off to be used as a stick. In another variation two bamboo sticks had to be fitted together by inserting one into the hollow end of the other so as to make the stick of adequate length. In still another experiment the fruit was hung from the ceiling of the cage, but so high that a box which was in the cage had to be placed under it. As a variation of this experiment the box was filled with stones which had to be taken out before the box could be moved. Again the fruit thus suspended could be reached by swinging towards it with a rope, which was likewise suspended from the ceiling at a distance of two meters. In a subsequent experiment the rope was laid on the floor, and it had to be replaced on the hook — which was accessible to the ape — before it could be used for purposes of swinging.

In struggling with these situations the apes naturally made errors, some of which Koehler calls " clever," and others he labels " stupid." For example, on one occasion an ape brought in a box and placed it against the wall

[1] W. Koehler, *The Mentality of Apes*, p. 4, quoted by K. Koffka, *The Growth of the Mind*, p. 181.

above the floor where it was in a position from which the fruit could easily be reached, if only the box could be made to stick to the wall. Koehler calls this a clever error because it showed a comprehension of the problem, even though an essential factor had been overlooked. This epithet applies also to the procedure of the ape who tried to obtain the fruit by means of two short sticks, his method being to lay the two sticks endwise, instead of inserting one into the other; so that by pushing with one of the sticks he made the other stick come into contact with the fruit. In this way the ape succeeded in reaching the fruit with the sticks, although this did not help him in bringing the fruit into the cage. By contrast a stupid error is illustrated by the behavior of a cat in Thorndike's experiments. The cat had learned to pull a string so as to release itself from the cage; and having learned this it went to the same spot and made the motion of pulling the string, in spite of the fact that the string had been hung in another part of the cage.

It may be remarked that the methods by which the apes sought to solve their problems were sometimes quite unexpected. In one instance the two sticks to be fitted together were too nearly of the same size, so the ape proceeded to whittle down the end of one stick with his teeth, apparently for the purpose of making it fit. This resulted in his breaking off a large splinter, which caused a change of plan. The splinter was inserted into the other uninjured end of the pole, which made it long enough to serve the purpose of reaching the fruit. On another occasion the ape led the keeper by the hand under the fruit, with the evident intention of using the keeper as a stepladder by climbing on his shoulder, as he had done on previous occasions. This time, however, the keeper knelt down at the critical moment, so that, after the ape had climbed up, the fruit was still beyond reach. The ape, as Koehler tells the incident, " climbs on to the man's shoulder after he has dragged him underneath the object, and the keeper quickly bends down. The animal gets off complaining, takes hold of the keeper by his seat with both hands, and tries with all his might to push him up. A surprising way of trying to improve the human implement." [2]

With one exception, all of the experiments mentioned, and others besides, were successfully performed by some one or more of the apes. As was perhaps to be expected, some of the apes proved to be distinctly superior to others in intelligence. The experiment in which all the apes failed required that a rope lying on the floor of the cage be hung on a hook in the roof of the cage so that it might be used as a means of swinging the animal within reach of the fruit. In these experiments there was no gradual sloping downward of the time-curve, as in the case of Thorndike's experiments with the cats, the reason being that Koehler's experiments were so arranged as to enable the animal to pick out the essential relationship beforehand. Ordinarily the successful performance meant that the animal was master of the situation at once. He could do the right thing on the next occasion with a minimum of fumbling. In terms of curves, his learning was represented, not by a gradual downward slope, but by a straight drop.

It is of interest in this connection to observe that the experiment in which stones had to be taken from a box before the box could be moved was performed in a way that exhibited a curious limitation of insight. Instead of

[2] W. Koehler, *The Mentality of Apes*, p. 146.

removing all the stones, the ape took out only as many as were necessary to make the box movable. The labor involved in moving the box with a quantity of stones still left inside was considerable, but the ape apparently did not grasp the fact that his labor would be lightened by the removal of the remaining stones. The stones were regarded as an obstacle to moving the box only as long as the box was too heavy to move. As soon as the box was movable, the remaining stones were ignored.

Learning, then, is a term that covers a variety of meanings. Sometimes the emphasis is on the co-ordination that is acquired, as in the case of the batsman who learns to hit the ball safely, or the golfer who learns to correct a fault, without, in either case, knowing how it has been done. All we can say is that there is an improvement in skill, together with a difference in the " feel " of the thing. Then there is the kind of learning in which the emphasis falls on this change in the " feel " or the quality of the experience; as when we learn to judge the speed of an automobile or to distrust certain persons, without being able to specify the clues on which we rely. Lastly, there is the kind of learning which is based on some trait or fact or relationship that can be analyzed out and offered as evidence, as when we infer from the appearance of a lawn that it needs sprinkling or when we abstain from coffee because it keeps us awake at night. The clear perception of relationships is what is sometimes designated as insight.

These differences in kinds of learning derive whatever significance they may have from the fact that they are connected with corresponding differences in the procedure by which they are acquired. They are primarily differences of emphasis. It seems safe to assume, on the one hand, that all learning involves some perception of relationship, however dim, and, on the other hand, that analysis, or insight into relationship, however extensive, never keeps abreast with the adaptive changes in our experience. Mind, as Dewey has told us, is "the power to understand things in terms of the use made of them." Understanding has to do with relationships. This understanding, however, may take various forms. It seems fair to describe the experience of the benighted pike in the tank as an obscure comprehension that the little fish were "to-be-let-alone." Some such quality of "futurity," therefore, inheres in all learning. It is worth noting that the expert who devotes himself to the business of analysis or the picking out of relationships does not thereby diminish the area of his unanalyzed experience. On the contrary, he increases it; he develops a kind of sixth sense or "instinct" or "intuition" which constantly outruns his ability to make clean-cut analyses and which guides him in situations that he cannot handle adequately by analysis. In other words, the expert never gets away from a certain resemblance to the pike. All this is reminiscent of the familiar advice given by an old judge to a young colleague, to the effect that a judge should make his decisions without giving the reasons therefor, because "the decisions are likely to be right, but the reasons are bound to be wrong."

All forms of learning, then, have a common element. They all involve a change in the experiential situation which gives greater control in relation to subsequent behavior. To the boy who has learned to swim, water has become a different medium, to which he responds differently. To the veteran salesman the reactions of his "prospects" when he approaches them take on the same kind of difference. The experiential situation has changed for them as truly as for the automobile mechanic who discovers that the trouble with an automobile is due to a defective carburetor. This change finds expression in the control of behavior, whether or not there is a *specific* reference to the future, in much the same way that the visual perception of a flame as " hot " controls behavior, without any such specific relationship as " flame *means* burn." All learning, then, is a change in experience such as to provide for increased control of behavior.[3]

We can now plot the curve of learning as it ordinarily goes on. It starts on the level of everyday living and it has to do with the changes made in things by our responses. These changes are speeded up and made more extensive by the process of analysis, or insight into relationships — a process in which the relationship of meaning or " pointing " is prominent and which aims to bring new elements into the picture. With familiarity this relationship of pointing drops out; the new elements become increasingly absorbed into the original experiences; recognition takes the place of inference. The experiences as thus modified become the basis for a repetition of the process; and thus experience continues to grow or to become enriched without any assignable limit.

This process of inference giving way to recognition is exemplified rather strikingly by language. When we first start to learn a foreign language, we rely extensively on the relationship, " this means that," (e.g., *cheval* means

---

[3] "We thus reach a technical definition of education: It is that reconstruction or reorganization of experience which adds to the meaning of experience, and which increases the ability to direct the course of subsequent experience." J. Dewey, *Democracy and Education*, p. 89.

*horse*). If we reach a point, however, where we can speak and think in terms of the new language, this relationship disappears. The words begin to *look* different and to *sound* different. This change in the quality or *feel* of words takes place in much the same way in the case of our mother tongue. As William James remarks:

> Our own language would sound very different to us if we heard it without understanding, as we hear a foreign tongue. Rises and falls of voice, odd sibilants and other consonants, would fall on our ear in a way of which we can now form no notion. Frenchmen say that English sounds to them like the *gazouillement des oiseaux* — an impression which it certainly makes on no native ear. Many of us English would describe the sound of Russian in similar terms. All of us are conscious of the strong inflections of voice and explosives and gutturals of German speech in a way in which no German can be conscious of them.[4]

The inference to be drawn is that the term "meaning" has different applications. In one sense the term denotes the function of pointing or symbolizing. To make a clear contrast between the thing and whatever is pointed to is to "intellectualize" the experience of the thing. When this contrast drops out, the thing is still considered to retain the meaning, but the term meaning is now used in a different sense. It is now a name for a certain quality of the total experience. To use an illustration, we avoid an onrushing automobile, and we ordinarily do so without the help of a specific relationship, such as "automobile means danger." The quality of danger has become a part of the automobile, in the same way as its shape or color; it remains, indeed, just as effective in the control of behavior, but meaning is now bet-

[4] W. James, *Principles of Psychology*, Vol. II, p. 80.

ter described as " appreciation " rather than " pointing." In the language of Dewey:

> Definiteness, depth, and variety of meaning attach to the objects of an experience just in the degree in which they have been previously thought about, even when present in an experience in which they do not evoke inferential procedures at all. Such terms as " meaning," " significance," " value " have a double sense. Sometimes they mean a function: the office of one thing representing another, or pointing to it as implied; the operation, in short, of serving as a sign. In the word " symbol " this meaning is practically exhaustive. But the terms also sometimes mean an inherent quality, a quality intrinsically characterizing the thing experienced and making it worth while. . . . In the situation which follows upon reflection, meanings are intrinsic; they have no instrumental or subservient office, — because they have no office at all. They are as much qualities of the objects in the situation as are red and black, hard and soft, square and round.[5]

If we turn now to the consideration of the implications contained in this general point of view for school procedures, we are at once confronted with what Dewey calls the principle of the continuity of experience. All learning, whether in school or out of school, has to do with the transformation of experience in the interests of better control. In order to bring about this transformation, it is necessary to do something that will produce the desired change. This contradicts the familiar assumption that pupils should go to school in order to draw upon a storehouse of knowledge, in somewhat the same way that a railroad car goes to the mine in order to take on a load of coal. The school, from the present point of view,

[5] J. Dewey, *Essays in Experimental Logic*, pp. 16, 17.

is simply a place which is especially designed to facilitate the business of securing the desired transformation of experience. It is a place where new experiences are provided in such a form as to best promote that reconstruction or reorganization of experience which is identified with education.

All this is but another way of saying that the school, ideally, is a place where pupils go in order to carry on certain activities, from which certain reconstructions or reorganizations of experience are expected to result. This emphasis on activities explains why *interest* occupies so prominent a place in the picture. It also explains the prominence given to " activity " programs, especially on the lower levels. For city children in particular the necessity of enabling them to get their hands on things is obvious, if we proceed on the theory that the character or quality of our experiences is determined by our responses. The principle involved here is not limited to the dealings of pupils with material objects. In this modern age the environment that is inescapably with us all the time is the social environment, and this environment, like the material environment, is all of one piece with our responses. We learn to recognize rights and duties, we learn to admire and to disapprove, we learn to recognize some things as complimentary and others as insulting, we learn to give support or co-operation in some situations and to withhold it in others. We learn, in brief, to act like social beings, according to our lights; and this learning, like all learning, relates to behavior. Social behavior must be so fashioned as to result in desirable insights and appreciations and habits. In other words, the school must provide for experiences in social relationships as well as for experiences with material things. The school should be the living embodiment of our highest ideal of social relationships.

School experiences, in brief, should be of such a kind as to widen and enrich and give greater meaning to life as it goes on in the out-of-school environment. To some degree this enrichment of experience goes on anyhow, whether a person goes to school or not. Learning does not normally come to a dead stop under any circumstances. Some circumstances, however, are more favorable than others, and even the most favorable circumstances in the out-of-school environment do not forward the business of learning as much as the conditions of modern life make necessary or desirable. A person who does not go to school, for example, is likely to pick up some of the elements of arithmetic and he may even acquire a certain acquaintance with a few printed words, but ordinarily such a person is listed in the census as illiterate. Hence the school is designed as a special made-to-order environment, so devised or organized that the activities which are carried on in it will do what the life outside does not do. The same applies to social relationships. The life of the school is designed to promote such attitudes as consideration for others, a sense of responsibility for the common good, respect for personal property, co-operation involving discussion and free give and take — in a word, the basic attitudes which in the outside world are all too frequently neglected or at best cultivated in a haphazard fashion.

The general idea back of all this is that the school, in making itself a special environment, must avoid the danger of separating itself from the life outside. An outstanding weakness of the traditional school has been that it devoted itself to matters which, from the standpoint of the pupil, bore no discernible relation to anything outside the school. This tendency was due, in large measure, to a misconception of the nature of learning. When schooling is regarded as a process of absorbing the funded knowledge of the past, or, in poetic phrase, " drinking at the fountain of learning," the connection of learning with living is left to chance. On the other hand, the theory that learning is a matter of reconstructing experience in the interests of better adaptation creates an insistence that the principle of the continuity of experience must be respected at all times. The application of this principle has led to a certain emphasis on incidental learning, to reliance on the project method, to studies of community life, and the like, so as to protect the organic continuity between the school and the larger life surrounding the school.

The difference in point of view regarding the nature of learning traces back, of course, to differences in the conception of mind. Dualism has tended to separate intellectual insight from both skill and appreciations, and to separate these latter from each other. The result has been a tendency to cultivate each of them in isolation from the others. Mathematics, for example, has to do with thinking; reading, spelling, etc., have to do with skills; poetry has to do with appreciation, and so on.[6] On the other hand, if we stress reconstruction of experience, in accordance with the conception of the " field " theory, it becomes apparent at once that such separation is essentially artificial. Thinking, appreciation, skill, and information are intimately interrelated. Thinking has to do with the removal of obstacles, and this involves an element of concern or value; else why take the trouble

[6] J. Dewey, *Democracy and Education*, Chap. XII.

to think at all?  The successful culmination of thinking
has an attendant esthetic quality, as when we speak in
mathematics of a " beautiful demonstration."  Thinking,
moreover, involves the gathering of data for the testing
of hypotheses, which in turn is related both to the acqui-
sition of information and to the development of skills or
techniques in observation, in analysis, and in the organization of material.  The point is that learning is neither a
matter of developing faculties nor of forming apperceptive masses according to a fixed procedure.  If we keep
our eye on the fact that learning is a reconstruction of
experience, which is a distinctive thing in the case of each
individual pupil, we avoid the danger of mechanizing the
learning process.  Learning as reconstruction combines
thinking, skill, information, and appreciation in a single
unitary process, and it is characterized by flexibility,
since it must constantly adapt itself to the circumstances
of the situation.   .

This flexibility is exemplified in the newer conception
of habit formation.  In the past habits were commonly
supposed to have a certain rigidity, as is required by the
reflex-arc concept and the notion of the " stamping in "
of S–R bonds.  If the " field " theory is to be trusted, the
reflex-arc concept is an oversimplification of the facts of
behavior.  The evidence indicates that even the simplest
behavior involves a reorganization of some range, i.e.,
that there is no such thing as exact repetition.  If so, it
follows that the ordinary notion of habit-formation must
be revised.  The essence of habit-formation is not repetition but smoothness of co-ordination.  Learning to play
golf, for example, is pretty much a matter of acquiring
such co-ordination.  The feet must be placed in a certain
way, there must be a certain grip on the club, the body

must move with a certain rhythm, the swing must follow through, and the eye must be kept on the ball. Taken separately the elements that enter into the total response are, for the most part, simple enough; it is the co-ordination of them that requires laborious practice. This co-ordination is a flexible thing, which can be adapted to various exigencies as they occur. In a similar way experience gives to the salesman, the teacher, the diner-out, a certain facility or resourcefulness in dealing with situations which is wholly mysterious if we think of habits as consisting of fixed connections, but which may be described as ease and flexibility of co-ordination. But if we describe habit in such terms, then habit is significant only in connection with the ends or purposes by which the co-ordinations are directed or controlled. Habit-formation must be linked up with learning as a process of reorganizing or reconstructing experience in a certain way, which means that the relation to ends must be constantly kept in view.

The central fact is that all normal behavior is controlled by ends, in some sense and to some extent. Our experiences change willy-nilly, and they change in ways that make for better adaptation. The infant that has been scratched by the cat is bound to see the cat differently from that moment on; a new relationship of "scratching" has been introduced; the infant's experience of the cat has been "reorganized." Frequently, however, the process of reorganization is more complicated. It may not be evident what the thing or the situation *means* or points to; and so it is necessary to have recourse to guessing or hypothesizing; after which prudence suggests that the guess should be verified or tested before we proceed to act on it. This whole process is called thinking, which may be defined most simply as the finding and testing of meanings. The great difference between the world of the civilized man and the world of the savage is the difference that is made by thinking. To the astronomer the comet in the sky is composed of certain materials; it travels at a certain rate and in accordance with the law of gravitation; to the savage it is an embodiment of fantastic superstitions and fears. The same kind of difference exists in other fields. It is clear, therefore, that the cultivation of effective thinking is a major responsibility of the schools. In terms of pragmatic theory, this thinking must relate itself at all times to the reconstruction of experience; the problems dealt with must be " real " problems in the sense that they present difficulties in the experience of the pupil which are of concern to him in the interests of better adaptation. " The sole direct path to enduring improvement in the methods of instruction and learning consists in centering upon the conditions which exact, promote, and test thinking. Thinking *is* the method of intelligent learning, of learning that employs and rewards mind." [7]

To summarize, the distinctive features of this theory of learning all flow from what Dewey calls the continuity of experience. According to this principle of continuity school experiences are educative only in so far as they serve to modify or " reconstruct " the background of experience which the pupil brings with him when he comes to school. This reconstruction goes on in any case, but our chief reliance in this connection is on thinking. A school operating on the basis of this theory will protect the continuity of the school with the life outside of the school and it will provide various kinds of ex-

[7] J. Dewey, *Democracy and Education*, p. 179.

periences, both with things and with social relations, so as to serve the overarching purpose of reconstruction. On the negative side it will avoid the fallacies of faculty psychology and rote learning and mechanistic conceptions of habit-formation; on the positive side it will stress insight and the practice of thinking which is required if these insights are to serve the purpose of giving our experience a new quality and a deeper meaning.

As every competent observer knows, this general point of view is far from being merely an academic theory. In one form or another its doctrines have taken root in practice, especially in connection with the movement known as progressive education, for which this theory is a kind of gospel. It is evident, however, that many questions are left unanswered. Granted that learning must find its orientation in the concept of adaptation or the control of experience, what kind of adaptation does it favor? Since our world is so largely a world of social relationships, a concept of adaptation or control is an empty thing, unless it symbolizes a concept of an ideal social order. What is the place in this educational program for such concepts as discipline, duty, the organization of subject matter, and indoctrination?

For a considerable period in the development of the progressive movements questions of this kind were generally disposed of by the simple process of ignoring them. The outstanding characteristic of the movement was an evangelistic zeal for the emancipation of childhood from the lockstep and regimentation of traditional education, which found a substitute for " progress " in such slogans as " interests " and " needs " and " growth." Of late years, however, these questions have come to the fore, which gives promise that an adequate program is in the making. It is becoming increasingly evident that the pragmatic conception of learning, however true, needs to be rounded out if it is to have effective application. This further development of the theory will form the topic of the next chapter.

## Bibliography

CHILDS, J. L., *Education and the Philosophy of Experimentalism*, Chaps. V, VI, VII.   Century Co.

DEWEY, J., *How We Think*, Chaps. I, IV.   D. C. Heath and Co.

DEWEY, J., *Human Nature and Conduct*, Part I.   Henry Holt & Co.

DEWEY, J., *The School and Society*.   University of Chicago Press.

KILPATRICK, W. H. (Editor), *The Educational Frontier*, Chaps. V, VI.   D. Appleton-Century Co.

KOEHLER, W., *The Mentality of Apes*, Chaps. I, II, III. Harcourt, Brace and Co.

# CHAPTER XVI

## Education and Social Outlook

WHEN viewed in terms of psychological theory, the history of education takes the form of a perennial struggle over the problems that grow out of the dualism of mind and matter. In pragmatic theory this dualism is superseded by the unity of the "field." Mind takes the form of a function within this field. It is a function of "leading" or "pointing," and the exercise of this function has to do with the transformation or reconstruction of the experiential situation. This process of reconstruction goes on inevitably; the school does not invent it, but undertakes rather to speed it up and to give it direction. Hence a well-considered school program is one built on the out-of-school experiences of the pupils, and it is designed to make these experiences richer and more meaningful. This general point of view has important bearings on the organization of the school, on classroom methods, and on the selection of subject matter, since the purpose of the school is not a cut-and-dried transmission of certain learnings, but rather the use of racial experience for the continuous improvement of present living.

All this, however, is only a start. Education, in whatever form, is concerned with the improvement of present living. The big issue is the question of what constitutes improvement. Our present task, therefore, is, first, to ascertain what ideal for improvement is implied in the pragmatic point of view, and, secondly, to indicate how this ideal bears on the operations of the school.

In approaching this question we may remind ourselves that the procedures of the earlier theories were determined by their conceptions of the nature of the individual who is to be educated.  The separation of the mind from the body at once raised the problem whence the patterns for education (or for improvement) were to be derived.  Rousseau asserted that these patterns were inherent in the individual mind.  Classicism looked for these patterns alternately in a principle of harmonious development and in the postulate of a transcendental truth which somehow gets itself reflected in our mundane lives.  Herbartianism had recourse to the Lesson Plan, which was supposed to follow psychological principles, but which was really a device for imposing patterns on the learner.  Behaviorism reduces the whole question of patterns to a process of conditioning, which does not pretend to be anything other than outright imposition.

All these points of view owe their character to the initial assumption of dualism.  If we reject this assumption from the outset, the whole perspective changes.  When we ask what education is for, we cannot look for patterns either to the inner structure of a substantive mind or to the outer structure of a transcendental reality.  The old contrast between the inner and the outer is superseded when we begin to think in terms of the field concept.  This contrast is now a contrast that arises within experience itself; it is not a contrast between mind on the one hand and matter on the other.  Thus the self, as was stated earlier (cf. pp. 112–115), is not conceived as an entity, but is identified with the values, the ideals, the more or less permanent interests which control conduct.  These values, ideals, interests arise within the context of experience. They are all tied up with the situations in which the experiencing organism lives and moves and has its being. They are, if you like, patterns or objectives for the improvement of living. This does not guarantee that they are good patterns, but it does indicate the limits within which we must operate. We are committed to the proposition that all patterns or ideals spring from the soil of experience, that they are created by man himself, and that they have no other purpose or meaning than to serve as guides for the continuous reorganization of experience. They are essentially experimental and are subject to continuous reconstruction in the light of new conditions. It is evident that this conception of selfhood and of what we may call spiritual values is a challenge to traditional points of view, which have become embedded in our outlook on life.

Before we undertake to explore this challenge or conflict further, let us try to elaborate the implications of this point of view. First of all, the self is not something that we are born with, but something that is acquired. A man's central interest may be to become a captain of industry, or a great scholar, or a crusader against the demon rum, or the champion pie eater of his community, or what not. There is a difference, of course, between a central interest and an exclusive interest. Every normal person maintains a variety of interests or values and so may be said to have a corresponding number of selves. His " real " or " deepest " self is not the only self, but it is the one which, in case of conflict, pushes the others aside and claims the right of way.

What form the development of selfhood is to take depends on the environment as much as on the individual organism. A savage in the forest could hardly become a journalist writing a daily syndicated column for the newspapers; an Eskimo in the far North could not be expected to become a Burbank or a scientist making laboratory studies in problems of heredity; the great explorers, like Columbus, could not have decided to become commercial or military aviators.   But while some doors are closed, others remain open.   The environment, therefore, plays a twofold role — it provides opportunities and it limits opportunities.   Moreover, these opportunities and limitations are both dependent to a tremendous extent on the social relationships which the environment provides.   A person growing up all by himself would have no occasion to distinguish between right and wrong, since this is a social relationship.   His esthetic sense would remain undeveloped.   He would have no language and so his thinking would remain rudimentary. He would scarcely rise to the human level at all, which means that no doors of any kind would be open to him.

These considerations seem to warrant the inference that patterns for the improvement of living must be concerned with social relationships.   Other things equal, a social organization with a rich content is better than one with a meagre content.   As Tennyson says: " Better fifty years of Europe than a cycle of Cathay."   Unfortunately, it is possible for a social group to possess rich cultural treasures without making these treasures accessible to all its members.   We have heard much about the glories of Greek civilization, but the Greeks had slaves who did not share in these glories.   The function of the slave was to enable others to profit by the achievements of the human mind.   To a considerable extent this was true of later periods, in which the serf and the peasant took the place of the slave.   In one form or another, there has always been great inequality of opportunity; and no one would care to say that such inequalities do not exist at the present time to a disturbing degree. From the point of view of the underdog, it is certainly true that patterns for the improvement of living must provide for wider participation in our common heritage. The aforesaid underdog has little reason to exult in the fact that we have great symphonies, marvelous educational facilities, highly improved methods of protecting health and combating disease, opportunities to have a share in remaking the social order which is so evidently in a state of transition — to exult in all this if it is not for him. What boots it that there are all these doors to the development of a deeply satisfying selfhood, if the doors are locked and barred?

But what about the other point of view, the point of view — to continue the same terminology — of the top-dog, i.e., of the person who enjoys a privileged position in the present scheme of things? For him the doors are open, and his unwillingness to surrender any of his advantages is entirely understandable. He finds it hard to view with equanimity the closing of any of these doors for him. History, so it is said, has no record of any privileged group that ever willingly gave up its privileges. For the person who is advantageously circumstanced there are a gratifyingly large number and variety of opportunities to cultivate interests or forms of selfhood — artistic, intellectual, industrial, political — the exploitation of which is roughly about what is meant by "the more abundant life." If he is generous, he would like to see the opportunities open to everybody, but he is naturally loath to be deprived of them himself.

There is, however, another angle to all this. A good

argument can be made to the effect that, in the long run, inequalities may be bad for the overprivileged as well as for the underprivileged. History seems to bear out this view. Before the French Revolution, for example, when the masses of the French people were reduced to a shockingly low level, the upper classes in France likewise presented a shocking picture, though in a very different way. They were incredibly callous to the sufferings of the common people; they exploited them in every way; they wasted the bloodstained money wrung from starving peasants in the idle pomp and glitter of a " social life " dominated by a corrupt and senselessly extravagant royal court. The degradation of the common people was avenged by a corresponding degradation of their rulers and masters.

The example is, of course, extreme, but the principle is of universal application. In terms of the development of selfhood it means that no one can escape from the necessity of integrating or harmonizing his various interests. The development of any particular kind of self may involve a price which no decent person can afford to pay. The French aristocrats developed to a high degree a certain polish or cultural veneer, but underneath that veneer there was often the moral insensitiveness of a gangster or murderer. The musician or artist who devotes himself to his talent at the expense of all consideration for relatives and friends, is a similar case; and perhaps the same can be said of a person like Rousseau, who wrote eloquent and moving documents about children, but sent his own offspring to a foundling home. Other illustrations might be drawn from the careers of businessmen, or from the lives of people who are so devout in their religion that they cease to be human. In all such cases the individual concerned closes certain doors to development by his own acts. The opportunity to develop selfhood still leaves us with the question as to the kind of selfhood that is to be developed.

We are once more confronted with the question of patterns. If we follow the lead of the pragmatic theory of mind, our general direction becomes fairly clear. In the first place, our general pattern or scheme of values must be derived from experience itself and not from any set of principles which claim authority on the ground that they have a cosmic origin and sanction. The pattern is something which man builds up for himself, by a process of creation or " invention." Second, such a pattern can have no test or validation save the fact that, in some sense or other, it serves to promote better adjustment. Third, this better adjustment, which is missed if any one type of selfhood is developed at the expense of the rest, must consist in some pattern of social relationships. A pattern is good in proportion as it provides a basis for the integration or harmonization of conflicting interests; it is bad if it permits some one of the interests to ride roughshod over all the rest.

A statement of this kind is perhaps too abstract to be very helpful. As an illustration of what is meant, let us take the case of a man whose attention is concentrated heavily on business success. Presently his employees come to him with certain legitimate grievances as to wages, hours, and working conditions. Our businessman, let us say, desires to be more than just a businessman; he wants to be a good citizen, a good neighbor, a good Christian. In terms of our present discussion, he has a variety of selves which he is concerned to protect. If this concern is real, he cannot be indifferent to the grievances presented to him, on the ground that business is business. Whether circumstances make it possible to do anything about them or not, he must at least take a sympathetic look.

Now suppose that he is in a position to do something about it and proceeds to do so. The situation thus created is interesting from the standpoint of educational theory. What happens then is a widening integration that leads to a different kind of selfhood on the part of the employer. His business interest becomes a medium for a wider expression of his moral self. In improving the physical surroundings of his employees his esthetic self may take a hand. As he becomes increasingly sensitive to the shortcomings of the present industrial system, he may see the need of legislation and thus bring his political self into play. With the new insight into the possibilities of human relationships that he gains through co-operation with his employees, the conception of the brotherhood of man may take on a new meaning and thus bring his religious self into the situation. All the doors are kept open. Instead of sacrificing the various kinds of selfhood to a single ruthless, imperialistic self, a process of integration takes place. Whether a person is engaged in business or in anything else, a type of integration is required for a good life which is essentially the same for everyone. It is an integration that rests on a certain social pattern for the development of selfhood. This pattern is essentially simple. It demands the integration of values on the basis of co-operation with mutual recognition of divergent interests.

In ordinary language, the development of a good self is a matter of overcoming selfishness. This is correct enough, but the nature of selfishness is usually misconceived. As a rule, selfishness is supposed to consist in placing one's own desires or values above those of others. Perhaps this conception of selfishness goes back to the mind-substance theory. We first think of the self as an entity with a content or nature of its own, and then we have the problem of reconciling the good of this self with the good of our fellows. How this reconciliation is to be brought about has never been explained satisfactorily. The case is different if we conceive of the mind in terms of " function." Adjustment to the social order then becomes a matter of identifying one's self with certain activities or concerns that are present in the environment. A selfhood is *built up*, and it is built up in terms of a social content. A mother, for example, identifies her selfhood with the good of her family, and a criminal identifies himself with the success or the program of his gang.

From this point of view selfishness does not consist in an opposition between an abstract individual or " self " and the social order, but in an opposition between different kinds of social living. In terms of our previous illustration, an employer is selfish if he refuses to widen his world. Perhaps he would not think of dealing dishonestly with his employees or his customers, even if he thought it would be safe to do so. But the fact that an employee has a sick wife, or is forced to accept a wretched standard of living, or is unable to educate his children, or is working very long hours, or is doing his work in very bad surroundings — all matters of this kind the employer may consider to be none of his concern. He will tell you, perhaps, that business is business. His selfishness consists in his insistence on confining his business life to a narrow framework. Unselfishness, on the other hand, lies in the disposition to widen this framework so as to take care of other interests also.  According to pragmatic philosophy, the underlying principle is to be converted into a conscious ideal or a philosophy of life.

It should be noted that the same thing applies essentially to the employees.  Co-operation cannot go very far if the employees are interested only in higher wages and shorter hours.  The spirit or attitude or morale of the employees is of the highest importance to the business, and all this is easily translatable into terms of an expanding and more highly integrated selfhood.  The employees can prevent waste and carelessness and soldiering on the job; they can gain a wider insight into the employer's problems; and, like the employer, they can extend this insight to political and religious matters.  The employees share with the employer in a process of growth — a process that is based on precisely the same principle.  A principle of this kind leads logically to participation also on the part of the consumer or the social order outside.  Viewed from this wider standpoint, there is opened up a road towards an ideal of business and industrial organization which is run for the benefit of the community as a whole and not primarily for the material benefit of the individuals that control it or are employed by it.

That there is a certain tendency in the direction of the ideal here presented can scarcely be doubted.  Religion, industry, government, and institutions generally are showing signs of becoming " socialized," in the sense of stressing co-operation on the basis of respect for divergent interests.  But this is by no means the same as saying that this ideal is being consciously adopted and set up as a test for progress.  We still have with us various other ideals or patterns for living, which reflect a different notion of what selfhood is like and of what constitutes a good life. The old and the new stand side by side in our living and in our thinking. Shall we take the final step and set up this ideal as a challenge to all others? If we do, we have on our hands a tremendous task of reinterpreting the civilization which we have inherited from the past.

One of these reinterpretations relates to the concepts of theology. These concepts took their form largely from the dualism of mind and matter. This dualism carried the direct implication that mind and spiritual values cannot be explained by matter. Since they had to be explained somehow, the concept of a supernatural realm was developed, and this realm was placed in sharp contrast with the everyday world of space and time, which is the world of practical life and of natural science. Out of this contrast grew the belief that man's chief business in this vale of wrath and tears is to prepare for a life after death. The tendency towards this view was strengthened by the fact that man's control over his environment was painfully limited. The methods of producing the necessities of life were crude and inadequate; the masses were condemned to live out their lives under what we have since learned to call an " economy of scarcity." For most people life meant unremitting toil, to say nothing of the lack of protection against diseases and against injustice and exploitation. In consequence heaven was conceived primarily as a place of rest and security, and religion centered on the method of preparing for it.

This newer conception of mind leaves no room for the division of reality into a natural and a supernatural realm. It holds that the world is all of one piece. The leadings

or pointings which are identified with mind are relationships between present experiences and future possible
experiences; they are not relationships between present
experiences and a reality beyond experience. Consequently this standpoint is in complete accord with
the present marked shift of emphasis in our churches
towards the importance of present living, of which
the functional conception of mind is the academic or
intellectual expression. The reorganization of life which
is forwarded by this function has to do with this
present life; it sets up an ideal of self-realization, or
self-fulfilment, or " the more abundant life " in terms of
the here and now. There is reason to believe that this
new emphasis comes closer to the spirit of the gospels than
the elaborate creeds of tradition. In theological language this emphasis points to a distinctive conception of
salvation. A reinterpretation seems to be on the way.

Another element or constituent of our spiritual heritage is the conception of culture. This conception traces
back to an aristocratic origin and is directed towards
self-cultivation in the dualistic sense of this term. Historically, the idea of culture has always been associated
with leisure, in contrast with vocation. In recent times
the trend has been away from this attitude; the very
word, culture, has taken on a flavor of effeminacy and
anemia, and so we tend to avoid it. By contrast there is
a growing emphasis on the importance of " functional "
education. The values of historic culture are not repudiated, but the conception of a purely individualistic and
"nonfunctional" type of education is increasingly
viewed with suspicion. We seem to be moving towards
a conception of culture which stresses the integration of
values, as illustrated by the case of our hypothetical em-

ployer in his relations to his employees and his community, and which seeks to arrive at a consistent and inclusive outlook on life. A reinterpretation of culture, away from the aristocratic tradition, is taking place.

A third need for reinterpretation arises in connection with our industrial system. In its origin our present system traces back to *laissez faire*. On the one hand this system was justified on the ground that free competition was the best way to develop resources and to secure both volume of production and a proper price level so as to place the fruits of production within the reach of all. On the other hand this system was justified on the ground that it encouraged initiative and resourcefulness and so constituted an invaluable means for "self-development." To most observers neither argument is adequate at the present time. Increased regulation has become a recognized necessity. With this recognition there is coming a growing insight into the importance of making this regulation take the form, as much as possible, of co-operative action on the part of the employer and the employee and the consumer as represented by government, if we are to escape the evils of bureaucracy and dictatorship.

The implication of this newer insight is far-reaching. Property rights, as measured by control, are being revised; the function of government, in promoting such joint control or regulation, is taking on a new meaning; and industry is becoming a means of self-development, not primarily through uncontrolled initiative, but through the participation of all concerned to make industry serve an increasingly wider range of common interests. All this points to a conception of shared control in industry, i.e., to the ideal of making industry contrib-

ute to the continuous development of all who are engaged in it, as well as providing a livelihood. Even if we
grant that the movement in this direction has not gone
very far, it is clearly on the way. Here again the opti-
mistic eye may discern the promise of a reinterpretation
that is inspired by a different social ideal.[1]

Unfortunately, the immediate effect of these changes
is a widespread confusion, which may have dangerous
consequences. The new has not displaced the old, but
exists side by side with it. Man's sole purpose is not to
prepare for a life after death; but this purpose is still
commonly recognized. Just what, then, is the relation of
this purpose to the more immediate purpose of making
this life worth while on its own account? The belief in
the supernatural is retained alongside of an implicit faith
in science, which insists on the supremacy of natural law.
How are these beliefs to be reconciled? We still believe
in culture although we reject its historic meaning. What
then does culture mean in a modern world? We must
make industry recognize the fact that its primary obligation is social service, and we must also protect the profit
motive. How are these to be harmonized? It is a curious fact that, while we have incomparably more educational facilities than we had in the past, we are also af-
flicted with more uncertainty and confusion than at any
previous time. A cynic might say that we have education which does not educate.

Widespread social changes are indubitably going on.
It would be absurd to attribute these changes to the speculations of theorists concerning mind and matter and
the nature of learning. It would be nearer the truth to

[1] Cf. W. Hard, "Labor and National Unity," the *Reader's Digest*,
November, 1939.

say the causal relationship works the other way. Men are progressively gaining greater control over their environment. This increased control has had a modifying influence on earlier ideals. It has made men less disposed to acquiesce in the shortcomings of this present life on the ground that the privations and sufferings which are endured here will be compensated for in a life beyond the grave. On the contrary, if things are not satisfactory, there is likely to be a clamor that something be done about it. We live in an atmosphere of science, which is making it increasingly difficult to think of the universe as sharply divided into a natural and a supernatural part. The control over nature has given to practical affairs an importance and a dignity which they did not have before; and this has correspondingly lessened our admiration for the ideal of self-cultivation. It is the business of theory to discover and formulate the deeper meanings or implications of such changes. The changes lead to philosophizing, and not the other way around. Philosophy in turn affects conduct, because if we can see what it is that we are doing we can be more intelligent about it.

At the present time there is a special need of becoming more intelligent about what is going on, since we are living in a period of accelerated change. New ideals and attitudes are coming in which are in conflict with the old. Unless we can gain some insight into the nature of this conflict we cannot claim to be intelligent about the business of living. A consideration of the various theories of learning can help us to formulate the underlying issue. There can be no doubt that the pragmatic view of learning is in line with certain present-day tendencies. The doctrine that learning is a genuinely creative process in that it is a process of reconstructing a " field " or an experiential situation so that the ongoing activities of the individual may be brought to fruition is in harmony with our creed of " respect for personality " and the right of the individual to self-expression or self-development. The doctrine that such self-expression must take account of the social context or setting, and that desirable self-expression is ultimately identical with a social ideal is a recognition of interdependence, which is becoming so prominent a fact in modern life. Shall we then go on and say that progress in the direction of such a social ideal is the final meaning of progress; in other words, that such progress is the test of what is good and bad, or of what is right and wrong?

Aye, there's the rub. Generally speaking, we approve of such progress, but to set up this conception of progress as an ultimate test is a very different matter. This conception brings with it a doctrine of salvation, a doctrine of culture, and a doctrine of industrial reconstruction. It is a whole way of life. The way of life which is handed down to us by tradition is built on different foundations. To adopt this way of life with a clear vision of what we are doing means an extensive reinterpretation of cherished beliefs. It is more tempting to adopt this ideal without surrendering these beliefs; we would like to be " progressive " without being made uncomfortable. Or, to put it more charitably, we give our approval to this generous social ideal without realizing its implications. Hence the current confusion, which has led some writers to call us a lost generation.

The moral of all this is that a sound conception of learning is of little avail unless the process of learning is guided by an equally sound conception of social progress. The opportunities for error, when this theory of learning is applied individualistically and not in the light of a social outlook, are all too numerous. The fact that learning is a process of reinterpreting or reconstructing experience by the individual has led to absurdities in "freedom" and pupil-planning, together with unpleasant by-products in the form of irresponsibility and bad manners, and a lack of significant organization in knowledge, and to the notion that social outlook is provided for if encouragement is given to group activities. There is a vast difference between the cultivation of social outlook and the transaction of business by committees. Social outlook in the present connection centers on the question of our standard for progress. Shall we say that the standard is the continuous organization of social relations in the direction of co-operation on the basis of mutual recognition of interests, or that it is something else?

Some such issue as this is what appears to be involved in the various theories of learning which have been surveyed in the preceding pages. The issue itself, however, is understandable apart from these theories. It is the issue of democracy, as this issue is shaping up under the conditions of twentieth-century living. Co-operation in itself is scarcely an issue. The totalitarian states of today are all examples of large-scale co-operation. What is important is, first, the end or purpose that is to be achieved, and, secondly, the appropriateness of the means to the end. In the case of totalitarianism the end is fixed by authority and the individual is subordinated to this end. The end may be the glory of race or of empire, or of a *Kultur* or of a creed, or what not. Once the end is accepted, the application of force or pressure to the conduct and the beliefs of the individual is justified, as long as the methods employed are in harmony with the end that is to be achieved.

Democracy likewise sets up an inclusive end, but it is of a distinctive kind. The democratic end is to promote common interests and purposes among men. As in the case of totalitarianism, there are occasions when it is necessary to have recourse to force or compulsion. If, for example, employers decline to consult with their employees on matters where such consultation is desirable there is nothing inherently wrong or undemocratic in passing legislation which requires such consultation. The justification for such legislation, however, does not lie in the easy assumption that an employer has been made democratically minded just because the law compels him to recognize, say, the union of his employees, but rather in the expectation that compulsion will result, in the course of time, in the spontaneous and voluntary " mutual recognition of interests " by both parties, which is of the essence of democracy. From the standpoint of democracy there is progress in so far as our institutions and organizations promote such recognition of interests, even if this leads to much fumbling and many mistakes. The pervading spirit cannot be secured by direct coercion. Men cannot be made to love one another by act of Parliament. Coercion, therefore, is warranted only in so far as it promotes the purpose of democracy.

All this has a specific bearing on the question of what may reasonably be expected of the schools in a democratic social order. If we grant the proposition that our patterns for living have become confused, this question can be answered without overmuch difficulty. The central task of these schools is to make their pupils intelligent with reference to the issue of what constitutes a good life. In order to do this it is necessary to bring the confusion into the light of day and to show that what lies behind it is a basic conflict between the conception of values as fixed and sacred, and the conception of values as experimental and subject to change, i.e., a conflict between the principle of authoritarianism and the principle of reliance on intelligence. Circumstances and events are conspiring to make this issue increasingly momentous. It is the task of the schools to bring it sharply to a focus. Is progress to be measured by a social ideal, such as has been indicated, or is it to be measured by something else? To make this a meaningful question, it is necessary to cultivate the insight that it is a question which involves a reinterpretation of our cultural heritage all along the line.

The question cannot be avoided by saying that the purpose of the schools is to develop individual capacity or talent, since this applies in some sense or other to all schools of whatever kind. The task of the democratic school is to develop individual capacity with a specific reference. This reference is to the issue of democracy as a whole way of life. This reference to democracy is of a twofold kind. A democratic school may be expected both to give actual experience in democratic living and to foster intellectual insight, or understanding of the principle on which democracy is based and which gives it a distinctive character.

When translated into practice, this conception of democracy requires, first of all, that the life of the school be made as perfect an embodiment of the democratic ideal as we are able to achieve. The school, then, is not a place either for the regimentation of pupils or for the indulgence or coddling of their whims or fancies. If we emphasize the proposition that the school is a form of social living, in which every pupil has both rights and responsibilities, we provide the same basis for the intelligent application of compulsion or discipline in school as out of school. The fact that discipline was so often applied ignorantly and vindictively is no excuse for an undiscriminating reaction against the whole notion of discipline. The big question is always whether the methods that we employ serve the end of promoting voluntary co-operation, a sense of social responsibility or duty, a disposition to consider others, and the like. Leaving room for discipline does not invalidate the proposition that the chief and direct way of promoting the spirit of democracy is to provide opportunity for the practice of it. Every school has numerous opportunities for participation on the part of the pupils in the management of affairs that are of common concern. The pupils should be invited to share responsibility in so far as they are capable of doing so, and they should be permitted to make mistakes, within reasonably safe limits. Democracy, like swimming, requires practice as well as theory.

It is important to bear in mind, however, that insight or intellectual comprehension must have a place, and a central place at that. This is a point which the dictatorships have not failed to recognize. In their systems of education the bearing of what is happening in the school on the ideology which is espoused by the government is never lost to sight. This bearing is just as important in a democracy as in a dictatorship. In the management of school affairs there is constant opportunity to direct attention to the underlying principle, so that it will be explicitly recognized in practice. On occasion the nature of the difference between democratic and undemocratic practices can be pointed out in terms of specific situations. Similar opportunities are afforded in connection with classroom activities — opportunities which are more frequently overlooked than recognized. To illustrate, a favorite project in elementary schools is the study of Indian life. The project undoubtedly has significant educational possibilities. What is of interest in the present connection is that it presents an opportunity to raise the question as to what makes a way of life good or bad, or why it is that one way of doing things — apart from differences made by technology — is better than another. This, of course, involves the basic principle of democracy, which can then be discussed on the level of competency of the pupils.

The concept of a democratic social order can and should be used as a central point of reference throughout the educational program, whether we happen to be dealing with special projects or problems or with more conventional subject matter areas. In the social sciences the history of the Greeks, for example, offers all kinds of opportunity to improve our thinking about democracy. There was much in Greek life that was democratic in spirit and much that was not. If we attempt to discriminate, we inevitably make constant comparisons between the life of the Greeks and our own times. Cross-fertilization is thus set up; and the study of Greek history becomes a means for a better understanding of our own day and age. Similarly the medieval period offers significant opportunities for the teacher who cares to avail himself of them. This period furnishes a splendid example of a civilization that was organized on the basis of an inclusive philosophy of life. It presents but a minimum of the confusions and uncertainties that afflict the modern man. We have by no means discarded the whole of this earlier outlook, but we are not always certain how much of this outlook we wish to retain nor how that which seems worth keeping fits in with our other beliefs and values. The principle of contrast can be used to give us a clearer comprehension of what is really at stake in our present world. When approached in this fashion the medieval period becomes invaluable material for a better understanding of our own times. It is not argued, of course, that any one period of history can give us all that we need to know about the present; but rather that each period of history can make an important and perhaps indispensable contribution.

The natural sciences can likewise make their contribution. Why has the conception of democracy had so hard a time in getting itself accepted? One reason, undoubtedly, was that the universe was divided into two parts, a natural world and a supernatural world, of which the latter overshadowed and dominated the former in the thinking of men. The supernatural world was regarded as a source of standards for values and for conduct. In such a setting, a democratic way of life could not possibly get a secure foothold, since it is essentially "naturalistic." Democracy as a way of life is committed to the proposition that man must place sole reliance on his unaided intelligence both for the discovery of methods for the exercise of control over his material and social environment and for construction of the ends to be achieved. A systematic study of science is necessary in order to understand the methods and the point of view of the scientist. Such study should be made with special reference to the purpose of gaining an appreciation of what is meant by the statement that for science the world is all of one piece, that the concept of mechanism is an artificial simplification of the facts in the interests of convenience, that the concepts of science generally are tools with which the scientist does his work, and that truth is a relative thing. These insights all have a direct connection with the pragmatic conception of mind and with a pragmatic outlook on life. In order to throw this outlook into relief, due account should be taken of the perpetually occurring collisions throughout the centuries between science and traditional thinking. By extending this general point of view to subjects like literature and the arts, we find grounds for doubting the idea that beauty is " objective " in a Platonic sense, although this idea has long prevailed. If we drop this idea, extensive changes in these subjects will result.

All this is but another way of saying that it is the task of the schools to develop individual capacity in a context that makes for progressive clarification of social outlook. Democracy is a problem at present because changes in conditions call for a new interpretation and a new application. We have been accustomed to thinking of democracy as essentially identical with the right of self-determination on the part of both individuals and groups. With respect to the individual, democracy in this country has meant primarily a minimum of interference by others. With respect to groups it has meant the right of autonomy, on the basis of majority opinion. This meaning of democracy has not been entirely superseded, and presumably never will be. But it does not take adequate account of the fact that we are now living in a world of extensive and growing interdependence. Both the individual and the group are tied up in all kinds of ways with the lives of others. It is for this reason that pledges of nonaggression will not settle international problems any more than they will settle the problems between capital and labor, or the problems of a family. The only solid basis for dealing with our modern problems lies in the cultivation of *common* interests and purposes, i.e., in co-operation on the basis of mutual recognition of divergent interests. Reliance on this principle for the determination of values and conduct constitutes the essential meaning of democracy. Twentieth-century democracy must be defined in such terms if it is to come to full fruition.

Curriculum making designed to secure this intellectual insight can be carried on most effectively by starting with the existing curricula and providing for continuous reinterpretation with reference to social outlook rather than in the introduction of sweeping changes from the start. Such changes do not necessarily and inherently constitute progress. On the contrary, they are likely to defeat our purpose. A school program can improve in the desired direction only to the extent that there is improvement in the social outlook of the teaching staff.

To repeat, the reconstruction of experience with reference to an ultimate standard of value is the outstanding concern of education. This concern or task is basic because democracy, as defined by pragmatic theory, is a challenge to every other system of belief and of education. Is this emphasis on the issue in itself an instance of indoctrination? There would be no point in denying that this formulation of the issue and the emphasis which is given to it betray a bias. This is inescapable. Every teacher has a bias of some kind. But there is an important difference with respect to purpose or aim. Education as here presented will not try to go beyond the purpose of making clear the nature of this challenge. It will not indoctrinate in the sense of trying to predetermine the beliefs of the pupils. Its purpose will be rather to promote the " reconstruction of experience " without any predetermination. It proceeds in the faith that if the issue is made clear, democracy will prevail in the end. Democracy must survive on these terms or it cannot survive at all. If it is to rest its case on the appeal to intelligence, it must trust the intelligence of the common man or else stultify itself by tolerating a contradiction between its theory and its practice, since indoctrination implies that the intelligence of the common man is not to be trusted. Pupils who do not accept the standpoint of democracy as here defined are nevertheless made more intelligent in so far as the issue is made clear, and where there is understanding there is generally a basis for sympathy and co-operation. The continuous extension of co-operation and common interests will eventually make such extension the ultimate ideal. At any rate, such is the faith of democracy.

## Bibliography

Counts, G. S., *The Prospects of American Democracy*, Chaps. XII, XIII. Reynal and Hitchcock.

Dewey, J., *Characters and Events*, Chap. on " Religion and Our Schools." Henry Holt & Co.

Dewey, J., *Freedom and Culture*, Chaps. V, VI, VII. G. P. Putnam's Sons.

Dewey, J., *Individualism, Old and New*. Minton, Balch.

Kilpatrick, W. H., *Education for a Changing Civilization*. Macmillan Co.

Kilpatrick, W. H. (Editor), *The Educational Frontier*, Chap. I. D. Appleton-Century Co.

Lynd, R. S., *Knowledge for What?* Chap. VI. Princeton University Press.

Yearbook of the John Dewey Society (W. H. Kilpatrick, Editor), Chap. XIII. D. Appleton-Century Co.

Yearbook of the John Dewey Society (Alberty and Bode, Editors), Chap. I. D. Appleton-Century Co.

# CHAPTER XVII

# The Present Situation

Our survey of theories regarding the nature of learning has indicated that methods of teaching are determined by our conception of mind. This is hardly a surprising discovery. It has also indicated that there is a close connection between our conception of mind and the conception of the aim or purpose of education. This is perhaps less clear, and so a brief retrospect may be in order.

If we start with the premise that reality consists of mind-substance and matter-substance, it follows at once that education can have no other purpose than to develop the potentialities of the mind; in other words, we are committed in advance to some form of the doctrine of formal discipline. The only point that remains to be settled relates to the pattern which is to be followed in developing the capacities of the mind. Here we find divergence of opinion. According to Rousseau, the pattern is inherent in the mind of the learner, since man was created in the image of God. According to Arnold, the pattern is set by the individual himself, as a matter of conscious purpose, and is to be found in the principle of harmonious development. According to classicism generally, the patterns are furnished by those writings which are generally regarded as classics. The pre-eminence accorded to the classics in the program of education is justified either by the claim that they exemplify so excellently the principle of harmonious development or else by the claim that they embody essential (i.e., transcendental) truth. Finally, the familiar, traditional doctrine of formal discipline skips the question of patterns altogether. It emphasizes *exercise* as the means for developing the powers of the mind, and it provides itself with such patterns as may be needed by smuggling them in at the back door.

The situation changes when the mind-substance is discarded in favor of mental states. Education now becomes an enterprise in developing apperceptive masses. As long as we are dealing with factual material, the patterns for apperception may be derived from science. When we go beyond this into the realm of values, the patterns are provided by the teacher as the representative of the social order by which the schools are maintained. In Behaviorism the situation is much the same. Apperception is, indeed, displaced by a physiological theory of habit and S–R bonds, but this difference is unimportant with respect to the question of patterns. Lastly, the pragmatic theory interprets the functional conception of mind as carrying the implication that all patterns are dependent on the central purpose of promoting democratic living. Stated in more familiar terminology, this theory has but one inclusive educational objective, viz., that of democratic living. No other objective can claim independent status, but must justify itself in terms of its contribution to this common end.

This brief summary seems to warrant the inference that, for education, the assumption which is made regarding the nature of mind by any given psychological doctrine is of outstanding importance. To many psychologists an inference of this kind is exceedingly unwelcome. The nature of mind constitutes a problem that is exceedingly complex. It cannot be solved by conducting experiments in a laboratory. It is not specifically a psychological problem, since it is tied up with the question of matter and this relates also to the physical sciences. Hence the spoken or unspoken attitude of many psychologists is that psychology had better concentrate on scientific studies of behavior and avoid what a bungling commentator once described as " the dry and troubled waters of metaphysics." The business of the psychologist is with the facts of conscious behavior, and it is then open to the theorist to interpret these facts as he may see fit.

This attitude accounts for the fact that so many of the books on psychology which are coming off the press at present pointedly abstain from taking position on the question of mind. These books are " behavioristic " in a different sense of the term, viz., in the sense that they study behavior, but without committing themselves on the question whether there is a dualistic mind or whether behavior can be explained adequately in terms of physics and chemistry. The justification offered is that psychology is a science and not a philosophy, and therefore it should stick to its knitting. It is the business of psychology to ascertain the facts with respect to sense perception, memory, problem-solving, etc., with special reliance on methods for the control of conditions. The psychologist does not need a theory of mind to do his work any more than the physiologist needs a theory of matter in order to ascertain the effect of drugs on the functions or the tissues of the body.

To some extent this attitude on the part of the psychologist is perhaps due to weariness from the perennial disputes as to the nature of mind. We can imagine that a distaste for theory has thus been induced in many psychologists who were not born with it. Moreover, psychology is still a young subject. It is only within comparatively recent times that it has emancipated itself from the domination of philosophy and set up its own housekeeping. It was naturally eager to become a science in its own right, and so it has imitated the other sciences in emphasizing laboratory procedures and techniques for making and recording observations. How well has it succeeded? William James, our most famous psychologist, once expressed the opinion that psychology is not really a science at all, but " a string of raw facts; a little gossip and wrangle about opinions; a little classification and generalization on the mere descriptive level; a strong prejudice that we *have* states of mind, and that our brain conditions them; but not a single law in the sense in which physics shows us laws, not a single proposition from which any consequence can causally be deduced. We don't even know the terms between which the elementary laws would obtain if we had them. This is no science, it is only the hope of a science." [1] A summarization of this kind naturally rankles and it helps us to understand the somewhat self-conscious insistence of psychology that it is an honest-to-goodness science — an attitude that expresses itself negatively in a repudiation of theorizing and positively in an emphasis on scientific techniques and procedures.

We may concede that considerable progress has been made in psychology since James expressed his opinion with regard to it. Whether this progress gives psychology a better claim to be rated as science is a question

[1] W. James, *Psychology* (*Briefer Course*), p. 468.

which we need not pause to consider. This question would naturally involve a definition as to what constitutes a science. Our concern is rather with the disposition of psychologists to draw a line between the study of behavior and underlying theory. There is much room for doubt whether this is the road to scientific status. It is not the road that was taken by the older and more established sciences. We need only point to the fact that the entire period of classical physics was dominated by a certain conception of matter. This conception was used constantly as a basis for theorizing. It was a perennial source of hypothesis and it defined the task of physics, which was to reduce all material phenomena to terms of mechanism. Even though it eventually proved untenable, the conception was an indispensable condition for the brilliant triumph of classical physics. Theory is the lifeblood of science. The closest approximation to this insight in psychology was presumably on the part of Behaviorism, which stepped out boldly with a theory of mind, viz., that " mind " is just a form of matter and motion. The fatal mistake of Behaviorism lay in the fact that it accepted uncritically the conception of matter evolved by classical physics, and held to this conception for a considerable time after leading physicists had reached the conclusion that it was untenable. Psychology has the same need as physics of a controlling theory for defining its problems and for guiding its interpretations.

The role of theory may be illustrated from the field of psychology itself. Lashley's studies of the learning of rats in a maze was inspired, as he himself states, by the theory that learning is a process of stamping in fixed connections in the nervous system. Koehler's work on apes

was intended to prove that learning centers on " insight,"
which at once leads to the right response, and that it is
not a matter of gradually sloughing off irrelevant responses, as was suggested by Thorndike's experiments
with hungry cats.   These experiments related to interpretation, which is to say that they raised the whole question as to the real facts in the case.   When an ape gets
himself a box to stand on, or when a cat learns to claw its
way out of a cage, just what is it that takes place?   Or,
to take another illustration, if experiments show that a
subject learns to behave in a certain way, as a result of
what has happened before, what is the meaning of this
fact?   Studies in learning are likely to be pointless unless they are conducted on a theory as to the nature of
learning.   We know that a sheet of paper which has been
creased will behave differently the next time, since it will
now tend to fold along the line of the crease.   Shall we
say that the paper has " learned " something, since it
shows the effect of previous happenings?   Under our
constitutional guarantee of freedom of speech, the psychologist has the right to call this an instance of learning,
but if he does, it cannot be claimed that he is being very
helpful.   He is duty bound to have a theory as to the nature of the change involved in learning.   In the long run,
he stays away from theory at the expense of being trivial.
To make his work really significant he must have a theory of learning, which is to say that he needs a theory as
to what is meant by mind.

Behaviorism rendered a service by raising this question
squarely.   In raising the question it presented a challenge,
which evoked considerable experimentation for the purpose of proving or disproving the behavioristic point of
view.   Not only so, but those experimenters who dis-

agreed with Behaviorism naturally tended to offer their own views as to learning and the nature of mind, which is, and must remain, the central problem of psychology.[2] This is an exceedingly hopeful sign. However, the movement in this direction still has a long way to go. It seems not to be generally realized that a theory of mind must have as a correlate a theory of matter. More specifically, the emphasis which is sometimes placed on the " organismic " character of human behavior will not get us out of the woods as long as the environment in which the human organism is placed is conceived in terms of mechanism. On this basis there is no possibility of identifying mind with a function of the environment.

At present, however, the disposition of psychologists to back away from theory, under the impression that they are being scientific when they are being merely superficial, appears to be widespread; and this is bound to impede the advance of psychology. It also means that people who study psychology do not get what they are entitled to get. The average student of psychology may get a variety of more or less interesting information, but he is not likely to get anything that will seriously disturb the conception of mind which is part of his cultural heritage. The student with a special interest in education is not likely to get anything that will eventually make him teach differently in any significant way. This is less true if the psychology that is studied emphasizes the importance of impulse and the connection between learning and doing. Such emphasis, however, makes no provision for a new insight into the relation between learning and educational ideals. It is only as we

[2] See, for example, K. Koffka, *The Growth of the Mind*, Chap. I; R. H. Wheeler, *The Science of Psychology*, Chap. 18.

achieve a reasonably comprehensive theory of learning that we are in a position to see the bearing of this theory on educational aims.

The need of reorientation in education is all too evident. The mind-substance theory has been discarded, but formal discipline and the opposition between culture and vocation still persist. Herbartianism belongs to the past, but lesson plans of the Herbartian type are still being stressed. Behaviorism is in the doghouse, but the old conception of habit is still with us. There is confusion both with respect to the nature of learning and with respect to educational aims. What is the teacher who is trying to be intelligent about his work to do about all this? The suggestion has been made that the teacher can get along by borrowing from psychology whatever is useful to him in any given situation, without bothering to get a consistent theory of learning, which is the business of the psychologist. In matters of drill and repetition, Behaviorism will come in handy; in problem-solving Dewey can be recommended; for self-expression through art the psychology of a substantive self may perhaps have something useful to offer. The teacher's loyalty belongs to " the concept of maximum all-around growth as the true goal of education," [3] and so he is entitled to use anything which will serve his purpose, without assuming any responsibility for theoretical consistency as regards psychological concepts.

The assumption back of all this is, of course, that such consistency has no bearing on the question of educational aims. In view of the fact that " maximum all-around

[3] H. Rugg, *Culture and Education in America*, p. 385. In this same connection we are told that " the insistent need today is an eclectic psychology upon which to base the reconstruction of our schools."

growth " is an empty phrase unless or until it is translated into terms of what the individual is and how he is
related to his environment, this assumption is somewhat
startling.  Every major psychological theory has had a
direct bearing on educational aims.  If we refuse to come
to terms with psychological theory, we are simply serv-
ing notice that we propose to determine educational ends
without being hampered by irritating questions as to the
nature of the individual, or of selfhood, or of creativeness.  In a procedure of this kind it may be predicted in
advance that the old familiar dualisms, such as culture
and vocation, the individual and the social, duty and interest, and the like, will again put in their appearance.
There is no effective way of getting rid of these except
by a reconsideration of the concept of mind; nor is there
much chance of envisaging clearly the problem of democracy in a modern world.

Another approach to the determination of educational
objectives without reference to the problem of mind or
of democracy is offered us in the name of science.  It
starts with the proposition that membership in the social
order requires proficiency in certain activities.  Occupations such as farming, plumbing, and bricklaying call for
a specifiable equipment in skills, information, and ideals.
These can be ascertained by scientific analysis.  Since the
whole of life is made up, ultimately, of specific activities,
all educational objectives are ascertainable in this way.
Analysis can reveal to us what it takes to be a good parent, a good neighbor, a good citizen, or a good church
member.  The blessed advent of science gives promise,
at long last, of escape from the vagaries of theorizing and
of individual predilections.  Scientific analysis rests its
case on hard, solid facts.  It enables us to ascertain educa-

tional objectives without recourse to speculation, and it also points the way to the selection of the curricular materials required for the realization of these objectives.

Here again we are confronted with a dubious assumption, viz., that the objectives need only be looked for hard enough and carefully enough in order to be found. As a matter of fact, the method is applicable only where there is no occasion to use it. Scientific analysis can indeed show that our social order requires a certain degree of literacy and that it needs farmers and plumbers, but this would be a demonstration of the obvious. We all approve of these objectives. The point at which we need help is where there is no agreement. Should life have its center in the things of this world or in the preparation for a hereafter? Is the good parent a person who believes in the suppression of desires or in kindly indulgence? Is the good citizen a person who leans towards a governmental policy of *laissez faire* or a person who favors a greater degree of collectivism? Does culture require an appreciation of literary classics and proficiency in modern languages? What are the hard, solid facts, in each case, upon which our judgments are to be based?

The plain fact is that it is as impossible to discover educational objectives by analysis as it is to discover gasoline engines or cellophane by such a process. In each case we are dealing, not with discovery, but with invention or sheer creation. Education, like invention, is primarily concerned, not with what is, but with what may be. Facts are of interest and importance simply as material or means to the end in view. There is much that a teacher needs to know, just as the inventor needs to take account of materials and conditions; but such knowledge does not reveal what kind of result is to be achieved. It is no accident that the " determination " of objectives in this fashion turns out in the end to be a compilation of opinions gathered from persons whom it pleases the investigator to regard as experts. The undertow of the position is in the direction of the " hired man " theory of teaching, which reduces the teacher to the status of being a mouthpiece for the ideas and sentiments of the curriculum-makers. With reference to civic education, for example, we are told that " there is no other field of training in which it is so necessary that the schools should be continuously, week by week, securing their commission from the community as to what they should do." [4]

The foregoing comments are not intended as in any sense disparagement of scientific method, except in so far as the claim is made that educational objectives can be determined by a process of simple fact-finding. How then are these objectives to be arrived at? In the passage just quoted the objectives are eventually set by the community. Broadly stated, the community supporting the school may and should decide on the objectives. This, in brief, is the position taken by Dr. T. H. Briggs, but with certain qualifications. His central thesis is that " the State supports free public schools to perpetuate itself and to promote its own interests." [5] The term " State," so it is explained, does not refer to a political unit of government, but to " the societal organization that has assumed responsibility for education. It may be a local school district, a municipality, a county, a political state, the entire population of the country, or any

---

[4] F. Bobbitt, *How to Make a Curriculum*, p. 122.
[5] T. H. Briggs, *The Great Investment*, p. 8.

combination of these." [6] Whatever the unit, its purpose in maintaining a school is to perpetuate itself and to promote its own interests.

Each school unit, whether small or large, is apparently to have the right to run its own show. This is quite in line with our historic conception of democracy. Let the people decide what kind of school they want. We are warned, indeed, that this is not " an implied argument for determining the school program by popular vote. Nothing could be more absurd " (p. 33). The school program, like a health program, is to be entrusted to experts. The public, through its representatives, decides questions of policy, or of objectives, and then it devolves upon the directors of the school to " select as manager someone who by training, experience and philosophy is considered competent to produce what is wanted. To him will be left decision as to details " (p. 35).

This is simple and understandable. But then comes a curious elaboration. First of all, it must be recognized that the small school unit is, so to speak, a historic accident. The trend at present is all towards the expansion of these units, which points ultimately to a common program for all our public schools. The underlying principle remains the same, but in the end the State that seeks to perpetuate itself and promote its own interests will and should be the nation as a whole.

With the school unit thus enlarged and made all-inclusive, it becomes necessary to differentiate our educational policy from those of totalitarian states, which likewise use education to perpetuate themselves and to promote their own interests. How are we to distinguish between the objectives of such states and our own objec-

[6] *Ibid.*, p. 13, footnote.

tives? It is clear that we are confronted at this point with the fact that there are " inevitable and eternal conflicts of philosophies of life " (p. 78). The educational objectives of the totalitarian states are sharply defined. What are the educational objectives of a democracy?

These objectives, unfortunately, have not yet been adequately ascertained (p. 97). There is, however, a large body of " generally agreed on details of the good State " (p. 49), so there is no occasion for worry. There is enough to go on. In other words, we can fall back on majority opinion or on the opinion of hand-picked " experts." Since the State is concerned to perpetuate itself and to promote its own interests, it is justified in adopting whatever means are appropriate to this end. It may use the schools to cultivate " loyalty to approved ideals," it may (and should) suppress private schools, it may exclude " immigrants who hold materially different philosophies of life," and it may demand that legislation pertaining to schools be approved by " experts " before it is adopted (pp. 82–95). In a word, it may behave precisely like a totalitarian state.

This is a disturbing conclusion. We start, innocently enough, with school units that are reminiscent of the days of the little red schoolhouse, and we lay down the principle that the local unit can manage its school as it may see fit. Then we enlarge the unit, so that ultimately it will include all the people, which means that the local units must be made to toe the mark. Here the lengthening shadows of the concentration camp begin to appear. By this time we need experts who, besides handling details, are also competent to decide on matters of policy, as, e.g., in connection with legislation. In order to qualify, these experts must have adequate training and experience and also the right philosophy, which means in this case "loyalty to approved ideals." Ideals that have not been generally approved must be discouraged or suppressed. In brief the schools must be run for the maintenance of the *status quo* and the protection of vested interests. As a matter of words, it is conceded that democracy is a genuine problem; as a matter of practice, the schools are expected to inhibit all further thinking about democracy. The whole argument is an excellent illustration of the danger that we may be induced to surrender our liberties in the name of a bigger and better democracy.

A different approach to the problem of objectives comes from the camp of those who call themselves the "essentialists." The argument that is advanced is to the effect that the whole question of objectives has already been decided before the tribunal of history. Men have had experience in associated living since they first became men — and even before that. These experiences have become crystallized into mores, customs, and institutions, the basic principles of which are as valid at one time as at another. "Courtesy and fair dealing are the same in the days of the automobile as in those of the horse-drawn vehicle." [7]   To quote another writer: "Frugality and thrift may not be so significant as they once were, but respect for life, respect for law, consideration for the feelings of others, and plain everyday honesty are still important. . . . These may not be eternal values, but one may venture a fairly confident prediction that they will be just as significant a thousand years from now as they have been in the past." [8]   This

[7] H. C. Morrison, *Basic Principles of Education*, p. 371.
[8] W. C. Bagley, *Education and Emergent Man*, pp. 151, 156.

being the case, the task of the school is clearly to exemplify and idealize these principles. If we can educate the oncoming generation in the spirit of these " eternal truths," the problem of democracy may be regarded as solved.

This is essentially an appeal to the " lessons of history." Let us grant that history has many and important lessons to teach. At the same time we should be mindful of the fact that there is always room for a lesson on these lessons. Just what is it that history teaches? Respect for life, for law, for property, and the like, are doubtless valuable principles, but to erect these principles into eternal truths or values is to invite trouble. The reason is simply that these eternal truths have a way of colliding with one another, and when this happens history does not tell us what we are to do about it.

Victor Hugo's story of Jean Valjean, in *Les Misérables*, is a case in point. It is a story of a man who got caught between two of these eternal truths, in a situation where they could not be reconciled. His sister's children were starving, and so respect for life — to say nothing of consideration for the feelings of others — prompted him to steal bread, since he had no money to buy it. On the other hand, the principles of respect for law and for property rights forbade the stealing. What was he to do? It seems clear that the unfortunate Valjean needed an " over-all " principle, in the form of a social ideal, by which to determine the applicability of the " eternal truths," in order to arrive at a rational solution of the trouble — a principle which history does not supply. Our American Revolution and the " underground railroad " of pre-Civil War days provide similar instances of conflicts, not to mention personal experiences which happen to all of us. History, at most, offers us competing social ideals, which must be interpreted and judged in the light of changing conditions. To refer once more to the analogy of the " field " concept, social living is not simply a matter of adaptation, but of perpetual reconstruction. If we accept the pragmatic theory of mind, this becomes an inevitable conclusion. The essentialist is no more likely to *find* his ideals for conduct by just looking for them than is the devotee of the classics.

During recent years still another approach to the problem of educating for democracy has been advocated. Assuming that some such ideal of democracy as has been presented in the preceding pages is desirable, the fact remains, so it is argued, that men must first be able to live in order to learn how to live well. In other words, the economic problem must be solved as a precondition for solving the problem of democracy. With millions of unemployed, with widespread economic insecurity, with a small privileged class controlling the means of production, there is little profit in talking about democracy as long as these conditions prevail. Economics is the basis of everything else. Education, therefore, must devote itself to the task of revealing the inequity, the needlessness, the brutality of existing conditions; and teachers must make common cause with the laboring class in order to hasten the coming of a humane industrial organization as an enduring basis for democratic living. Whether we are willing to admit it or not, we find ourselves engaged in a class struggle, and in this struggle there are no neutrals. Devotion to the ideal of democracy requires us to be partisans in the fight.

The question at issue here does not concern the ideal

of democracy, nor yet the necessity of an extensive reconstruction of the existing economic and industrial order, but rather the ways and means of achieving the desired end.  In a class struggle there may be complete
absence of democracy in both camps.  The fact that one
group is numerically stronger than another does not automatically make its cause a democratic one.  It is not
necessary to go far back into history to show that a majority can be just as brutal and tyrannical as a minority.
A good, practical test of a democracy, in fact, may be
found in the treatment of minorities.  Educationally it
makes a world of difference whether one class is to be
superseded by another or a new basis of co-operation is
to be provided which will supersede both classes.  If we
stress co-operation, with such use of force as may be expedient to achieve this end, the whole situation changes.
Let us grant that a privileged minority will not volun-
tarily consent to surrender its privileges.  It can be compelled to make repeated concessions, in accordance with
the requirements of a progressively widening program of
co-operation, and it should be made to do so.  The point
is that co-operation must be kept central, with economic
readjustments as an integral part of the program.  It is
precisely this emphasis on co-operation which makes the
program educational and democratic.  To work for reconstruction apart from such emphasis is to inflame passions which, by themselves, interfere with the extension
of democracy.  It exemplifies the old saying about pour-
ing out the baby with the bath.
    It is precisely this spirit of democracy for which the
schools must assume specific responsibility — in the organization of school life, in community relations, and in
the promotion of insight or understanding of the mean-

ing of democracy. As a professional group the teachers need to organize for the protection of educational interests. Whenever educational issues arise, they will join forces with any other group that is like-minded with them on the particular issue which is involved. Presumably such co-operation will occur more frequently with labor groups than with other organizations, and so provision should be made for easy and prompt united action whenever such action is desirable. This is very different, however, from membership by teachers' unions in larger organizations that have at best but a minor interest in education. The public has a right to object to the use of the classroom for other than educational purposes, and the advocacy of economic reconstruction, save as an application of democracy — which is an educational end — is a misuse of the teacher's calling. In sticking to his calling, the teacher does not withdraw from the struggle for social improvement, but contributes an educational solution for problems and conflicts which is provided by neither of the parties engaged in the class struggle and which is not always welcomed by either. The teacher as a citizen has wide latitude in the matter of joining organizations; in his professional capacity he cannot be officially allied with one group without doing injury to the cause of education.

What, then, is the " cause " or the central purpose of education? If we approach this question in the perspective afforded by the examination of the various theories of learning, the answer should be clear. Each of these theories, as we have seen, has significant bearing upon the scale of values or program for living by which progress — in the individual and in the social group — is to be measured. The newer developments in both the natural sciences and the social order point to the conclusion that standards of value and conduct are flexible and changing products of everyday experience and are to be judged by no other test than the enrichment of human life here and now. This is the wider meaning of the term democracy, a meaning which transforms it from a political concept into a whole way of life. This conception of values and conduct has never prevailed in the past. It cannot prevail now except at the price of extensive reconstruction in our beliefs and attitudes and institutions. The central task of education, then, is to impart a realizing sense that we stand at a fork in the road. This reconstruction of experience is something that the individual must do for himself. There must be no indoctrination in the sense that the outcome is to be prescribed. A democratic philosophy of education rests on the faith that if the oncoming generation is given an opportunity to see the basic issue, democracy will win. It must win on these terms or it cannot win at all.

There is a very real sense in which it may be said that nothing else really matters. Our present civilization is full of conflicts which imperil its future. To a considerable extent these conflicts have their origin in the fact that men are making new demands on life. They crave opportunity for larger self-expression, for the richer living which our control over the forces of nature has made possible. In education this demand has led to a greater recognition of childhood, particularly as expressed in the movement commonly known as progressive education. The conflicts arise because this newer demand brings with it a conception of human living which has not, so far, been sharply formulated and made current; we still think too much in terms of the old categories, which means that we do not see clearly what it is that we want. Hence the function of the school is not merely to conserve the values of the past, but to provide for the continuous reinterpretation of our cultural heritage so as to make it the servant and not the master of our lives.

## Bibliography

BAGLEY, W. C., *Education and Emergent Man*, Chap. XI. Thomas Nelson and Sons.

BOBBITT, F., *How to Make a Curriculum*, Chap. VII. Houghton Mifflin Co.

BRIGGS, T. H., *The Great Investment*. Harvard University Press.

COUNTS, G. S., *Dare the School Build a New Social Order?* John Day Co.

HEIDBREDER, E., *Seven Psychologies*, Chap. I. D. Appleton-Century Co.

INDEX

# Index